THE SCARECROW AUTHOR BIBLIOGRAPHIES

Cy commencement de ceste iiie partie sieuuat la
zoute des princesses qui devant sont Et pius
les dames et damoiselles de court et hors nous
conuiet si comme nous promismes plier des
femmes destat des ates/ Cest assauoir a celles qui sont mariees
aux clercs gens de conseil de rois ou de princes ou gardat iustice
on en diuers offices/ Et aussi a celles qui sont mariees aux
bourgois des ates et bonnes villes qui en aucun pais sont appellez
nobles quant ils sont de buuaise coiuers/ Et apres dirons aux autres estas des femmes affin q toutes se sentent de nre doctrine
Et si q la auons touchie plusieurs fois ce deuat Cest nre entete
q toutes ce q recorde auons aux dames autretat aux vertus

CHRISTINE DE PIZAN:

A Bibliography

second edition

by
EDITH YENAL

Scarecrow Author Bibliographies, No. 63

The Scarecrow Press, Inc.
Metuchen, N.J., & London
1989

Frontispiece: From Le Livre des Trois Vertus, by Christine de Pizan; Ms. 427, folio #72R. Reprinted by permission of The Beinecke Rare Book and Manuscript Library, Yale University.

348744

c U

British Library Cataloguing-in-Publication data available

Library of Congress Cataloging-in-Publication Data

Yenal, Edith.
    Christine de Pizan : a bibliography / by Edith Yenal. -- 2nd ed.
        p.   cm. -- (Scarecrow author bibliographies ; no. 63)
    Includes bibliographical references.
    ISBN 0-8108-2248-2
    1. Christine, de Pisan, ca. 1364-ca. 1431--Bibliography.
I. Title. II. Series.
Z8693.7.Y45   1989
[PQ1575.Z5]
016.841'2--dc20   89-10718

To

DAPHNE
in memoriam
and to
Sacit, Emre, Kem, and Renée

• CONTENTS •

• PREFACE TO THE SECOND EDITION •

This manual is a revised and enlarged edition of the Christine bibliography first published in 1982. It contains more than 840 numbered entries as opposed to the 346 of the previous volume. Most items listed have brief descriptive or critical annotations that indicate, among other things, how the item relates to Christine de Pizan and what it says about her.

This second edition also has some new, supplementary material which researchers may find useful. It includes not only three indexes--for Scholars, Manuscripts, and Individual Works--but two appendixes. Appendix A features a selection of Christine de Pizan's contemporaries; Appendix B lists forthcoming studies and addenda. The edition has been completely reorganized and given a simpler, more streamlined format. Sections entitled Dissertations, Literary Histories, and Brief Mentions were eliminated and the material incorporated into existing headings.

Bibliographical coverage for the second edition ranges over a period of five hundred years, from the fifteenth century to the late twentieth. The closing date for entries in this edition is April 1988, whereas for the first edition it was almost a decade earlier (March 1978). Items coming to my attention after the deadline or upon completion of the typescript are listed in Appendix B. As in the preceding work, the approach here is chronological (by date of publication and date of composition for Christine's writings), then alphabetical by author, editor, translator. The previous Introduction, though rewritten and shortened, has been retained for the benefit of students and nonspecialists who are not acquainted with the life or work of this medieval author.

Part I of the bibliography deals with the original texts

of Christine de Pizan. It lists all of Christine's published
and unpublished writings, provides a summary for each work,
gives the work's main textual sources and manuscripts (up-
dated after Angus J. Kennedy 742), furnishes citations for
the various editions and translations, and presents notes and
critical studies relating to the work. Part II comprises surveys of Christine de Pizan's life and writings, full-length
bio-literary studies, and general criticism. Part III covers
Special Topics, being subdivided into six headings: (a)
Manuscripts and Manuscript Illumination, (b) Style and Language, (c) Poetics, (d) Political and Educational Ideas, (e)
Chivalry and Courtly Love, (f) Humanism. Manuscript Catalogs are not included in this bibliography since these are
more than adequately covered in Angus J. Kennedy's Bibliographical Guide, 742, pp. 20-28. Part V, Miscellanea, contains items of lesser research value than the material listed
in the preceding sections. For Parts IV, VI, VII no comment
seems necessary since the subject-headings are self-explana-
tory.

A word of explanation is in order however about the
items below:

1. NAME. It will be noted that the name "Christine
de Pisan" has been changed in this edition to "Christine de
Pizan" in order to conform to what is now the accepted (and
correct) spelling of Christine's surname.

2. PERSONS CITED. Names of Christine de Pizan's
contemporaries that are cited in the Introduction or annotations are keyed to Appendix A.

3. SPECIAL ISSUES. Where an entire issue is ex-
clusively devoted to Christine de Pizan and her works, as
is the case with #636, each paper in the collection is treated
as a separate, numbered entry and listed under the author's
name (except for items in Appendix B). The issue itself
appears under the name of its editor.

4. CRITICAL REVIEWS. A sampling of review articles
with brief comments is provided in Part VIII. Full citations
to reviews not personally seen appear directly beneath the
item being reviewed.

5. UPDATING AND UPGRADING. Although the main

concern of the second edition has been to fill existing gaps and bring the bibliography up to date, I have also endeavored to upgrade the earlier material. Hence, every item of the first edition has been reviewed and, in most cases, rewritten. Old errors were corrected, annotations made more concise or expanded to include additional information, and citations checked for accuracy. Furthermore, an attempt has been made to respond to the criticism of the previous book and to implement reviewers' suggestions whenever feasible.

Despite these revisions it is possible that some problems have still been overlooked. But if this new volume has succeeded in supplying readers with the essential titles on our author and given them a bibliographical overview of the field, then my task will have been accomplished.

In closing, I would like to thank all the scholars who have taken time out from their busy schedules to reply to my inquiries and letters: Drs. Barbara K. Altmann, Kevin Brownlee, Sheila Delany, Thelma S. Fenster, Glenda K. McLeod, Ann Hunter McMillan, Christine M. Reno, Earl Jeffrey Richards, and Charity Cannon Willard. My special thanks must go to Professor Nadia Margolis for her interest and help and for calling my attention to many of the items that appear in this work.

Edith Yenal
Garden City, NY
April 1989

• ABBREVIATIONS •

AB	Art Bulletin
ASNSL	Archiv für das Studium der Neuern Sprachen und Literaturen
BEC	Bibliothèque de l'École des Chartes
BF	Les Bonnes Feuilles
BHR	Bibliothèque d'humanisme et Renaissance
BL	British Library
BN	Bibliothèque Nationale
BN f.fr.	Bibliothèque Nationale fonds française
BR	Bibliothèque Royale
BSED	Bulletin de la Société des Études Dantesques
BTAM	Bulletin de Théologie Ancienne et Médiévale
CDU	Centre de Documentation Universitaire
CH, CdP	Christine, Christine de Pizan
CN	Cultura Neolatina
CNRS	Centre Nationale de la Recherche Scientifique
CPFEHR	Culture et politique en France à l'époque de l'humanisme et de la Renaissance. (For full citation see #570.)
CR	Critical Review
CUER MA	Cahiers du Centre Universitaire d'Études et de Recherches Médiévales d'Aix en Provence
DAI	Dissertation Abstracts International
EC	L'Esprit Créateur
EETS	Early English Text Society
EHR	English Historical Review
ELN	English Language Notes

e.s.	extra series
FCS	Fifteenth Century Studies
FR	French Review
FS	French Studies
GBA	Gazette des Beaux-Arts
GSLI	Giornale Storico della Letteratura Italiana
HLB	Harvard Library Bulletin
IFW	Ideals for Women in the Works of Christine de Pizan (For full citation see #636.)
JHI	Journal of the History of Ideas
JMH	Journal of Medieval History
JMRS	Journal of Medieval and Renaissance Studies
LR	Les Lettres Romanes
MA	Le Moyen Age
MAe	Medium Aevum
M & H	Medievalia et Humanistica
MF	Le Moyen Français
MLAA	Modern Language Association of America
MLN	Modern Language Notes
MLR	Modern Language Review
MP	Modern Philology
MR	Marche Romane
MS	Mediaeval Studies
n.d.	no date
NMS	Nottingham Medieval Studies
n.p.	no page numbers
n.p.p.	no place of publication
n.pub.	no publisher
n.s.	new series
nouv. acq. fr.	nouvelles acquisitions françaises
NYTBR	New York Times Book Review
o.s.	old series
PMLA	Publications of the Modern Language Association of America
PQ	Philological Quarterly

Quarrel	the quarrel over the Roman de la Rose
RBPH	Revue Belge de Philologie et d'Histoire
RDM	Revue des Deux Mondes
RES	Revue of English Studies
RH	Revue Historique
RJ	Romanistisches Jahrbuch
RLC	Revue de Littérature Comparée
RLM	Revue des Lettres Modernes
RLMC	Rivista di Letterature Moderne e Comparate
RLR	Revue de linguistique roman
RM	Revue Mondiale
RN	Romance Notes
Roman	Le Roman de la Rose
RPh	Romance Philology
RQ	Renaissance Quarterly
RQH	Revue des questions historiques
RR	Romanic Review
RSH	Revue des Sciences Humaines
SATF	Société des Anciens Textes Français
SF	Studi Francesi
SM	Studi Medievali
SMSRQF	Seconda Miscellanea di Studi e Ricerche sul Quattrocento Francese. (For full citation see #443.)
ZFSL	Zeitschrift für Französische Sprachen und Literatur
ZRP	Zeitschrift für Romanische Philologie

• INTRODUCTION •

I.

Christine de Pizan's current revival has brought her new international fame and unprecedented popularity in this country.
Indeed, since this bibliography was first compiled over a decade ago Christine seems to have inspired a whole host of
publications, both scholarly and popular, and become the subject of lengthy essays, journal articles, lectures, as well as
a significant number of works in book form. These include
a newly edited text of the Cent ballades d'amant et de dame
(Cerquiglini 1982, #310); two editions of the previously unedited Epistre de la prison de vie humaine (Kennedy 1984,
#345, Wisman 1984, #729); two full-length biographies (Per-
noud 1982, #447, Willard 1984, #450); three modern renditions
of the Livre de la cité des dames--in English (Richards 1982,
#234), French (Hicks and Moreau 1986, #235), and German
(Zimmerman 1986, #236)--and one of the Livre des trois vertus (Lawson 1985, #266), with a critical edition of this text
soon to be released by the Bibliothèque du XVe Siècle (ed.
C. C. Willard), and an iconographical study that sheds new
light on the miniatures and political ideology of the Epistre
d'Othea (Hindman 1986, #84).

Although three of Christine's works remain presently
still unedited (#292, #315, #348), and others are available only
in old or inadequate editions, the 1980s have nevertheless
considerably widened the scope of Pizan studies and given us
a second look at Christine and her artistic achievement. Just
how remarkable that achievement was will be seen in the brief
review that follows.

II.

As is often noted, Christine de Pizan was one of the best-

xv

known and most celebrated literary figures in fifteenth-century France and perhaps in all of late medieval Europe. Her long and illustrious career spanned more than three decades during which she was actively involved in worldly affairs, addressing the crucial problems of her time.

Educator of princes, social and political commentator, and royal historian, Christine spoke with a forceful voice on important issues earning respect in aristocratic and learned circles alike. She occupies a unique place in French letters as both a writer and an intellectual arbiter. Largely self-educated and possessing an invincible spirit, she managed to rise above exceptionally difficult circumstances to become a versatile and highly accomplished lyric poet, a prolific nonfiction writer, and a productive scholar who won further renown for her feminism and participation in the quarrel over the <u>Roman de la Rose</u> (c. 1236-1267). Her pivotal role in that famous dispute placed her at the center of controversy and debate at a time when women were scarcely allowed to have an opinion let alone express it openly in public. As an author of both verse and prose, Christine wrote on a variety of subjects in different genres, making contributions not only to her contemporaries but to the history of ideas.

Born in Venice, Italy, c. 1364 into a Bolognese family of academic background, Christine de Pizan was reared near the court of Charles V (see #798) in Paris where her father, Tommaso di Benvenuto da Pizzano, held a post as an astrologer-physician. He was at the same time a practicing alchemist suspected of having accidentally poisoned members of the royal family (Thorndike, #677, pp. 614-15). In 1380 at age fifteen, Christine was married to a young court notary from Picardy named Etienne de Castel. At twenty-five she suddenly found herself widowed and left with an aging mother, a niece, and several small children to support: a daughter born in 1381, a son who seems to have died in infancy, and another son born around 1385. Christine's two brothers, Paolo and Aghinolfo, had in the meantime returned to their native Italy to claim a family inheritance.

Her husband's untimely death (in 1390 during an epidemic) proved to be the turning point of Christine's life. As we have learned from her autobiographical writings, this tragic event led not only to her literary career but to a life of study and learning. She would apply herself to both with a singular passion, becoming the very model of scholarship and erudition.

Christine turned to writing for personal as well as economic reasons. Other than being left a small sum of money from her husband's estate (which she was unable to collect for years and then only after prolonged litigation) no financial provisions had been made for her--neither by her father, who had died in virtual poverty between 1388 and 1389, nor by her husband. Not able to live by her pen alone, Christine is believed to have found employment as a copyist in the medieval book trade. Her familiarity with manuscripts and bookmaking later enabled her to supervise the production and illustration of her own manuscripts.

Her career began a few years after Etienne's death, probably around 1393, with a series of poems lamenting her widowhood. These now form part of a collection entitled Cent ballades, Virelais, Rondeaux (Roy, #702). Rueful and melancholy, they tell of the loneliness she suffered as a despondent young widow. After composing her poèmes de veuvage, Christine wrote on chivalry and courtly love. With the courtly love poems she almost immediately attracted the attention of important members of the French royal court and became what her biographer has called a "society poet" (Willard, #450, p. 70). Her admirers included not only such ducal benefactors as Philip and John of Burgundy (#823, #814), Louis of Orleans (#815), and that renowned collector of illuminated manuscripts, Jean of Berry (#812), but the king of France, Charles VI (#799) and his consort, queen Isabeau of Bavaria (#811).

From 1399 to 1405 Christine brought out several love debates, the Débat de deux amans (c. 1400, #39) and the Livre des trois jugemens (c. 1400, #45); a pastourelle, the Dit de la pastoure (1403, #185); and a long courtly romance, the Livre du duc des vrais amans (1404-1405, #224), in which she upholds marriage and cautions women about the "dangers" of courtly love. Viewing courtly love from a uniquely feminine perspective, Christine often portrayed it as a disillusioning if not traumatic experience for women.

After 1404 she seems less interested in courtly themes, turning instead toward larger and more serious subjects, and increasingly toward prose and didactic writing. The earliest compositions signaling this change are the Livre du chemin de long estude (1402-1403, #154) and the Livre de la mutacion de Fortune (1403, #174). These two encyclopedic works, though still in verse, contain social criticism and reveal

Christine's considerable knowledge of history and geography.
In the Chemin de long estude she undertakes an allegorical
voyage that is analogous to Dante's journey in the Divine
Comedy. In the Mutacion de Fortune she presents a universal history and introduces the theme of poverty, a theme not
very extensively treated in French literature prior to Christine (see Woledge, #181).

It was with long philosophical compositions like the Mutacion and Long estude--as well as with her autobiographical
Avision (1405, #284) and treatises on government, peace, and
military strategy--that Christine acquired a reputation as a
scholar and came to be compared to Boethius, whose Consolatione Philosophiae she had read and drawn inspiration from.
On the basis (presumably) of her learned Mutacion, which
she presented to the regent Philip of Burgundy (#823) in
January 1404, he commissioned her to write the official biography of his late brother, king Charles V (#798). Com-
pleted on November 30, 1404, the Livre des fais et bonnes
meurs du sage roy Charles V (#192) chronicles well-known
figures and events from Charles's reign. It is the only history Christine ever wrote.

As stated earlier, Christine was both successful and prolific. By 1405 she had already written over a dozen major
pieces and by the end of her career filled scores of manuscripts. Altogether she left some three hundred ballades,
sixty-three rondeaux, sixteen virelais, two lais, and a collection of seventy jeux à vendre, not to mention the allegories,
epistolary works, and didactic treatises cited below. Her collected writings are preserved at the British Library, London
in MS Harley 4431, the so-called Queen's (Isabeau, #811) manuscript. Famed for its frontispiece and outstanding miniatures,
of which there are 130, Harley is codicologically important
having been identified as an autograph manuscript.

Following the conventions of her day, Christine often
placed her ideas in an archaic allegorical framework. However, her message was always timely. She tried above all to
imbue her aristocratic patrons with a sense of justice and ap-
peal to their nobler instincts. In an age where courtly love
was the dominant literary theme, Christine offered her readers
a series of moral precepts, the Enseignemens moraux (1400-
1401, #93). In the Livre du chemin de long estude (1402-
1403, #154) she set out to popularize science; in the Livre de

la paix (1412-1413, #336), politics. The Livre de la prod'
hommie de l'homme (c. 1405-1406, #393) deals with virtue and
vice; the Epistre d'Othea (c. 1400, #46) with the ideals of
knighthood.

In the Epistre d'Othea as in other didactic works, Christine uses models from mythology and the classics. Her attempt to revive the spirit of antiquity is what linked her to
the movement of humanism. Because her writings were among
the earliest in France to embrace a humanistic philosophy modern scholars have come to view Christine as one of the first
humanists of the French Renaissance (in #302, #455, #572).
Her humanistic thinking is especially evident in the political
treatise the Livre du corps de policie (1406-1407, #295), which
falls into the same class of didactic works as Erasmus's The
Education of a Christian Prince (1516). But as the late Diane
Bornstein has pointed out, Policie is, ironically, more often
associated with chivalric idealism than with humanism (#302,
pp. 112-13).

As we know, Christine had occasion to correspond with
the early French humanists at the beginning of the fifteenth
century when she became involved in a literary dispute over
the most popular work of the Middle Ages, the Roman de la
Rose (c. 1236-1276). Backed by Jean Gerson (#807), the in-
fluential Chancellor of the University of Paris; Guillaume de
Tignonville, the Provost of Paris; and the Marshal Boucicaut
(#794), she accused the author of the second part of the Roman, Jean de Meun, of misogyny and immorality. De Muen's
apologists--the Provost of Lille, Jean de Montreuil (#820), and
two royal secretaries named Pierre and Gontier Col (#803)--
tried unsuccessfully to get Christine to recant. They wrote
rude letters to her but she in turn replied with irony and
wit. Refusing consistently to let these eminent humanists
convert or intimidate her, she would on the contrary continue
to denounce the sexist writings of Jean de Meun to the very
end.

It was under these somewhat unusual circumstances that
Christine de Pizan became the first woman of her age to come
forward and defend her sex, publicly and in writing, against
the foremost intellectuals in France; and further, to raise
questions about women that would be debated for the next
five centuries--starting with the querelle des femmes in the
Renaissance and continuing to our own day.

xix

Christine presents her eloquent defense of women in four different works: in the Epistre au dieu d'Amours (1399, #16), an epistle in verse in which she attacks clerics and misogynic authors; in the Dit de la Rose (1402, #146), a poem defending women's honor and condemning the practice of defaming them; in the Epistres sur le Roman de la Rose (1401-1403, #107), a collection of polemical letters issuing from the above quarrel; and in the Livre de la cité des dames (1405, #227), her most explicit feminist piece. The latter has probably contributed more to Christine's reputation as a feminist than any other single work. Besides being one of the first histories of women, it is the only writing in which she specifically asks for the right to an education for women. In the Livre des trois vertus (1405, #259), a follow-up to the Cité, Christine does not attempt to justify or rehabilitate women; instead, she outlines their roles and responsibilities in society. Although the two latter works differ in style and content, the notion that women can and have made contributions to the world is implicit in both. Acutely aware of women's low status in medieval society, Christine was determined to redefine the female image and help women gain greater self-confidence and self-esteem.

Yet not all of Christine's ideas on women were progressive, as critics who charge her with conservatism are quick to point out (in #609, #637, #644, #662). Even in the Cité des dames, a book that clearly tries to elevate and dignify women, instances of female subservience can still be found. A case in point is the Griselda tale, which appears in Part II, chaps. 11.1 and 50.1-4 of the Cité (Richards, #234). In none of Christine's writings are women urged to abandon their traditional roles or strike out in new directions. Christine did not recommend, for instance, that women enter "men's" professions as she herself had done; nor did she ever propose equal rights for women. To claim that she was a feminist in any modern sense would therefore be misleading.

However, whether one views Christine de Pizan as a feminist trailblazer or as a defender of the status quo, her ideas on women were entirely consistent with her humanistic attitudes and beliefs. In the end, Christine was both a humanist and a humanitarian concerned with the dignity and worth of all human beings.

While Christine's final work still pays homage to a woman, she would devote the latter part of her career to the causes

of her adopted country rather than her sex. Her writings
on the political affairs of France--with which she deals in the
Epistre à la reine (1405, #280), the Lamentacion sur les maux
de la France (1410, #334), and again in the Livre de la paix
(1412-1413, #336)--these form an important genre within the
body of her work. They not only reflect the political realities
of fifteenth-century France but chart her literary development,
showing how her writings evolved from the first love lyrics
penned for her patrons' diversion to the later prose works
in which she analyzes French society.

After writing the Epistre de la prison de vie humaine
(1414-1418, #344), a consolatory letter destined for her friend
the duchess Marie of Berry, she composed a religious piece
based on the Scriptures, the Heures de contemplation sur la
Passion de Nostre Seigneur (c. 1420-1424, #348). Christine's
career came to a close with a tribute to France's national
heroine, Joan of Arc (#813). Her lengthy poem Ditié de
Jehanne d'Arc (#349) is said to have been the only work in
French to appear before Joan's condemnation and burning at
the stake in 1431. Written in exile from the Poissy convent
to which she had fled a decade earlier to escape the bloody
French civil war, the Ditié is Christine's last-known work.
Upon its completion on July 31, 1429, she vanishes from sight.
It is thought she died sometime around 1430 at the age of
sixty-five, but her actual date of death has never been con-
firmed.

During her own lifetime and in the century after her
death, Christine de Pizan was held in high esteem. In England the advent of printing created a vogue for her work,
resulting in the translation and publication of five of her
books: The Epistle of Othea to Hector, or, the Boke of
Knyghthode (Scrope, c. 1440-1459, #52), The Morale Proverbs
of Christyne (Woodville, 1478, #97), The Boke of the Fayt of
Armes and of Chyualrye (Caxton, 1489 or 1490, #318), The
Boke of the Cyte of Ladyes (Anslay, between 1509 and 1521,
#231), and The Body of Polycye (Skot, 1521, #297). William
Caxton himself (#797) had translated one and printed two of
these volumes at his Westminster Abbey press in London in
the final years of the fifteenth century. Among other English-
men expressing an interest in Christine were the Earl of Salisbury (see #445) and kings Henry IV, Edward IV, and Henry
VII, as well as the English writers William Worcester and
Thomas Hoccleve (#810); in short, many of the notables of

the day. Nor was her fame solely confined to France or England, as already indicated. In Flanders, Italy, Spain, and Portugal her works were copied and translated.

After the sixteenth century, however, when literary tastes began to change, Christine fell into relative obscurity. The majority of her writings remained thus in manuscript for over three hundred years. It was not until the eighteenth century that a handful of such French scholars as Boivin le Cadet (#373), the abbé Lebeuf (#195), and Mlle. de Kéralio (#700) finally rediscovered Christine and published extracts from her works. In the nineteenth century Raimon Thomassy and his Essai sur les écrits politiques de Christine de Pisan (1838, #701) contributed greatly to the revival of interest in Christine, as did the work of her first modern editor, Maurice Roy, whose three-volume edition of the Oeuvres poétiques de Christine de Pisan (#702) was published in Paris from 1886 to 1896.

During the first quarter of the twentieth century, there appeared a number of feminist studies on Christine by the French and German scholars Rose Rigaud (#585), Dora Melegari (#587), and Mathilde Kastenberg (#583), as well as surveys of her writings by Fred P. Henry (#386), Carl Baerwolff (#557), and the noted Belgian jurist Ernest Nys (#546). These publications were to be followed in 1927 by Marie-Josèphe Pinet's Christine de Pisan ... étude biographique et littéraire (Paris, #398), a pioneering work of 463 pages which despite its flaws has since become a classic.

While it is true that Christine de Pizan has always enjoyed a certain international following, she did not really attract a sizable readership until the women's movement began calling attention to her in 1960. By the early 1970s her name was appearing frequently in women's literature. Latter-day feminists were eager to claim Christine and make her into one of their "mothers to think back through"--a phrase borrowed from Virginia Woolf but more recently taken up by the Canadian scholar Sheila Delany (#644, #662), who considers Christine too conservative to be a role model for modern women authors. Just the same, feminist critics view this medieval writer as part of their literary heritage and as a major figure in women's history.

Aside from being indebted to contemporary feminism,

Christine's current popularity owes something too to inter-disciplinary scholarship and its present fascination with the later Middle Ages. This resurging interest in the medieval period has helped further the cause of Pizan studies, bring-ing Christine de Pizan critical attention not only from femi-nists or traditional students of French language and litera-ture, but from scholars in every field: medievalists, liter-ary and cultural historians, art historians (for the illuminated manuscripts), political scientists and, not least, bibliographers.

Old-time French critics like Gustave Lanson, who once contemptuously dismissed Christine as an "insufferable blue-stocking" (#390, p. 167) but whose opinions are now no longer taken seriously (Hicks and Moreau, #235, p. 17), seem clearly to have been overruled by modern scholarship. For today, as previously noted, Christine de Pizan is recognized as a world-class author. Her writings, half a millennium after her death, continue thus to be read, edited, translated, and an-thologized, as the present volume so graphically demonstrates. If some of her works seem dated now--those on chivalry and courtly love especially--others, with more universal themes, appear surprisingly modern. What Christine had to say about the human condition (in the Mutacion, #174; Avision, #284; Vie humaine, #344) is still relevant, as are her observations on ethics and morality, good and bad rulers, loss and be-reavement, misogyny, the eternal battle of the sexes, and a number of other subjects.

In grappling with these fundamental questions, Christine de Pizan has shown herself to be an innovative and critical thinker. History will remember her not only as France's "first woman of letters" but as a committed writer whose teachings and moral influence were perhaps as significant as her liter-ary achievement.

INDIVIDUAL WORKS: PRIMARY AND
SECONDARY SOURCES

1 CENT BALLADES (1399-1402)
This collection of short lyrics dates from the late fourteenth,
early fifteenth centuries. With the exception of Nos. XXI-XLIX
and LXV-LXXXVIII, the ballades were composed as individual pieces
and then arranged as a series of one hundred consecutive poems.
Many are courtly love poems. The first twenty, the so-called
poèmes de veuvage, deal with CH's bereavement and widowhood.
They reflect her profound anguish and poignantly express her
feelings about the untimely death of her young husband, Etienne
de Castel. The remainder of the collection is devoted to the theme
of love and various other topics: secret grief, adulterous affairs, jealous husbands, gossipers, Charles VI's mental illness
(No. XCV), greetings to friends, and patriotic, religious, and
mythological subjects. Meditative and moralizing poems are included too.

MANUSCRIPTS:
Chantilly, Musée Condé 492, ff. 2^r-22^V.
London, BL Harley 4431, ff. 4^r-21^r.
Paris, Arsenal 3295, ff. 3^r-44^V.
_____, BN f.fr. 604, ff. 2^r-18^r.
_____, ___ ____ 835, ff. 1^r-16^V, 18^{r-V}.
_____, ___ ____ 12779, ff. 1^r-21^V.
_____, ___ Moreau 1686, ff. 1^r-42^V.

EDITION:
See Roy 702, I, pp. 1-100.

NOTES AND STUDIES:
See also Abry 409, DuBos 704, Laidlaw 494, Le Gentil 411, Moulin
714, Tabarlet-Schock 538, Varty 715, Wilkins 519, 721, Willard
539.

2 Le Roux de Lincy, Antoine Jean Victor. "Complainte sur la folie
de Charles VI, par Christine de Pisan." BEC, I (1839-1840),
374-76.

Prints a ballade from Mouchet, Bibliothèque Royale MS 6, f. 20v° in which CH talks about Charles VI's (799) mental illness. Considers the poem significant as historical commentary but not as literature.

3   Le Roux de Lincy, Antoine Jean Victor.   "Trois ballades de Christine de Pisan sur le combat de sept français contre sept anglais, en 1402."   BEC, I (1839-1840), 376-88.
     First printing of the "Montendre" ballades, composed by CH on 9 May 1402 in commemoration of a joust held in that town.

4   Bertoni, Giulio.   Lingua e Pensiero.   (Studi e Saggi Linguistica). Florence: Leo S. Olschki, 1932.
     Makes analysis of the vocabulary, grammar, syntax in the Cent ballades, pp. 111-19.

5   Urwin, Kenneth.   "The 59th English Ballade of Charles of Orleans."   MLR, XXXVIII (1943), 129-32.
     Compares similarities between CH's ballade "Seulete suy" and the 59th ballade in The English Poems of Charles of Orleans (ed. R. Steele and M. Day, Oxford, 1941-1946), arguing that although Orleans (800) appears to have been conscious of his French model, his development after the first strophe is not that of CH.

6   Cigada, Sergio.   "Christine de Pisan e la traduzione inglese delle poesi di Charles d'Orléans."   Aevum, XXXII (1958), 509-16.
     On Orleans's (800) poem "Alone am y" as probable English translation of CH's "Seulete suy" (Roy 702, I, 12).   CR's:
        SF, 8 (1959), 293
        LR, XIV (1960), 262-63

7   Poirion, Daniel.   "Création poétique et composition romanesque dans les premiers poèmes de Charles d'Orléans."   RSH, XC (1958), 185-211.
     Sees CH as one of Orleans's (800) early influences.   The latter not only based one of his English poems on her ballade "Seulete suy" but arranged his poetry in sequence of one hundred consecutive poems after her Cent ballades.

8   Fox, John.   "Charles d'Orléans, poète anglais."   Romania, LXXXVI (1965), 433-62.
     Finds similarities between CH's ballade "Seulete suy" and Orleans's (800) "Alone am y" but notes that despite strong resemblance Orleans's poem is not literal translation of CH's.

9. Deschaux, Robert.   "La poésie lyrique en France à la fin du Moyen Âge.   Jalons pour l'étude de quelques ballades."   Recherches et Travaux.   Bulletin.   (Univ. de Grenoble), XVII (1978), 1-9.
     On pp. 2-5 compares the love poems of CH, Machaut (816), and Deschamps (804).

10 Robbins, Rossell Hope. "The Middle English Court Love Lyrics."
   In The Interpretation of Medieval Lyric Poetry. Ed. W. T. H.
   Jackson. New York: Columbia Univ. Press, 1980, pp. 224-33.
       Cites the Cent ballades, p. 231 n. 73, as example of poetry
   written in a sequential time frame.

11 VIRELAIS (1399-1402)
   CH wrote sixteen virelais. Their subject matter ranges from
   personal sorrow, in No. I, to St. Valentine's Day, in No. X.
   In Virelai XV she tells us that, for the sake of others and to
   alleviate her own pain, she will henceforth compose more cheerful
   verse.

   MANUSCRIPTS:
   Chantilly, Musée Condé 492, ff. 23^r-26^v.
   London, BL Harley 4431, ff. 21^r-24^r.
   Paris, Arsenal 3295, ff. 45^r-52^r.
   _____, BN f.fr. 604, ff. 18^r-20^v.
   _____, ___ _____ 835, ff. 17^r-^{v}, 19^r-20^v.
   _____, ___ _____ 12779, ff. 21 (bis)^r-24^v.
   _____, ___ Moreau 1686, ff. 43^r-50^r.

   EDITION:
   See Roy 702, I, pp. 101-18.

   ANTHOLOGIES:
   See Moulin 714, Varty 715, Wilkins 721.

12 RONDEAUX (1399-1402)
   CH wrote sixty-three rondeaux. In the first group she continues
   to lament her widowhood but after Rondeau XI the poems become
   less personal. Love, often depicted from a woman's point of
   view, seems to be a favorite and recurring theme. The collection also includes rondeaux composed in a more serious vein.

   MANUSCRIPTS:
   Chantilly, Musée Condé 492, ff. 41^r-47^r.
   London, BL Harley 4431, ff. 28^v-34^r.
   Paris, Arsenal 3295, ff. 77^v-89^v.
   _____, BN f.fr.604, ff. 32^r-36^v.
   _____, ___ _____ 835, ff. 25^r-31^r.
   _____, ___ _____ 12779, ff. 39^r-45^r.
   _____, ___ Moreau 1686, ff. 75^v-87^v.

   EDITION:
   See Roy 702, I, pp. 147-85.

   STUDIES, ANTHOLOGIES:
   See Calvez 540; Françon 520, 522, 525, 537; Garey 531, 534;

Laidlaw 494; Moulin 714; Tabarlet-Schock 538; Varty 715; Wilkins 519, 721.

13 BALADES D'ESTRANGE FAÇON (1399-1402)
This group of poems comprises four ballades whose form is indicated by their title: Balade retrograde qui se dit a droit et a rebours, Balade a rimes reprises, Balade a responses, Balade a vers a responces.

MANUSCRIPTS:
Chantilly, Musée Condé 492, ff. 26^v-27^r, 32^v.
London, BL Harley 4431, ff. 24^r-25^r.
Paris, Arsenal 3295, ff. 52^r-53^v, 64^r-^{v}.
_____, BN f.fr. 604, ff. 20^v-21^r, 25^v.
_____, ___ _____ 835, ff. 21^r-^{v}.
_____, ___ _____ 12779, ff. 24^v-25^r, 30^v.
_____, ___ Moreau 1686, ff. 50^r-51^v, 62^r-^{v}.

EDITION:
See Roy 702, I, pp. 119-24.

14 LAIS (1399-1402)
CH wrote two lais, one with 266 lines the other with 246.

MANUSCRIPTS:
Chantilly, Musée Condé 492, ff. 37^r-41^r.
London, BL Harley 4431, ff. 25^r-28^v.
Paris, Arsenal 3295, ff. 73^r-77^r.
_____, BN f.fr. 604, ff. 28^v-32^r.
_____, ___ _____ 835, ff. 21^v-25^r.
_____, ___ _____ 12779, ff. 37^r-39^r.
_____, ___ Moreau 1686, ff. 71^r-75^r.

EDITION:
See Roy 702, I, pp. 125-45.

15 JEUX A VENDRE (1399-1402)
This verse-form served as a type of entertainment for the upper classes in the fourteenth and fifteenth centuries. It usually involved two players one of whom would offer an item for sale and another who would reply with a witticism, compliment, or advice. CH wrote seventy jeux.

MANUSCRIPTS:
Chantilly, Musée Condé 492, ff. 47^v-51^r.
London, BL Harley 4431, ff. 34^v-37^r.
Paris, Arsenal 3295, ff. 90^r-96^v.
_____, BN f.fr. 604, ff. 36^v-39^v.

_____, __ _____ 835, ff. 31^r-34^r.
_____, __ _____ 12779, ff. 45^v-48^v.
_____, __ Moreau 1686, ff. 88^r-94^v.

EDITION:
See Roy 702, I, pp. 187-205.

16 L'EPISTRE AU DIEU D'AMOURS (1 May 1399)
An allegorical poem that can be read both as a feminist response
to Jean de Meun's part of the Roman de la Rose and as a witty
commentary on courtly pretensions. Written in decasyllabic verse
with rhyming couplets, it is cast in form of a letter in which
Cupid, the God of Love, answers women's complaints about dis-
loyal men. Cupid conveys the women's grievances to an assembly
of gods. After describing the kind of outrages men inflict upon
women, an attack is made on writers who frequently malign women,
most notably Ovid (and his Ars Amatoria) and Jean de Meun,
whose cynical portrayal of women in the second part of the Roman de la Rose deeply offended CH. At the end of the epistle,
the God of Love issues a decree banishing all false lovers from
his court. CH appears in the poem as a royal secretary at the
court.

TEXTUAL SOURCE:
Heroïdes, Ovid; French translation of, in the Histoire ancienne
jusqu'à César.

MANUSCRIPTS:
Chantilly, Musée Condé 492, ff. 67^v-73^v.
London, BL Harley 4431, ff. 51^r-56^v.
_____, Westminster Abbey Library MS 21, ff. 52^a-64^b.
Paris, Arsenal 3295, ff. 128^r-140^v.
_____, BN f.fr. 604, ff. 51^v-56^v.
_____, __ _____ 835, ff. 45^r-50^r.
_____, __ _____ 12779, ff. 65^v-71^v.
_____, __ Moreau 1686, ff. 126^r-138^v.

EDITIONS:
See Roy 702, II, pp. 1-27.

17 Le Contre-Romant de la Rose nommé Gratia Dei. n.p., n.pub.,
n.d.
An early printed edition of the epistre.

18 Fenster, Thelma S., ed. and trans. Christine de Pizan's
'Epistre au dieu d'Amours,' and 'Dit de la Rose,' with Thomas
Hoccleve's 'Letter of Cupid.' Leiden, Holland: E. J. Brill,
date not set.
Dual-language editions of the Epistre and Dit. Contains the
texts, an Introduction, a discussion on the manuscripts and
versification, and an explanation on the establishment of the

texts.   Both editions have textual notes and notes on the contents.   Includes Table of Proper Names and glossary.   The section on Hoccleve provides an Introduction, notes, an edition of
the original Middle English poem and a Modern English translation
of it.   Also, a glossary.   (Source of Reference: Thelma S.
Fenster, Fordham Univ., NY; typed, signed letter to E. Y. dated
17 March 1988).

TRANSLATIONS:

19 Hoccleve, Thomas.   The Letter of Cupid.   In The Works of
    Geoffrey Chaucer.   Ed. John Urry.   London: B. Lintot, 1721.
        Hoccleve's Letter, printed here on pp. 534-37, is a loose
    English translation of CH's epistle.

20 Furnivall, Frederick James, ed.   Hoccleve's Works.   I. The
    Minor Poems in the Phillipps MS 8151 (Cheltenham) and the Dur-
    ham MS III.9.   (EETS, e.s. LXI).   London: Kegan Paul, Trench,
    Trubner, 1892.
        The Letter of Cupid is printed on pp. 72-92.

21 Hoccleve, Thomas.   The Letter of Cupid.   In The Complete
    Works of Geoffrey Chaucer.   Ed. W. W. Skeat.   Supplementary
    volume.   Oxford: Clarendon Press, 1897.
        The Letter is on pp. 217-32.

22 Gollancz, Israel, ed.   Hoccleve's Works.   II. The Minor Poems
    in the Ashburnham MS Addit. 133.   London: Oxford Univ.
    Press, 1925.
        The Letter appears on pp. 20-33.

23 Ritchie, W. Tod., ed.   The Bannatyne Manuscript Written in
    Tyme of Pest by George Bannatyne.   Edinburgh/London: William
    Blackwood, 1930.
        Vol. IV, 49-64, prints Hoccleve's Letter of Cupid.

NOTES AND STUDIES:
See also Brownlee 145, Grimal 132, Melegari 587, Rigaud 585,
Tiffen 510.

24 Neilson, William Allan.   The Origins and Sources of the 'Court
    of Love.'   1899; rpt. New York: Russell & Russell, 1967.   CdP:
    pp. 83-85, 149, 195-96, 242.
        Prints lines from Dieu d'Amours to demonstrate that CH's
    Cupid was conceived as a feudal sovereign; also to show that
    she was familiar with the Statutes of Love.

25 Frappier, Jean, ed.   Jean Lemaire de Belges' 'Les Epîtres de
    l'Amant Vert.'   Lille: Giard; Geneva: Droz, 1948.
        Introduction comments on the rhyme schemes of Dieu d'Amours
    and Epistre à Eustache Morel, pp. xxv-xxvi.

26 Robbins, Harry W., trans. and ed. The 'Romance of the Rose'
    by Guillaume de Lorris and Jean de Meun. New York: E. P.
    Dutton, 1962.
        The Introduction, by Charles W. Dunn, makes comment about
    Dieu d'Amours, p. xxvi.

27 Pearsall, Derek Albert. "The English Chaucerians." In Chaucer
    and Chaucerians. (Critical Studies on Middle English Literature.)
    University, AL: Univ. of Alabama Press, 1967. pp. 201-39.
        Hoccleve's Letter of Cupid is supposed to show that he "could
    laugh at women as well as at himself," p. 225. D. Bornstein
    strongly disagrees, see 35.

28 Mitchell, Jerome. Thomas Hoccleve: A Study in Early Fifteenth-
    Century English Poetic. Urbana: Univ. of Illinois Press, 1968.
    CdP: p. 20, 22-23, 50, 53, 59, 72, 77-84, 95.
        Describes Hoccleve's Letter of Cupid as a loose though not
    literal translation of CH's Epistre. Both works are considered
    "typical run-of-the-mill courtly poems," p. 84.

29 Tupper, Frederick. Types of Society in Medieval Literature.
    New York: Biblo & Tannen, 1968. CdP: pp. 124-26, 135.
        Includes analysis of CH's defense of women as reflected in
    Dieu d'Amours and the Cité des dames.

30 Fleming, John V. "Hoccleve's Letter of Cupid and the 'Quarrel'
    over the Roman de la Rose." MAe, XL (1971), 21-40.
        Describes Hoccleve's Letter as a "scholarly Chaucerian's re-
    sponse" to the Quarrel arguing, unlike Bornstein in 35, that it
    does not violate the spirit or intent of CH's epistle.

31 Hartung, Albert E. A Manual of the Writings of Middle English
    1050-1500. New Haven, CT: Connecticut Academy of Arts and
    Science, 1972.
        Vol. III, 747, carries notice on Thomas Hoccleve acknowledg-
    ing that his Letter of Cupid is an adaptation of CH's Epistre.

32 Angenot, Marc. Les Champions des femmes: examen du dis-
    cours sur la supériorité des femmes 1400-1800. Montreal:
    Presses de l'Univ. de Québec, 1977.
        Several paragraphs devoted to CH and her Epistre in a dis-
    cussion on pro- and antifeminist medieval literature, pp. 15-16.

33 Waller, Martha S. "Christine de Pisan's Epistle of the God of
    Love and the Medieval Image of Woman." Christianity and Litera-
    ture, XXVII (Winter 1978), 41-52.
        Discusses CH's epistle with reference to the Roman de la Rose,
    the Gospels, and medieval literature.

34 Fyler, John M. Chaucer and Ovid. New Haven, CT: Yale
    Univ. Press, 1979.
        Passing reference to CH and the Epistre on p. 99.

35   Bornstein, Diane. "Anti-feminism in Thomas Hoccleve's Transla-
     tion of Christine de Pizan's Epistre au dieu d'Amours." ELN,
     XIX (1981), 7-14.
         Demonstrates that Hoccleve's Letter of Cupid not only vio-
     lates spirit and intent of CH's Epistre but that he made his
     Letter into a parody of feminism rather than presenting it as
     the serious defense (of women) CH meant it to be.

36   Seymour, M. C. Selections from Hoccleve. Oxford: Clarendon
     Press, 1981.
         The Introduction (p. xii, xiii) notes that Hoccleve's Letter
     of Cupid is loose translation of CH's Epistre.

37   Willard, Charity Cannon. "A New Look at Christine de Pizan's
     Epistre au dieu d'Amours." In SMSRQF (1981), 71-92.
         Complete reassessment of the Epistre with special focus on
     (a) its models, content, importance in CH's career; (b) signifi-
     cance in Rose debate; (c) link with humanism; and (d) place
     in posterity. Feels the epistle should be read as a witty attack
     on the hypocrisies practiced by the Cour Amoureuse rather than
     as a defense of women. CR: 787.

38   Mitchell, Jerome. "Hoccleve Studies, 1965-1981." In Fifteenth
     Century Studies: Recent Essays. Ed. Robert F. Yaeger. Ham-
     den, CT: Archon Books, 1984. pp. 49-63.
         Carries an announcement (p. 53) re Douglas J. McMillan's
     forthcoming edition of the Letter of Cupid to be published to-
     gether with CH's original epistre. See Fenster 18 for latest
     edition of this work.

39   LE DÉBAT DE DEUX AMANS (c. 1400)
     A poetic debate in which a knight and a squire present their
     views on love. The knight sees love as an illness that can turn
     even wise men into fools and bring them sorrow. A young woman
     has a different opinion on the subject. Maintaining that men
     suffer less for love than they purport to, she complains about
     lovers not being what they once used to be but agrees with
     the knight on love's being blind. The squire differs with both.
     For him love is an ennobling experience. In an eloquent speech
     defending it, he explains why love is a source of delight and
     knightly fulfillment. After all sides have stated their positions
     the argument is submitted to Louis of Orleans (815), to whom
     the work is dedicated.

     MANUSCRIPTS:
     Brussels, BR 11034, 39 ff.
     Chantilly, Musée Condé 492, ff. 51^V-67^r.
     London, BL Harley 4431, ff. 58^V-71^r.
     Paris, Arsenal 3295, ff. 97^r-127^V.
     _____, BN f.fr. 604, ff. 39^V-51^V.

_____, ___ _____ 835, ff. 52^r-64^r.
_____, ___ _____ 1740, 32 ff.
_____, ___ _____ 12779, ff. 50^r-65^r.
_____, ___ Moreau 1686, ff. 95^r-125^v.

EDITION:
See Roy 702, II, pp. 49-109.

NOTES AND STUDIES:
See also Bailly 408, Champion 509, Riesch 588, Sallier 58, Tiffen 510, Willard 564.

40 Hoepffner, Ernest, ed. Oeuvres de Guillaume de Machaut (816). 3 vols. SATF, 1908-1921; rpt. New York: Johnson Reprint, 1965.
    In Vol. I, vi-vii, the editor deals with CH's Débat and her indebtedness to Machaut.

41 Crane, Thomas Frederick. Italian Social Customs in the Sixteenth Century and their Influence on the Literatures of Europe. New Haven, CT: Yale Univ. Press, 1920.
    Page 47 calls attention to important similarities between central theme in CH's Débat and Pietro Bembo's Gli Asolani, written about a century later.

42 Schilperoort, Johanna Catharina. Guillaume de Machaut et Christine de Pisan: étude comparative. The Hague: H. P. de Swart, 1936.
    Establishes that two of CH's works--the Débat de deux amans (1401) and Dit de Poissy (1400)--were modeled, respectively, after Machaut's Jugement dou roy de Navarre (1349) and his Jugement dou roy de Behaigne (c. 1346), as first reported by Pugh in 89.

43 Willard, Charity Cannon. "A Re-examination of Le débat de deux amants." BF, III (Fall 1974), 73-88.
    After closely analyzing this text and comparing CH with her French predecessors and later Italian writers, the author concludes that the Débat is more consistent with the dolce stil nuovo of Dante than with the traditional view of fine amour. CR: SF, 57 (1975), 527.

44 Guillaume de Machaut: poète et compositeur. (Actes et Colloques, XXIII). Paris: Klincksieck, 1982. CdP: p. 26, 34 n. 48, 61, 63, 136, 141, 241, 249, 261, 340.
    Assorted references to CH in a collection of essays presented at 1978 Machaut Colloquim. See especially paper by Cerquiglini on the Débat.

45 LE LIVRE DES TROIS JUGEMENS (c. 1400)
    This poem is dedicated to Jean de Werchin, the seneschal of

Hainault. The seneschal is appointed to preside over a love debate in which three plaintiffs air their grievances. In the first
case a jilted lady argues that she did not break her vows to a
former lover by taking on a new love. In the second instance
an eager knight, prevented from seeing his beloved by a jealous
husband, wants to know if loving another woman constituted
disloyalty. In the third situation a young woman, whose chevalier
had left her for someone of nobler birth, refuses to accept his
renewed proposals even though he has come to realize that she
is the more virtuous of the two women. Implicit in all three
arguments is the question of loyalty.

MANUSCRIPTS:
Chantilly, Musée Condé 492, ff. 79^V-91^V.
London, BL Harley 4431, ff. 71^V-81^r.
Paris, Arsenal 3295, ff. 151^V-175^V.
_____, BN f.fr. 604, ff. 60^V-70^r.
_____, __ _____ 835, ff. 64^r-73^V.
_____, __ _____ 12779, ff. 77^V-89^V.
_____, __ Moreau 1686, ff. 149^V-173^V.

EDITION:
See Roy 702, II, pp. 111-57.

NOTES AND STUDY:
See Bailly 408, Riesch 588, Willard 564.

46 L'EPISTRE D'OTHEA (L'Epistre d'Othea la deesse, que elle envoya
    a Hector de Troye quant il estoit en l'age de quinze ans) c.
    1400
    A didactic prose work with verse passages. It is extant in an
    exceptionally large number of manuscripts, some famous for their
    beautiful illuminations. The narrative is presented in form of a
    letter written by Othea, the Goddess of Prudence, to Hector of
    Troy. Intended as a spiritual guide to knighthood, it is composed
    of one hundred short chapters each comprising a Texte (in
    quatrains), a Glose, and an Allegorie. The Texte tells a story
    about a mythological hero or heroine from which the knight is
    supposed to draw a moral lesson. The Glose explains and rein-
    forces the Texte with a saying by an ancient philosopher. The
    Allegorie comments on the spiritual significance of the Texte,
    adding a citation from the Scriptures or Church Fathers. This
    work and its miniatures can also be read as a political allegory--
    see Hindman 84.

TEXTUAL SOURCES:
Chapelets des vertus
De claris mulieribus, Boccaccio (793)
Dits moreaux des philosophes, a translation by Guillaume de
    Tignonville of John of Procida's Dicta Philosophorum

Flores bibliorum, for Biblical quotations
Golden Legend, Jacobus de Voragine
Histoire ancienne jusqu'à César, for history and mythology
Inferno, Dante
Manipulus florum, Thomas Hibernicus
Ovide moralisé, for mythology

MANUSCRIPTS:

Beauvais, Bibliothèque Municipale 9, ff. 1^V-52^r.
Brussels, BR 4373-76, ff. 55^r-130^V.
_____, __ 9392, ff. 1^r-105^r.
_____, __ 9559-64, ff. 7^r-74^r.
_____, __ 11102, ff. 1^r-93^r.
_____, __ 11103, ff. 1^r-92^r.
_____, __ 11244-51, ff. 108^r-176^r.
_____, __ IV 1114, ff. 123^r-166^r.
Cambridge, Fitzwilliam Museum Add. 49, CFM 22, ff. 1^r-63^V.
_____, Newnham College 070 6, ff. 1^r-51^V.
Chantilly, Musée Condé 492, ff. 108^V-148^r.
_____, _____ 495, ff. 3^r-116^V.
_____, _____ 496, ff. 1^r-92^r.
Cologny (Geneva), Bibliotheca Bodmeriana 49, 151 ff.
Erlangen, Universitätsbibliothek 2361, ff. 3^r-126^r.
Lille, Bibliothèque Municipale 175 (formerly 391), ff. 1^r-100^r.
_____, _____ 335 (formerly 392), ff. 2^r-58^V.
London, BL Harley 219, ff. 106^r-147^r.
_____, __ _____ 4431, ff. 95^r-141^V.
_____, __ Royal 14. E. II, ff. 295^r-331^V.
_____, __ _____ 17. E. IV, ff. 272^r-316^V.
New York, Pierpont Morgan Library 929, ff. 1^r-104^r.
Oxford, Bodley 421, ff. 1^r-67^V.
_____, _____ Laud. misc. 570, ff. 24^r-92^V.
Paris, Arsenal 3295, ff. 209^r-278^V.
_____, BN f.fr. 604, ff. 83^r-111^V.
_____, __ _____ 606, ff. 1^r-46^V.
_____, __ _____ 848, ff. 1^r-20^r.
_____, __ _____ 1185, ff. 1^r-97^r.
_____, __ _____ 1186, ff. 2^r-54^V.
_____, __ _____ 1187, ff. 5^r-53^r.
_____, __ _____ 1644, ff. 1^r-58^r.
_____, __ _____ 2141, ff. 1^r-110^r.
_____, __ _____ 5026, ff. 1^r-38^V.
_____, __ _____ 12438, ff. 1^r-97^V.
_____, __ _____ 12779, ff. 106^V-141^r.
_____, __ _____ 15214, ff. 1^r-39^V.
_____, __ _____ 22986, ff. 145^r-185^V.
_____, __ _____ 25559, ff. 1^r-126^V.
_____, __ nouv. acq. fr. 6458, ff. 1^r-94^V.
_____, __ _____ 7518, ff. 1^r-47^r.
_____, __ _____ 10059, ff. 65^r-113^r.
_____, __ Moreau 1686, ff. 208^r-277^V.

_____ , ___ lat. 6482, ff. 201^r-218^v.
Rome, Biblioteca Apostolica Vaticana Reg. lat. 1323, ff. 36^r-63^v.
Stockholm, Kungliga Biblioteket Vu 22, ff. 101^r-112^v.
The Hague, Koninklijke Bibliotheek 74.G.27, ff. 1^r-96^r.

EDITIONS:

47 Les cent histoires de Troye lepistre de Othea deesse de prudence
    envoyee a l'esprit chevalereux Hector de Troy avec cent hys-
    toires. Paris: Philippe Pigouchet. n.d.
        Edition is undated but of the fifteenth century. The name
    "Othea" has been relegated to the subtitle and no mention is made
    of Hector's age as in the original work. The name given the au-
    thor is "Chrestienne."

48 S'ensuyt l'epistre de Othea, deesse de Prudence, moralisee ...
    par Christine de Pisan. Paris: la veuve Trepperel, c. 1518.
        A second copy of this edition may have been issued by the
    widow Trepperel around 1521.

49 Les cent hystoires de Troye. Paris: Philippe Le Noir, 1522.
        Early printed edition.

50 L'epistre de Othea. Rouen: Raulin Gaultier. n.d.
        This undated edition is known to have been produced before
    1534, the year Gaultier ceased printing.

51 Loukopoulos, Halina Didyky. "Classical Mythology in the Works
    of Christine de Pisan, with an edition of L'Epistre Othea from
    the Manuscript Harley 4431." Ph.D. Wayne State 1977. DAI,
    XXXVIII (1978), 6706A.
        Appendix A of this unpublished dissertation contains a critical
    edition in French of the epistre; Appendix B is a historical and
    linguistic study of Harley 4431; Appendix C is a glossary of
    difficult words; Appendix D is an index of mythological names.
    The main body of the thesis deals with the mythological content
    of CH's courtly poetry and didactic writings. Forty-seven pages
    are devoted to the literary background, sources, and classical
    myths in the Othea.
    CR: SF, 81 (1983), 539.

TRANSLATIONS:

52 Scrope, Stephen. The Epistle of Othea to Hector, or, the Boke
    of Knyghthode. c. 1440-1459.
        Scrope's Middle English translation does not use CH's original
    title nor give her name as author except obliquely in the Pre-
    face, where he states that the book was composed by the doctors
    of the University of Paris at the instigation of the "fulle wyse
    gentylwoman of Frawnce called Dame Cristine." (See Bühler 56,
    pp. xxv-xxvi, and 67 on question of which of the original French
    manuscripts Scrope used for his translation.)

53 Here foloweth the C. hystoryes of Troye, Lepistre de Othea
    deesse de Prudence envoyee a l'esprit chevalereux Hector de
    Troye London: Robert Wyer, c. 1540.
        An English translation by the printer Robert Wyer. Title is
    taken from Pigouchet 47.

54 Warner, George F., ed. The Epistle of Othea to Hector, or the
    Boke of Knyghthode: translated from the French of Christine
    de Pisan, with a dedication to Sir John Fastolf, K.G., by Stephen
    Scrope, esquire. (The Roxburghe Club, CXXXXI). London:
    J. B. Nichols & Sons, 1904.
        Based on Longleat 253, a manuscript preserved in the library
    of the Marquis of Bath, this English edition comprises the text
    of the Othea (pp. 1-114), a glossary (pp. 115-24), an index of
    proper names (pp. 125-28), and an introduction (pp. ix-xlvii).
    It speculates on Scrope's relationship to Sir John Fastolf, com-
    pares a second translation of the epistle to the present one, and
    offers an explanation as to why Scrope might have withheld CH's
    full name and title from his translation. Warner introduces in-
    ternal evidence here suggesting that the second translation was
    made by Robert Wyer (53), an Englishman hitherto known only
    as a printer. Includes reproductions from Longleat 253 and
    Harley 4431.

55 Gordon, James D., ed. The Epistle of Othea to Hector: A
    'Lytil Bibell of Knyghthod', edited from Harleian MS 838. Ph.D.
    Pennsylvania. Philadelphia: Private printing, 1942.
        This edition is based on a fifteenth-century English transla-
    tion probably made by Anthony Babygnton. It contains the text
    of the Othea (pp. 1-145), notes (pp. 147-58), a glossary (pp.
    159-68), an index to the text (pp. 169-72), and a bibliography
    (pp. lxiv-lxv). The Introduction (pp. i-lxiii) deals with the
    origin of the name Othea; the significance of Hector; the struc-
    ture, content, and narrative sources of the epistle; and its date
    of composition. Gordon also discusses the phonology and charac-
    teristics of the text and evaluates Babyngton as a translator.

56 Bühler, Curt Ferdinand, ed. The 'Epistle of Othea' translated
    from the French Text of Christine de Pisan by Stephen Scrope.
    (EETS, o.s. CCLXIV). Oxford: Oxford Univ. Press, 1970.
        Critical edition of Scrope's Middle English translation after
    Cambridge, St. John's College, MS H.5. It includes an Intro-
    duction (pp. xi-xxxii); a bibliography (pp. xxxiii-xxxvii); the
    text (pp. 3-120); an appendix containing the "Preface in Long-
    leat MS" (pp. 121-24); an appendix with a note by A. I. Doyle
    on the base manuscript (pp. 125-27); notes on the edition (pp.
    128-96); an index of Biblical quotations (pp. 197-99); an index
    of patristic quotations (pp. 200-01); a glossary (pp. 202-31);
    and index of proper names (pp. 232-36). The Introduction covers
    the dedications, choice of text, manuscripts, translations, sources,
    and principle of editing. It also analyzes the main textual

differences between Scrope's translation and those attributed to
Babyngton (55) and Wyer (53). On pp. xxv-xxvi and in Bühler
67, the editor speculates as to which of the original French manu-
scripts Scrope might have used for his English translation. This
is a highly regarded scholarly work. CR's: 751. See also:
　RQ, XXIV (1971), 355-56
　RES, XXIII (August 1972), 327
　MLR, LXIX (1974), 367

NOTES AND STUDIES:
See also Chesney 464; Hindman 484; Meiss 474, 478; Mombello
475, 502; Reno 635; Van den Gheyn 462; Willard 442.

57　Goujet, l'abbé. Bibliothèque française ou histoire de la littéra-
　　ture française. Paris: Mariette & Guerrin, 1745. IX, 422-25.
　　　Presents extracts from Othea and discusses the epistle's com-
　　position, sources, and message.

58　Sallier, l'abbé. "Notice de deux ouvrages manuscrits de Chris-
　　tine de Pisan, dans lesquels il se trouve quelques particularités
　　de l'histoire de Louis duc d'Orléans, fils de Charles V." Mém-
　　oires de Littérature, tirez des Registres de l'Académie des In-
　　scriptions et Belles Lettres. XVII. Paris: Imprimerie Royale,
　　1751. pp. 515-25.
　　　The two works under discussion are the Epistre d'Othea and
　　the Débat de deux amans.

59　Plomer, Henry Robert. Robert Wyer, Printer and Bookseller.
　　London: Bibliographical Society, 1897.
　　　Contains material on Wyer's English translation of the Epistre.

60　MacCracken, Henry Noble. "An Unknown Middle English Transla-
　　tion of L'Epître d'Othéa." MLN, XXIV (1909), 122-23.
　　　Identifies Anthony Babyngton as the translator of a third,
　　hitherto unknown, English translation of the Epître (which be-
　　came basis for Gordon's 1909 edition; see 55).

61　Campbell, P. G. C. (Percy Gerald Cadogan) 'L'Epître d'Othéa':
　　étude sur les sources de Christine de Pisan. Paris: Champion,
　　1924.
　　　Exhaustive study on CH's sources. Devotes 121 pages to
　　identifying the latter and 53 pages to epistle's title, date of
　　composition, dedications, format, early editions and text. For
　　a partial listing of Othea's sources, see 46. See also 64 and 65.
　　CR: 753.

62　Wells, William. "A Simile in Christine de Pisan for Christ's Con-
　　ception." Journal of the Warburg Institute (London), II (1938-
　　1939), 68-69.
　　　Explains the significance of having the third Article of the
　　Creed (which refers to conception of Christ) appended to the 25th
　　chapter of the Epistre.

63 Bühler, Curt Ferdinand, ed. The Dicts and Sayings of the
Philosophers: The Translations Made by Stephen Scrope, William
Worcester, and an Anonymous Translator. London: EETS, 1941.
   In the Introduction Bühler explores the relationship between
Stephen Scrope, Sir John Fastolf, William Worcester and the texts
of the Othea and the Boke of Noblesse.

64 _____ . "The Fleurs de toutes vertus and Christine de Pisan's
L'Epître d'Othéa." PMLA, LXII (1947), 32-44.
   Thinks CH used a French translation of the Fiore di vertù
as a source and model for the Othea. See also Bühler 65.

65 _____ . "The Fleurs de toutes vertus." PMLA, LXIV (1949),
600-01.
   Changes title of an Othea source from Fleurs (64) to Chapelet
des vertus.

66 _____ . "Wirk alle thyng by conseil." Speculum, XXIV (1949),
410-12.
   "Wirk" is a proverb translated from the Latin Omnia fac cum
consilio which appears in both Chaucer and CH's Othea.

67 _____ . "Sir John Fastolf's Manuscripts of the Epître d'Othéa
and Stephen Scrope's Translation of this Text." Scriptorium,
III (1949), 123-28.
   Thinks Scrope made his English translation of the Othea from
a "sister text" to Oxford, Bodley Laud. misc. 570. This MS was
prepared for Sir John Fastolf, Scrope's mentor, in 1450 or 1454.
For more on the Scrope translation see Bühler's Introduction to
56, plus 54 and 464.

68 _____ . "The Apostles and the Creed." Speculum, XXVIII
(1953), 335-39.
   Explains how CH assigned certain sections of the Creed to
each of the twelve Apostles in the Othea and compares her arrangement with the traditional one noted by M. R. James, Wil-
helm Molsdorf (in Christliche Symbolik der mittelalterlichen Kunst,
Leipzig, 1926), and others.

69 _____ . "Christine de Pisan and a Saying Attributed to Socrates." PQ, XXXIII (1954), 418-20.
   Reflects on how various Othea translators have rendered the
phrase "Et dist socrates cellui qui porte le faissel d'enuie a peine
perpetuelle" in English.

70 _____ . "The Revisions and Dedications of the Epistle of
Othea." Anglia, LXXVI (1958), 266-70.
   Suggests that Scrope's English translation of the Othea may
have been altered by William Worcester.

71 Scherer, Margaret R. The Legends of Troy in Art and Literature.

New York/London: Phaidon Press, 1963. Plates. CdP: p. 8.
98f, 154, 162, 226.
Scattered but significant references to the Othea and its
ancient sources. Plates 5, 79, 126, and 136 show how illustrators reworked Greek and Roman myths to reinforce CH's didactic
message.

72 Mombello, Gianni. "Per un' edizione critica dell' Epistre Othea
di Christine de Pizan." SF, 24 (1964), 401-17; 25 (1965), 1-12.
Studies the manuscripts, dedications, extant editions, audience, imitators, and philological criticism concerning the Othea
in preparation for a critical edition that was never published.

73 Tuve, Rosemond. Allegorical Imagery: Some Mediaeval Books
and their Posterity.   Princeton: Princeton Univ. Press, 1966.
CdP: p. 4, 4n, 33-45, 49, 51, 52, 54, 55, 65, 71, 133, 134,
172, 183n, 229, 236, 262n, 265, 266, 274, 284, 284n, 285-311,
320, 321n, 330-32.
This classic work on the meaning of allegory abounds in
references to CH and the Othea, which the author uses to show
how allegory works. Tuve sees the epistle as an important didactic tool for the training of ideal knight. CR: 781. See also
SF, 34 (1968), 124-25.

74 Bühler, Curt Ferdinand. "The Assembly of Gods and Christine
de Pisan." ELN, IV (June 1967), 251-54.
The anonymous poet who wrote the Assembly (c. 1468) may
have been inspired by CH's Epistre (c. 1400).

75 Mombello, Gianni. La tradizione manoscritta dell' 'Epistre Othea'
di Christine de Pizan: Prolegomeni all' edizione del testo. (Mem-
orie dell'Accademia delle Scienze di Torino. Classe di Scienze
Morali, Storiche e Filologiche: Serie 4^{a}, XV). Turin: Accademia delle Scienze, 1967.
Exhaustive 400-page codicological study of the Epistre. It
offers brief introduction (pp. 1-8), a minutely detailed description (pp. 9-287) and classification (pp. 289-328) of the manuscripts, and summary of the findings (pp. 328-42). Fully docu-
mented with tables, appendices, and various indexes: for manuscripts cited, incunabula, scribes, manuscript owners, catalogs,
authors and modern personages. CR: 772. See also:
Paideia, XXIV (1969), 106
RLMC, XXIII (1970), 155-56

76 _____. "Recherches sur l'origine du nom de la Déesse Othea."
Atti della Accademia delle Scienze di Torino, II Classe di Scienze
Morali, Storiche e Filologiche, CIII, 2 (July-December 1969),
343-75.
Reviews what earlier critics said about the name Othea and
offers new hypothesis as to its origin.

77 Friedman, John Block. Orpheus in the Middle Ages. Cambridge,
    MA: Harvard Univ. Press, 1970. CdP: p. 72, 120, 155, 172,
    175.
        Contains references to CH's treatment of Orpheus in the Othea
    and Avision; also includes black-and-white illustrations of Orpheus
    and Eurydice from the Epistle.

78 Jung, Marc-René. Études sur le poème allégorique en France
    au Moyen Âge. Berne: Francke, 1971. CdP: pp. 12-13, 23,
    80 n. 30, 277.
        Characterizes the Othea as an atypical medieval allegory on
    the basis of its not manifesting the usual Christian spirit.

79 Bühler, Curt Ferdinand. Early Books and Manuscripts: Forty
    Years of Research. New York: Grolier Club and Pierpont Mor-
    gan Library, 1973.
        Includes two textual studies of the Othea (pp. 412-27) re-
    printed from Bühler 64 and 65.

80 Ignatius, Mary Ann. "Manuscript Format and Text Structure:
    Christine de Pizan's Epistre Othea." Studies in Medieval Culture,
    XII (1978), 121-24.
        Discusses Othea as a work of visual art and experiment in
    form.

81 Hindman, Sandra L. "Politics and Painting in Christine de
    Pizan's Epistre d'Othéa." Fourteenth International Congress on
    Medieval Studies, 3-6 May 1979, Kalamazoo, MI.
        Presents preliminary research for 84.

82 Ignatius, Mary Ann. "Christine de Pizan's Epistre Othea: An
    Experiment in Literary Form." M & H, n.s. IX (1979), 127-42.
        Detailed analysis of epistle's formal structure and visual ele-
    ments. The latter believed to be the reason for its great popu-
    larity during Middle Ages. CR: 762.

83 Johnson, L. Stanley. "The Medieval Hector: A Double Tradi-
    tion." Mediaevalia, V (1979), 165-82.
        Places Othea's Hector in tradition of Lydgate and writers who
    have rendered him as "both brave and wise and foolish," p. 171.

84 Hindman, Sandra L. Christine de Pizan's 'Epistre Othéa': Paint-
    ing and Politics at the Court of Charles VI. (Studies and Texts,
    77). Toronto: Pontifical Institute of Mediaeval Studies, 1986.
        Important new study on the textual and pictorial content of
    the Othea. Not only reinterprets the paintings but offers fresh
    insights into their political meaning. Hindman indicates that the
    pictures were meant to amplify the political views in text and
    can be read as political allegory. Documentation includes Epi-
    logue: Historical Legacy, pp. 183-88; Appendix: Concordance of
    the Subjects of Miniatures in the Othea and their Antecedents,

with description and table of the MSS, pp. 189-203; an extensive
bibliography, pp. 204-22; index pp. 223-29; four color plates
and ninety-four figures.

85   LE LIVRE DU DIT DE POISSY (April 1400)
A narrative poem of 2,075 lines, divided into two parts. In the
first the poet recalls a visit she made with friends to the Domini-
can Convent of Saint-Louis in Poissy, where her daughter lived
as a nun. CH describes how, on a bright April morning, the
group rode on horseback along the Seine and through the forest
of Saint-Germain. Their arrival at the royal convent marks the
end of the prologue. The narrative continues with an account
of life at the priory which includes some colorful vignettes of
the convent's residents, a sketch of CH's happy reunion with
her daughter, and a description of the cloister and its grounds.
The second part of the poem presents a love debate in the tradition of Machaut. It involves two of CH's traveling companions.
The question being debated is which of the two young people
might be suffering the greater misfortune, the woman whose
lover was captured during the Battle of Nicopolis or the squire
who was rejected by his lady. As no decision can be reached
the parties arrange, through CH, to have their case heard by
the seneschal of Hainault (i.e., Jean de Werchin). The latter
is one of three possible candidates to whom the poem may have
been dedicated, the other two being the Marshall Boucicaut (794)
and Jean de Châteaumorand.

MANUSCRIPTS:
Chantilly, Musée Condé 492, ff. 92^r-108^r.
London, BL Harley 4431, ff. 81^r-94^r.
Paris, Arsenal 3295, ff. 176^r-208^v.
_____, BN f.fr. 604, ff. 70^r-82^v.
_____, ___ _____ 835, ff. 74^r-86^v.
_____, ___ _____ 12779, ff. 90^r-106^r.
_____, ___ Moreau 1686, ff. 174^r-206^v.

EDITIONS:
See Roy 702, II, pp. 159-222.

86   Pougin, Paul. "Le Dit de Poissy de Christine de Pisan. Description du prieuré de Poissy en 1400." BEC, XVIII (1857),
535-55; also pub. as 23-page offprint Paris: Firmin-Didot, 1857.
     Critical examination of poem with partial edition of text.

87   Bories, Edmond. Histoire de la ville de Poissy, ornée de 160
gravures d'après les dessins de l'auteur. 1901; rpt. Poissy:
Imprimerie de Poissy, 1925.
     Prints text of Poissy and discusses CH's stay in that town.

88   Altmann, Barbara K., ed. "Christine de Pizan's Livre du dit

de Poissy: An Analysis and Critical Edition." Ph.D. Toronto 1988.

New, unpublished dissertation consisting of an Introduction (pp. 1-15) and the thesis proper: Part I, Christine and the Tradition of the "Débat Amoureux" (pp. 16-43), Historical Aspects of the Dit de Poissy (pp. 44-55), Structure of the Poem (pp. 56-78), notes to Part I (pp. 79-92); Part II, Summary of the Contents of the Dit de Poissy (pp. 93-95), Language (pp. 96-99), Versification (pp. 100-03), Establishment of the Text (pp. 104-05), Manuscripts (pp. 106-18), notes to Part II (pp. 119-30); Part III, an edition of Le Livre du Dit de Poissy (pp. 131-220), textual notes (pp. 221-43); works cited. (Source of Reference: Barbara K. Altmann, Univ. of Toronto, Canada; typed, signed letter to E. Y., undated but c. 6 September 1988.)

STUDIES:
See also Favier 423, Kemp-Welch 586, Schilperoort 42, Wieland 375, Willard 564.

89 Pugh, Annie Reese. "Le Jugement du roi de Behaigne de Guillaume de Machaut et le Dit de Poissy de Christine de Pisan." Romania, XXIII (1894), 581-86.
Discusses CH's borrowings from Machaut (816) in Poissy and other works.

90 Binais, A. M. "Glossaire des vieux mots employés par Christine de Pisan dans le Livre du Dit de Poissy." M.A. Leeds 1926.

91 Kells, Kathleen. "Christine de Pisan's Le Dit de Poissy: An Exploration of an Alternative Life-Style for Aristocratic Women in Fifteenth-Century France." Paper presented at International Congress on Medieval Studies, Western Michigan Univ., 10 May 1985.
Poissy seen as a coherent and thematically unified piece of work connected by "Christine's concern for the place of women in fifteenth-century French Society."

92 Altmann, Barbara K. "Diversity and Coherence in Christine de Pizan's Dit de Poissy." French Forum, XII (September 1987), 261-71.
A close reading of the text reveals that CH's Dit was conceived as a diptych in which structural, lexical, and thematic elements establish a link between its two disparate parts. An earlier version of this original paper was presented at Fifth Triennial Congress of the International Courtly Literature Society, Dalfsen, The Netherlands, 9-16 August 1986. See also author's new ed. of Poissy, 88.

93 LES ENSEIGNEMENS MORAUX (1400-1401)
A series of precepts and aphorisms destined for CH's son, Jean
de Castel. The teachings in this and the next work (96) were
collected from popular sayings and such ancient texts as the
Distics of Cato. They follow in tradition of writers such as
Raymon Lull (1232-1316), who used proverbs for didactic purposes.
Text is composed of 113 quatrains.

MANUSCRIPTS:
Brussels, BR IV 1114, ff. 167^r-170^r.
Chantilly, Musée Condé 492, ff. 156^V-160^V.
Clermont-Ferrand, Bibliothèque Municipale 249, ff. 39^r-50^r.
Dresden, Sächsische Landesbibliothek (formerly Königliche Bibliothek) Oc 62, ff. 111^V-113^r.
London, BL Harley 4431, ff. 261^V-265^r.
_____, ___ Add. 17446, ff. 24^r-34^r.
Paris, Arsenal 3295, ff. 294^V-303^r.
_____, BN f.fr. 604, ff. 118^r-120^V.
_____, ___ ___ 836, ff. 42^r-45^V.
_____, ___ ___ 1181, ff. 10^V-19^V.
_____, ___ ___ 1551, ff. 52^r-59^r.
_____, ___ ___ 1623, ff. 98^r-102^V.
_____, ___ ___ 2239, ff. 18-30.
_____, ___ ___ 2307, ff. 7^r-21^V.
_____, ___ ___ 12779, ff. 149^V-153^V.
_____, ___ ___ 24439, ff. 15^r-24^r.
_____, ___ ___ 25434, ff. 116^V-131^V.
_____, ___ Moreau 1686, ff. 279^r-287^V.
_____, Bibliothèque Sainte-Geneviève 2879, ff. 47^V-54^r.
Rome, Biblioteca Apostolica Vaticana Ottobonian 2523, ff. 58^r-59^r.
Stockholm, Kungliga Biblioteket Vu 22, ff. 249^r-252^V.

EDITION:
See Roy 702, III, pp. 27-44.

NOTE AND STUDY:
See also Bartsch 340, Wieland 375.

94 Tilander, Gunnar. "Chansons inédites tirées de deux manuscrits de Modus." Neuphilologische Mitteilungen, XXXIV (1933),
187-88.
    Deals with the Enseignemens moraux in Dresden MS Oc 62, f.
111 which is similar to a copy contained in Rome, Vaticana MS
Ottobonian 2523 mentioned by E. Langlois in the Mélanges d'Arch-
éologie et d'Histoire, V (1885), 74-76.

95 Gabriel, Astrick Ladislas. The Educational Ideas of Vincent of
Beauvais. 1956; 2nd ed. South Bend, IN: Univ. of Notre Dame
Press, 1962. CdP: p. 44, 58, n.3, 60.
    Vincent of Beauvais influenced CH's views on the moral training

of women. In her Enseignemens moraux (Roy 702, III, p. 39)
she recommends him to her son.

96 LES PROVERBES MORAUX (1400-1401)
A sequel to 93. The Proverbes consist of 101 couplets.

MANUSCRIPTS:
Grenoble, Bibliothèque Municipale 871 (MS 319), ff. 1-4^V.
London, BL Harley 4431, ff. 259^V-261^V.
Paris, BN f.fr. 605, ff. 3^V-5^V.
_____, ___ _____ 812, ff. 264-266.
_____, ___ _____ 1990, incipit f. 106.

EDITION:
See Roy 702, III, pp. 45-57.

TRANSLATIONS:

97 The Morale Prouerbes of Christyne. Westminster: W. Caxton,
1478.
      This four-leaf folio contains the translation that Anthony
Woodville, the second Earl Rivers (also known as Anthony Wyde-
ville and Antoin Wideuylle), made for the Prince of Wales in the
fifteenth century.

98 Morall Prouerbes of Christyne. In Chaucer, Here begynneth
the boke of fame. London: R. Pynson [1526].
      Richard Pynson was the king's printer. Here he reprints
Woodville's translation of CH's proverbs together with a work
by Chaucer.

99 The Morale Prouerbes of Cristyne. In Thomas Frognall Dibdin,
Typographical Antiquities. London: W. Miller, 1810-1819.
      Prints excerpts from Woodville's translation, pp. 72-77.

100 The Morale Prouerbes of Cristyne. In Thomas Frognall Dibdin,
Bibliotheca Spenceriana. London: Shakespeare Press, IV,
1815.
      Reprint of Woodville's translation, pp. 218-24.

101 Morale Prouerbes, composed in French by Cristyne de Pisan,
translated by the Earl Rivers, and reprinted from the original
edition of William Caxton, A.D. 1478, with introductory remarks
by William Blades. London: Blades, East and Blades, 1859.
      An edition of Woodville's translation. It contains six un-
numbered pages of commentary by William Blades, the facsimile
edition and, on facing pages, French and English renditions of
the text in modern print. Blades states that he wanted this
volume to be executed in "close imitation" of the original by
William Caxton.

102   The Morale Prouerbes of Christyne. (The English Experience,
      CCXLI). Amsterdam/New York: Da Capo Press, Theatrvm
      Orbis Terrarvm Ltd., 1970.
          Facsimile of Caxton's 1478 edition. It has four unsigned
      leaves reproduced from Manchester, John Rylands Library MS
      M 3 3EH. Head of title reads: "Christine du Castel."

      NOTES:
      See also Lownsberry 404.

103   Walton, Thomas. "Notes sur le manuscrit 871 de la Biblio-
      thèque Municipale de Grenoble." Romania, LIV (1928), 465-75.
          Indicates that couplets 47 and 57-79 (except 77) of CH's
      Proverbes in Grenoble 871, ff. 1-108, are missing.

104   Bühler, Curt Ferdinand. "A Caxton Ghost--Made and Laid."
      Bibliographical Society of America. Papers, LIX (1965), 316.
          Argues that the English translation of CH's Trésor de la
      cité des dames (Livre des trois vertus), purported to have been
      printed by William Caxton and cited by Paulin Paris, never
      existed. Trésor may have been mistaken for the Moral Proverbs
      which were printed by Caxton (see 797).

105   Blake, N. F. Caxton and his World. London: André Deutsch,
      1969. CdP: p. 67, 87, 98, 234.
          Situates CH's Proverbs and Book of Fayttes of Armes and
      of Chyualrye within Caxton's output.

106   Painter, George D. William Caxton: A Biography. New York:
      G. P. Putnam's, 1977. CdP: pp. 90-91, 95, 95 n.2, 151 n.1,
      163, 169-70, 173, 174, 180 n.2, 211, 214.
          Modern specialist in fifteenth-century printing describes
      every known Caxton (797) edition and makes repeated refer-
      ences to CH's works as part of his output. Page 211 shows
      that her Moral Proverbs were among first English language books
      to be printed by Caxton--on 20 February 1478--at his West-
      minster Press in London.

107   LES EPISTRES SUR LE ROMAN DE LA ROSE (1401-1403)
      This collection of letters represents the correspondence that
      was exchanged between CdP, Jean de Montreuil (820), Jean
      Gerson (807), and Pierre and Gontier Col (803) during their
      famous quarrel over the Roman de la Rose (c. 1236-1276). What
      originally began as a literary discussion between CH, de Mon-
      treuil and a third (unknown) party, turned into a debate on
      women when CH accused Jean de Meun, author of the second
      part of the Roman, of misogyny and immorality. Her strong
      feminist stand in this controversy (the starting point of the
      querelle des femmes) made CH not only the first medieval woman
      to publicly defend her sex, but earned her a lasting reputation
      as women's champion and intellectual arbiter.

MANUSCRIPTS:
Berkeley, University of California UCB 109, 41 ff.
Brussels, BR 9559-9564 (9561), ff. 97^r-109^V.
Chantilly, Musée Condé 492, ff. 148^V-156^r.
London, BL Harley 4431, ff. 237^r-254^r.
Paris, Arsenal 3295, ff. 279^r-294^r.
_____, BN f.fr. 604, ff. 112^r-117^r.
_____, __ _____ 835, ff. 87^r-103^V.
_____, __ _____ 1563, ff. 178^r-199^r.
_____, __ _____ 12779, ff. 141^V-149^r.
_____, __ Moreau 1686, ff. 289^r-304^r.

EDITIONS:

108 Beck, Friedrich, ed. Les epistres sur le 'Roman de la Rose'
von Christine de Pisan nach drei Pariser Handschriften bear-
beitet und zum ersten Mal veröffentlicht. Neuburg: Griess-
mayerische Buchdruckerei, 1888.
    First publication of the Rose letters--now superseded by
Hicks 111. Beck's claim that a certain letter of Gontier Col's (803)
was missing is disproven by A. Piaget, 113, who located it in
BN f.fr. 1563. Piaget also calls attention to errors in Beck's
chronology and identification of persons.

109 Ward, Charles Frederick, ed. "The Epistles on the Romance
of the Rose and other Documents in the Debate." Ph.D. Chicago 1911.
    This edition has been replaced by Hicks 111. It offers a
discussion on the Quarrel and manuscripts (pp. 3-12), a bibliography (pp. 12-15), and the printed texts including letters by
CH (pp. 16-28, 32-37, 83-111), Gontier Col (pp. 29-31), Jean
Gerson (pp. 38-55, 76-82), Pierre Col (pp. 56-76, 112-13), and
Jean de Montreuil (pp. 114-17).

110 Langlois, Ernest. "Le traité de Gerson contre le Roman de la
Rose." Romania, XLV (1918-1919), 23-48.
    Publishes Gerson's Traité, based on three BN manuscripts,
and lists fifteen pieces relevant to the Quarrel including letters by CH, Jean de Montreuil (820), Pierre and Gontier Col
(803), and Guillaume de Tignonville. Now superseded by Hicks
111.

111 Hicks, Eric, ed. Christine de Pisan, Jean Gerson, Jean de
Montreuil, Gontier et Pierre Col. Le Débat sur le 'Roman de la
Rose.' Édition critique, introduction, traductions, notes. (Bibliothèque du XVe Siècle, XLIII). Paris: Champion, 1977. CdP:
pp. 5-26, 49-57, 115-50, 157-59, 187-94.
    Important critical edition known for its impeccable scholar-
ship and exhaustiveness. Based on the actual manuscripts, it
is the first study ever to print the entire set of documents from
the debate (pp. 5-175). In addition to the texts it offers a

lengthy Introduction of nearly one hundred pages. The latter
gives a complete synthesis of the Quarrel (pp. ix-xxiii), a history of the received ideas on the Roman and Quarrel (pp. xxiv-
li), a Chronology (pp. li-liv), a detailed analysis of the MSS
(pp. lv-lxix), a Catalogue Codicologique (pp. lxx-xcii), and
plan of the edition (pp. xciii-xcix). Hicks establishes here
that it was Jean de Montreuil (820) and not CH (as popularly
believed) who inspired the debate. Appendices contain selections from Gerson's Poenitemini sermons and extracts from the
Cité des dames, transcribed from BN f.fr. 607. Also, the
Latin texts with translation into Modern French by the editor
(on facing pages, pp. 179-94), followed by extensive Notes (pp.
197-233). Does not include CH's Epistre au dieu d'Amours
(1399) as it predates Quarrel. CR's: 761.

TRANSLATION:

112 Baird, Joseph L., and John R. Kane, trans. La Querelle de
la Rose: Letters and Documents. (Univ. of North Carolina
Studies in the Romance Languages and Literatures, CXCIX).
Chapel Hill: Univ. of North Carolina, Department of Romance
Languages, 1978.
     An English translation, not an editing of the texts, of twenty-
three letters and documents associated with the Debate. The
texts are presented chronologically instead of following the dos-
siers in the manuscripts as in Hicks 111. Includes Introduction,
pp. 11-31, and bibliography, pp. 275-76. Also, part of CH's
Epistre au dieu d'Amours. CR: 745. See also: SF, 69 (1979),
545.

NOTES AND STUDIES:
See also Boldingh-Goemans 407; Broc 584; Richardson 592, Chap.
I; Rigaud 585.

113 Piaget, Arthur. "Chronologie des Epistres sur le Roman de la
Rose." In Études romanes dédiées à Gaston Paris. Paris:
Bouillon, 1891. pp. 113-20.
     Reconstructs chronology of the letters exchanged between
CH, Jean de Montreuil (820), Pierre and Gontier Col (803),
and Jean Gerson (807) during Rose debate. Now superseded
by Hicks 111.

114 Le Duc, Alma. Gontier Col and the French Pre-Renaissance.
Lancaster, PA: New Era Printing, 1918; rpt. from RR, VII
(1916), 414-57; VIII (1917), 145-65, 290-306.
     Makes the point that Gontier Col (803) will be remembered,
if at all, as the man who wrote rude letters to CH during the
Rose quarrel.

115 Faral, Edmond. "Le Roman de la Rose et la pensée française
au XIIIe siècle." RDM, XCVI (1926), 430-57.

Discusses Roman's influence on the Middle Ages, taking the
opportunity of making sarcastic remarks about CH, p. 444.

116 Thuasne, Louis. Le Roman le la Rose. (Les Grandes Evéne-
ments Littéraires). Paris: Société française d'Éditions Littéraires et Techniques, 1929.
 Various references to CH and the Quarrel, pp. 49-52, 154-
55. Claims the Roman de la Rose had no serious challengers
until CH and Gerson (807) attacked it in fifteenth century.

117 Coville, Alfred. Gontier et Pierre Col et l'humanisme en France
au temps de Charles VI. Paris: Droz, 1934.
 Chap. X (pp. 191-228) deals with Rose quarrel. It makes
frequent reference to CH and tells who wrote what, to whom,
when. Coville credits CH with starting the Quarrel and making
significant contributions to it, but later study by Hicks (111)
indicates that it was Jean de Montreuil (820) who initiated first
phase of the debate.

118 Telle, Emile V. L'Oeuvre de Marguerite d'Angoulême reine de
Navarre et la Querelle des femmes. Toulouse: Lion, 1937;
rpt. Geneva: Slatkine, 1969.
 Chapter I deals with the controversy over Roman de la Rose
and CH's attempt to turn a clerical debate on marriage into debate on women.

119 High, Gilbert. The Classical Tradition: Greek and Roman Influences on Western Literature. n.pub., 1949; reissued New
York: Oxford Univ. Press, 1971.
 Makes passing reference to CH's opposition to the Roman de
la Rose, p. 69.

120 Gunn, Allan M. F. The Mirror of Love: A Reinterpretation of
'The Romance of the Rose.' Lubbock: Texas Tech Press, 1952.
CdP: pp. viii, 38, 39-41, 409, 432n, 463.
 Reinterprets Roman from a literary rather than philosophical
standpoint. Gunn argues that CH's reaction to poem constitutes
proof of its being a unified piece of work with both parts re-
volving around the subject of love.

121 Mourin, Louis. Jean Gerson prédicateur français. Rijksuniversiteit te Gent...113e Aflevering Bruges: De Tempel, 1952.
 Pages 124-26 outline sequence of events in Rose debate, nam-
ing CH as one of the correspondents.

122 Lieberman, Max. "Chronologie Gersonienne." Romania, LXXXIII
(1962), 52-89.
 Prints text of Gerson's (807) sermon containing first allusion
to the Roman de la Rose and makes references to CH as Gerson's
ally in Quarrel. Also prints passage from one of her epistles to
Jean de Montreuil (820) from ed. Ward, 109, p. 17.

123 Robertson, Durant Wait, Jr. A Preface to Chaucer: Studies
     in Medieval Perspectives. Princeton, NJ: Princeton Univ.
     Press, 1963. CdP: p. 21, 85, 361 ff, 363, 364, 389, 454, 460.
         Chapter IV discusses Roman de la Rose and CH's attitude
     toward its explicit sexual references. The author sees her at-
     tack on the Roman as marking a transition in medieval sensi-
     bilities.

124 Fleming, John V. "The Moral Reputation of the Roman de la
  . Rose before 1400." RPh, XVIII (1964-1965), 430-35.
         Thinks that Gerson's (807) and CH's attack on the Roman
     points to new critical view of poem.

125 _____ . The 'Roman de la Rose': A Study in Allegory and
     Iconography. Princeton, NJ: Princeton Univ. Press, 1969.
     CdP: p. vi, 12, 47, 135, 237.
         Characterizes CH as "minor" poet and suggests that her con-
     tributions to the Quarrel were exaggerated by modern feminists.
     These arguments refuted by Baird and Kane, who present dif-
     ferent view of CH, in 131 and 140.

126 Stone, Donald, Jr. France in the Sixteenth Century: A Medi-
     eval Society Transformed. Englewood Cliffs, NJ: Prentice-Hall,
     1969.
         Traces tradition of the querelle des femmes to the Rose de-
     bate and CH's and Gerson's (807) involvement in it, pp. 52-53.

127 Potansky, Peter. Der Streit um den Rosenroman. (Münchener
     Romanistiche Arbeiten, Heft XXXIII). Munich: Wilhelm Fink,
     1972.
         Complete assessment of Quarrel with biographical sketches of
     all participants (CH, pp. 24-28); a chronology; and close analy-
     sis of the letters. Deals with debate's cultural implications and
     critically examines many of CH's and Gerson's (807) writings.
     In last section, "Christine und die Frauenfrage" (pp. 224-32),
     discusses her role as defender of women. See Hicks's critique
     of Potansky in 134.

128 Batany, Jean. Approches du 'Roman de la Rose': ensemble
     de l'oeuvre et vers 8227 à 12456. Montreal/Brussels/Paris:
     Bordas, 1973.
         CH and feminist reaction to Roman de la Rose discussed in
     Chap. IV. Includes a good bibliography of various Roman edi-
     tions, pp. 7-12.

129 Cohen, Gustave. Le Roman de la Rose. Paris: CDU, 1973.
         CH and her defense of women mentioned in the Conclusion.

130 Poirion, Daniel. Le Roman de la Rose. (Connaisance des Let-
     tres). Paris: Hatier, 1973.

CH and Rose quarrel cited in the conclusion (p. 204) of this well-known work.

131 Baird, Joseph, and John R. Kane. "La Querelle de la Rose: In defense of the Opponents." FR, XLVIII (1974), 298-307.
A refutation of Fleming and his claim, in 125, that CH's role in Quarrel was exaggerated by modern feminists. Her contributions seen as significant.

132 Grimal, Pierre, ed. L'Histoire mondiale de la femme. 4 vols. Paris: Nouvelle Librairie de France, 1974.
Volume II of this illustrated history of women contains article by Yves Lefèvre, "La Femme au moyen âge en France dans la vie littéraire et spirituelle" (pp. 79-134), which briefly discusses the Epistre au dieu d'Amours and CH's role in Rose debate. Includes reproduction of the frontispiece from Harley 4431 and BN f.fr. 607. Also, portraits of queen Isabeau (811) and Jeanne de Bourbon.

133 Hicks, Eric. "The 'Querelle de la Rose' in the Roman de la Rose." BF, III (Fall 1974), 152-69.
Tries to reconstruct contents of Jean de Montreuil's (820) lost treatise from CH's reply to him. Hicks sees an analogy between the treatise and the argument of the Rose, suggesting that the poem contains "a proxy Christine" (p. 155) to present the other side of the argument.

134 _____. "De l'histoire littéraire comme cosmogonie: la Querelle du Roman de la Rose." Critique, XXXII, 348 (May 1976), 510-19.
Reviews Potansky's (127) and Poirion's (130) books and examines Gerson's (807) role in Quarrel, speculating as to whether he was the "notable clerc" CH refers to in one of her letters. This article now incorporated in Hicks 111.

135 _____, and Ezio Ornato. "Jean de Montreuil et le débat sur le Roman de la Rose." Romania, XCVIII (1977), 36-64, 186-220.
Important redating of documents belonging to first phase of Quarrel. Focusing on de Montreuil's (820) contribution the study covers the Epître 103, CUM UT DANT; Relation entre les Epîtres 103 et 116; Destinaire de l'Epître 103; Nicolas de Clamanges et le "Notable Clerc" de Christine de Pizan, and other relevant topics. Also presents evidence suggesting that CH actively promoted second phase of Quarrel. Chronological table included. CR: 759.

136 Monter, E. William. "The Pedestal and the Stake: Courtly Love and Witchcraft." In Becoming Visible: Women in European History. Ed. Renate Bridenthal and Claudia Koonz. Boston: Houghton Mifflin, 1977. pp. 119-36.

Includes casual remarks about CH and the quarrel over the
Roman; also, on Burgundian Court of Love.

137   Furr, Grover Carr, III.   "The Quarrel of the Roman de la Rose
      and Fourteenth Century Humanism."   Ph.D. Princeton 1979.
      DAI, XXXIX (1979), 6115-16A.
      Includes discussion on CH.

138   Badel, Pierre-Yves.   Le 'Roman de la Rose' au XIVe siècle:
      étude de la réception de l'oeuvre.   (Publications Romanes et
      Français, CLIII).   Geneva: Droz, 1980.
      Comprehensive study of the Roman's influence in fourteenth-
      century France, with full account of Quarrel and CH's role in
      it (pp. 411-47).   Badel makes the point that only Guillaume De-
      guilleville, Jean Gerson (807) and CH really understood what
      Jean de Meun was trying to say.   CR: 744.   See also: MLR,
      LXXXVI (1981), 957.

139   Ott, Karl August.   Der Rosenroman.   (Erträge der Forschung,
      CILV).   Darmstadt: Wissenschaftliche Buchgeselschaft, 1980.
      Pages 34-40 discuss the Quarrel, the individuals associated
      with it, and its historical meaning.   Bibliography, pp. 192-215.

140   Baird, Joseph L.   "Pierre Col and the Querelle de la Rose."
      PQ, LX (1981), 273-86.
      Feels modern scholarship has been too heavy-handed in its
      approach to Quarrel; suggests latter be reevaluated in terms of
      its tone and implied attitude.

141   Hicks, Eric.   "La tradition manuscrite des épîtres sur la Rose."
      In SMSRQF (1981), 93-123.
      Another outstanding contribution on the Epistres by Hicks.
      Reexamines the manuscript sources and documents relating to
      Quarrel; establishes correct chronology; sorts out intricate text-
      ual problems; explains function and organization within the manu-
      scripts of the different dossiers; and, finally, puts everything
      into proper literary and historical perspective.   Also sheds light
      on hitherto unrecognized role of CH as epitres editor.   This
      study, on which 111 is based, was supposed to have been pub-
      lished before the book.   CR: 760.   See also: Speculum, LX
      (1985), 229-30.

142   Moody, Helen Fletcher.   "The Debate of the Rose: The Querelle
      des Femmes as Court Poetry."   Ph.D. California, Berkeley 1981.
      DAI, XLII (1982), 3153A.
      In concluding chapter examines CH's role in quarrel over the
      Roman.

143   Richards, Earl Jeffrey.   Dante and the 'Roman de la Rose':
      An Investigation into the Vernacular Narrative Context of the
      'Commedia.'   Tübingen: Max Niemeyer, 1981.

Reviews history of attempts to find parallels between the
Roman and Commedia, starting with CH's remarks in the Quarrel
and Laurent de Premierfait's comparison made around 1410. On
p. 73 prints CH's explicit reference to Dante in her 20 October
1402 letter to Pierre Col (803).

144 Luria, Maxwell. A Readers' Guide to the 'Roman de la Rose.'
Hamden, CT: Archon Books, 1982. CdP: pp. 4-5, 11, 24,
52, 54, 63-65, 68, 183-202, 268n.
     Very good manual for nonspecialist. Part I deals with Ro-
man's authors, manuscripts, and editions; also with Quarrel and
the literary-critical issues it raised. Parts II and III provide
analytical outline of the poem, with narrative summary in English
and glossary of personifications. Part IV (pp. 183-202) prints
some of CH's and Pierre Col's (803) letters. Includes bibliographies.

145 Brownlee, Kevin. "Discourses of the Self: Christine de Pizan
and the Rose." RR, LXXIX (1988), 199-221.
     Lengthy psychological and literary analysis of CH's early
engagement with the Roman de la Rose. The author sees her
involvement with the Roman as an "extended act of self-legitima-
tion" (p. 200) and the Epistres as the culmination of her long
struggle with this work both as a reader and writer. Deals
also with the Epistre au dieu d'Amours and Dit le la Rose.

146 LE DIT DE LA ROSE (14 February 1402)
This poem was composed on St. Valentine's Day as a tribute to
Charles VI's Court of Love, and dedicated to duke Louis of
Orleans (815). It depicts a social gathering held at the duke's
Parisian court, to which CH had been invited. After giving a
poetic description of the evening's festivities, CH tells how
there suddenly appeared among the guests the beautiful Goddess
of Loyalty. She had been sent by the God of Love to found the
Order of the Rose and to distribute roses to each guest pledg-
ing loyalty to the opposite sex. When the celebration is over
CH retires to her room. She falls asleep and has a vision.
Loyalty appears once more to say that the God of Love was
concerned about men who speak ill of women. The Order of
the Rose has been established to put an end to such bad practices. Before departing, Loyalty leaves a charter of the Order
on CH's pillow. She must now go and spread the word, insti-
tuting the Order of the Rose wherever men of good will can be
found.

MANUSCRIPTS:
Chantilly, Musée Condé 492, ff. 74^r-79^r.
Paris, Arsenal 3295, ff. 141^r-151^r.
_____, BN f.fr. 604, ff. 56^v-60^v.
_____, __ ____ 12779, ff. 72^r-77^r.
_____, __ Moreau 1686, ff. 139^r-149^r.

EDITIONS:
See Roy 702, II, pp. 29-48.

147   Heuckenkamp, Ferdinand, ed. 'Le Dit de la rose' von Christine
      de Pisan. Ph.D. Vereinigen Friedrichs-Universität. Halle a.s.:
      Buchdruckerei des Waisenhauses, 1891.
         The text (pp. 1-19) is based on BN f.fr. 604. It is preceded
      by a four-page Introduction, which discusses the Order of the
      Rose and various personalities associated with the Quarrel.

      TRANSLATION:
      See Fenster 18.

      STUDY:
      See also Brownlee 145, Champion 509, Dow 594, Tiffen 510.

148   Willard, Charity Cannon. "Christine de Pizan and The Order
      of the Rose." In IFW (1981), 51-67.
         Complete analysis of the Dit and the circumstances surround-
      ing its composition. Sees poem as a "significant turning point
      in Christine's literary career" (p. 63) but expresses doubts as
      to the Order's actual existence. CR: SF, 78 (1982), 529.

149   L'OROYSON NOSTRE SEIGNEUR (1402-1403)
      A prayer of sixty quatrains recalling the life and Passion of
      Christ our Lord.

      MANUSCRIPTS:
      Chantilly, Musée Condé 492, ff. 164^r-165^v.
      London, BL Harley 4431, ff. 257^r-258^r.
      Paris, BN f.fr. 604, ff. 121^r-^{v}.
      _____, ___ _____ 836, ff. 63^r-65^r.

      EDITION:
      See Roy 702, III, pp. 15-26.

150   L'OROYSON NOSTRE DAME (1402-1403)
      A prayer of eighteen stanzas. Expressing concern about the
      state of the French kingdom, it invokes the names of the Virgin
      Mary, the king and queen of France, the entire royal family,
      and persons of various estates and circumstances.

      MANUSCRIPTS:
      Chantilly, Musée Condé 492, ff. 161^r-162^v.
      London, BL Harley 4431, ff. 265^r-266^v.
      Paris, Arsenal 3295, ff. 303^v-307^r.
      _____, BN f.fr. 836, ff. 45^v-47^r.
      _____, ___ _____ 12779, ff. 154^r-155^v.

EDITIONS:
See Roy 702, III, pp. 1-9; see also Thomassy 701.

151 L'Oroyson Nostre Dame. Utrecht: De Roos, 1942.
A 22-page offprint from Roy (above) with lay-out by J. van
Krimpen.

TRANSLATION:

152 Misrahi, Jean, and Margaret Marks, trans. 'L'Oroyson Nostre
Dame': Prayer to our Lady by Christine de Pisan. New York:
Kurt H. Volk, 1953.
French and English texts are printed in adjacent columns.

153 LES QUINZE JOYES NOSTRE DAME (1402-1403)
A poem to the Virgin Mary asking her to pray for CH.

MANUSCRIPTS:
Chantilly, Musée Condé 492, ff. 163^{r}-^{v}.
London, BL Harley 4431, ff. 267^{r}-^{v}.
Paris, Arsenal 3295, ff. 307^{v}-308^{v}.
_____, BN f.fr. 836, ff. 47^{r}-48^{r}.
_____, ___ _____ 12779, ff. 156^{r}-^{v}.

EDITION:
See Roy 702, III, pp. 11-14.

154 LE LIVRE DU CHEMIN DE LONG ESTUDE (written between 5
October 1402 and 20 March 1403)
An allegorical poem inspired by Dante, Boethius, and the Roman de la Rose. Its 6,392 lines recount a dream-vision in which
the poet and her guide, the Cumean sibyl, undertake an imagi-
nary voyage. After making a tour of the Orient and Middle
East, they rise to the heavens where they survey the firmament.
The Cumean sibyl shows CH cosmological events like a comet,
the sun, the stars, the planets. Eventually they arrive at the
Court of Reason. There they see the four queens who rule the
world: Wealth, Wisdom, Chivalry, and Nobility. Reason, the
reigning queen, is seated in the center. She has received a
complaint from mother Earth about the vices of her children and
now wants the four queens to find a solution for these troubling
problems. The queens suggest that a universal monarch be
found who would rule the world and reestablish order. In
selecting such a monarch each queen nominates a candidate with
her own attributes: Nobility chooses a noble prince; Chivalry,
a valiant knight; Wealth, a rich man; Wisdom someone learned,
a philosopher-king like the late Charles V. As no immediate
agreement can be reached, the choice of a ruler is left to a
court of earthly judges. These turn out to be none other than

the French princes. CH is appointed as Reason's messenger
and descends to earth to await the outcome of the princes' decision. The poem ends with CH's mother knocking on her bed-
room door to awaken her from her dream.

TEXTUAL SOURCES:
De Consolatione Philosophiae, Boethius.
Divine Comedy, Dante (CH took her title for Long estude from
    the first Canto of the Inferno where Dante tells Virgil that
    he read the Aeneid with "long study"--The Portable Dante,
    ed. P. Milano, New York, 1969, p. 6).
Manipulus florum, Thomas Hibernicus.
Policraticus, John of Salisbury.
Travels, John Mandeville.

MANUSCRIPTS:
Berlin, Königliche Bibliothek fr. 133 (disappeared 1939-1945).
Brussels, BR 10982, 100 ff.
_____, ___ 10983, 96 ff.
Chantilly, Musée Condé 492-493, ff. 184^r-231^v.
London, BL Harley 4431, ff. 178^a-219^c.
Paris, BN f.fr. 604, ff. 122^r-160^v.
_____, ___ _____ 836, ff. 1-41^v.
_____, ___ _____ 1188, 101 ff.
_____, ___ _____ 1643, 93 ff.

EDITIONS:

155 Le chemin de long estude de dame Christine de Pise ou est
     descrit le debat esmeu au parlement de Raison, pour l'élection
     du Prince digne de gouverner le monde. Traduit de langue
     Romanne en prose Françoyse, par Jan Chaperon, dit lassé de
     Repos. Paris: Estienne Groulleau, 1549.
         Early printed prose edition by Jean Chaperon. He states in
     the Preface that he wanted to make CH's text more understand-
     able for 16th century readers.

156 Püschell, Robert, ed. Le Livre du chemin de long estude par
     Christine de Pisan, publié pour la première fois d'après sept
     manuscrits de Paris, de Bruxelles et de Berlin. Berlin: R.
     Damköhler, 1881; Paris: Le Soudier, n.d.; new ed. Berlin:
     Hettler, 1887; rpt. of 1887 ed. Geneva: Slatkine, 1974.
         This text (pp. 1-270) is based on seven of the nine extant
     manuscripts: Paris, BN f.fr. 1643, 836, 1188, 604; Brussels,
     BR 10982, 10983; and Berlin, Königliche Bibliothek fr. 133.
     Püschell's Introduction deals with dialect, versification, and the
     manuscripts. Includes glossary.

157 Eargle, Patricia Bonin. "An Edition of Christine de Pisan's
     Livre du chemin de lonc estude." Ph.D. Georgia 1973. DAI,
     XXXIV (1974), 5167A.

The Introduction provides an overview of CdP, pp. 1-14; a bibliography, pp. 15-16; a discussion of the work, pp. 17-21; and a description of the manuscripts, pp. 22-24. The text, pp. 25-318 (based on Harley 4431 with variants from the remaining manuscripts), is followed by a glossary, pp. 320-47, and a list of works consulted, pp. 348-50.

NOTES AND STUDIES:
See also Beltran 306, Blanchard 454, Cropp 444, Joukovsky-Micha 425, Patch 177, Wieland 375, Willard 442.

158 Beck, Friedrich (Frederico). "Un imitazione dantesca nell'antica letteratura francesca." L'Alighieri, II (1890), 381-84.
Discusses Dante's influence on CH and Long estude.

159 Toynbee, Paget. "Christine de Pisan and Sir John Maundeville." Romania, XXI (1892), 228-39.
Traces ll. 1191-1568 in Long estude (1402-1403) to the Travels of Sir John Maundeville (1356).

160 Hauvette, Henri. "Dante dans la poésie française de la Renaissance." Annales de l'Université de Grenoble, XI (1899), 137-64; rpt. in Hauvette, Études sur la 'Divine Comédie': la composition du poème et son rayonnement, Paris: Champion, 1922. pp. 149-53.
Prints excerpts from Long estude to show CH's indebtedness to Dante.

161 Farinelli, Arturo. "Dante nell'opere di Christine de Pisan." In Aus romanischen Sprachen und Literaturen: Festschrift Heinrich Morf zur Feier seiner fünfundzwanzigjährigen Lehrtätigkeit von seinen Schülern dargebracht. Halle: Max Niemeyer, 1905, pp. 117-52; rpt. in Farinelli, Dante e la Francia dall'Età Media al secolo di Voltaire, Milan: Hoepli, 1908, I, 146-92.
One of first studies to show Dante's influence on CH in Long estude and other works. It was Farinelli who was responsible for crediting CH with being first French writer to cite Dante and for perpetuating idea that she actually "discovered" and introduced him to France in the fifteenth century. This claim disputed by G. di Stefano in 168, pp. 159-61.

162 Merkel, Maria. "Le Chemin de long estude, primo tentativo di imitazione dantesca in Francia." Rassegna nazionale, XXXII (1921), 189-211, 243-58.
Early study on CH's borrowings from Dante.

163 Picco, Francesco. Dame de Francia e poeti d'Italia. Turin: Lattes, 1921.
Deals with Dante's influence on CH and Long estude.

164 Friederich, Werner P. Dante's Fame Abroad: 1350-1850. (Univ.

of North Carolina Studies in Comparative Literature, II).
Chapel Hill: Univ. of North Carolina Press, 1950. CdP: p.
25, 58-59, 60.
   Identifies elements of Dante in CH's works and discusses
traits they had in common.

165   Rickard, Peter. Britain in Medieval French Literature 1100-
      1500. Cambridge: Cambridge Univ. Press, 1956. CdP: p.
      119, 180-81, 241, 245.
         Finds evidence of British influence in Long estude and the
      Autres ballades XXII, the first being indebted to the Poli-
      craticus of John of Salisbury, the second to the Travels of
      Sir John Maundeville.

166   Petroni, Liano. "La prima segnalazione di Dante in Francia."
      In Dante e Bologna nei tempi di Dante. Bologna: Commissione
      per i testi di lingua, 1967. pp. 375-82.
         One of the major studies to suggest that CH was first French
      writer to cite Dante. This claim subsequently challenged by
      G. di Stefano in 168, pp. 159-61. Dante's influence to be seen
      in Long estude and other works.

167   Batard, Yvonne. "Dante et Christine de Pisan (1364-1430)."
      In Missions et démarches de la critique: mélanges offerts au
      Professeur J. A. Vier. (Publications de l'Univ. de Haute-
      Bretagne). Paris: C. Klincksieck, 1973, pp. 345-51; rpt. in
      Dante nel pensiero e nella esegesi dei secoli XIV et XV. (Con-
      gresso nazionale di studi danteschi, Melfi 1974). Florence:
      Leo S. Olschki, 1975. pp. 271-76.
         Notes that while frequently using Dantean images (in Long
      estude, Mutacion), CH seems to lack the Italian poet's vision.

168   Di Stefano, Giuseppe. "Alain Chartier ambassadeur à Venice."
      In CPFEHR (1974), 155-68.
         See pp. 159-61 where the author identifies Philippe de
      Mézières (819) as first French writer to cite Dante--in his
      Songe du vieil pelerin (1389). This honor had previously been
      bestowed upon CH by Arturo Farinelli (161), but di Stefano now
      shows that de Mézière's reference to Dante in Songe antedates
      her writings, both the Epistres sur le Roman de la Rose (1401-
      1403) and Long estude (1402-1403).

169   Gompertz, Stéphane. "Le voyage allégorique chez Christine
      de Pisan." In Voyage, quête, pèlerinage dans la littérature et
      la civilisation médiévales. Sénéfiance, II. (Cahiers du CUER
      MA). Paris: Champion, 1976. pp. 197-208.
         Comparative study of the allegorical voyages in the Livre de
      la mutacion de Fortune and Long estude. CH's "voyages"
      thought to differ from those of her predecessors in that she
      makes use of an authorial "I." CR: SF, 63 (1977), 519.

170 Richards, Earl Jeffrey. "Christine de Pizan and Dante: A
     Reexamination." ASNSL, CCXXII, 137 (1985), 100-11.
        Presents a "balanced evaluation of Christine's reception of
     Dante which both considers the positive aspects of Christine's
     use of Dante and analyzes the limitations of this reception"
     (p. 101). Richards indicates that CH was a significant though
     hitherto underestimated interpreter of the Italian poet. CR:
     SF, 92 (1987), 271

171 AUTRES BALLADES (Ballades de divers propos) 1402-1407
     The Autres ballades consist of fifty-three poems. They deal
     with different themes. In Ballade XII, CH pays homage to the
     knights of Marshal Boucicaut's Ordre de l'Escu Vert à la Dame
     Blanche (794). Ballades XXIX, XXX, XXXI celebrate a joust
     held at Montendre in 1402 (on these, see 3). Several poems in
     the collection were written for the nobility: No. XXIX for
     Louis of Orleans (815); No. XXXVI for queen Isabeau of France
     (811); Nos. II, II, XXI for the French knight Charles d'Albret.
     Ballade XLII records the death of CH's patron, duke Philip of
     Burgundy (823)--on this poem, see 172.

     MANUSCRIPTS:
     Chantilly, Musée Condé 492, ff. 27^r-34^V.
     London, BL Harley 4431, ff. 37^V-48^r.
     Paris, Arsenal 3295, ff. 53^V-68^V.
     _____, BN f.fr. 604, ff. 21^r-27^r.
     _____, ___ ____ 835, ff. 34^r-44^V.
     _____, ___ _____ 12779 ff. 25^r-32^V.
     _____, ___ Moreau 1686, ff. 51^V-66^V.

     EDITION:,
     See Roy 702, I, pp. 207-69.

     STUDIES:

172 Coville, Alfred. "Sur une ballade de Christine de Pisan." In
     Entre camarades (Société des Anciens Élèves de la Faculté des
     Lettres de l'Université de Paris) Paris: Félix Alcan, 1901.
     pp. 181-94.
        Deals with Autres ballades XLII (Roy 702, I, pp. 255-57)
     which CH wrote to commemorate the death, on 27 April 1404,
     of her patron Philip the Bold (823).

173 Lecoy, Felix. "Note sur quelques ballades de Christine de
     Pisan." In Fin du Moyen Âge et Renaissance: mélanges de
     philologie française offerts à Robert Guiette. Antwerp: De
     Nederlandsche Boekhandel, 1961. pp. 107-14; rpt. in MF,
     XII (1983), 43-49.
        Informative study which explains how CH edited the Autres
     ballades. Lecoy suggests that Roy (702, I, pp. 207-69) should

have printed fifty instead of fifty-three ballades since CH pur-
posely dropped three ballades from her 1407-1410 Collection.
CR: SF, 18 (1962), 529.

174 LE LIVRE DE LA MUTACION DE FORTUNE (1403)
An allegorical poem consisting of a prose section and 23,636
lines of octosyllabic rhyming couplets. It is one of CH's longest and most important poetic compositions. Divided into seven
parts, it recounts the poet's encounter with the Goddess of
Fortune, traces the role of Fortune in human affairs, and presents a universal history.
    Part I (ll. 1-1460) offers an autobiographical account in
which CH allegorizes significant events in her life and introduces the reader to the person who compiled this book. It is
here that we learn about her traumatic "mutacion." Assuming
the dual role of author and protagonist, CH describes how she
was brought into Fortune's employ. She blames the capricious
Goddess for taking away her beloved husband and for trans-
forming her against her will into a man, but credits her sexual
transformation with making a writer of her.
    In Part II (ll. 1461-4272) the scene shifts to the revolving
Castle of Fortune and to the allegorical figures guarding the
entrance to it. This section deals with the residents and
prospective residents of the castle, the latter being so consumed
with a desire for worldly goods that they can barely wait to
reach the Gate of Wealth. The majority of those already in-
side seems to pursue the paths of Pride and Spite rather than
the loftier but more difficult paths of Knowledge and Righteous-
ness. Fortune herself lives in the castle along with her two
brothers, Eure and Meseur, who govern it.
    Part III (ll. 4273-7052) considers the castle's other inhabi-
tants among whom are the great and powerful from CH's own era.
There is a discussion on the great schism of the Church, the
corruption of churchmen, and the Papacy. CH takes the opportunity here of making some humorous remarks about the two
Popes quarreling over the chair of St. Peter. After lamenting
the fate of Richard II of England, to whom Fortune had not
been kind, she mentions the conflict between the Guelphs and
the Ghibellines of Italy and evokes her birthplace, Venice.
This is followed by a favorable assessment of Italians as opposed
to an unfavorable estimate given the French. The latter are
censured for their vices, especially for the sins of sloth, pride,
and envy, and for their pejorative treatment of women. Nobles
as well as commoners are chastised for excessive drinking, and
merchants are further accused of engaging in dishonest practices.
    Part IV (ll. 7053-8748) gives a description of the physical
features of the Castle of Fortune. One of its great chambers
is the Hall of Fame where magnificent murals illustrate the ex-
ploits of princes. Various branches of knowledge are represented here: Theology, Physics, Mathematics, Music, Geometry,

Astronomy, Ethics, Economics, Politics, Grammar, and Rhetoric.
Following some observations on Fortune's effect on civilization
CH narrates a universal history, beginning with the biblical
story of the Creation and culminating with an account of the
Jews and the fall of Jerusalem (in prose).

Part V (ll. 8749-13,456) is a survey of ancient history covering the kingdoms of Assyria, Persia, Egypt, and Greece, with
special reference to the women of these cultures.

Part VI (ll. 13,457-18,244) turns to mythology and relates
the stories of the Amazons, Ulysses, Hercules, the Trojan Wars,
and the destruction of Troy.

Part VII (ll. 18,245-23,636) deals with the Roman empire and
tells about Aeneas and Augustus. It chronicles the Carthaginian,
Spanish, and Teutonic Wars and recalls the deeds of Alexander
the Great.

CH's history of the world goes up to the fifteenth century,
concluding with contemporary persons and events. Toward the
end of the poem (ll. 23,277-23,594) she cites well-known European leaders with whom she or her family has had some connection. After mentioning Louis I of Hungary, the duke of Milan,
Edward III, and again Richard II of England, she names the
kings of France: John II, Charles V (798), and Charles VI
(799). Also mentioned are her patrons, Louis of Orleans (815)
and the dukes of Berry (812) and Burgundy (823), to whom
this work was presented on 4 January 1404.

TEXTUAL SOURCES:
Acerba, Cecco Ascoli
Anticlaudianus, Alain de Lille
De Consolatione Philosophiae, Boethius
Divine Comedy, Dante
Etymologiae, Isidore de Seville
Faits des Romains (probably)
Flores chronicorum, Bernard Gui
Histoire ancienne jusqu'à César
Historia de proeliis
Livre du trésor, Brunetto Latini
Mappemonde
Ovide moralisé
Panthere d'Amours, Nicole de Margival
Roman de Fauvel
Roman de la Rose, Guillaume de Lorris and Jean de Meun
Solatium ludi scacchorum, Jacques de Cessoles; Jean de Vignai's
     translation of

MANUSCRIPTS:
Brussels, BR 9508, 190 ff.
Chantilly, Musée Condé 493, ff. 232^r-427^r.
_____, _____ 494, 177 ff.
Munich, Bayerische Staatsbibliothek Cod. gall. 11, 140 ff.
Paris, Arsenal 3172, 301 ff.

_____, BN f.fr. 603, ff. 81–242.
_____, ___ ____   604, ff. 160^V–314.
_____, ___ ____   24530, 181 ff.
_____, ___ nouv. acq. fr. 14852, 2 ff.
The Hague, Koninklijke Bibliotheek 78. d. 42, 170 ff.
Private Collection: M. Pierre Bérès, 178 ff., formerly in library of Sir Sidney Cockerell.

EDITION:

175   Solente, Suzanne, ed.   Le Livre de la mutacion de Fortune par Christine de Pisan.   (SATF).   4 vols.   Paris: Picard, 1959–1966.
       First unabridged edition of one of CH's major works.   Vol. I contains first two parts of the text (pp. 7–153), explanatory notes (pp. 156–65), and a solid Introduction.   It provides a discussion on the author and date of composition (pp. ix–xi), an analysis of the poem (pp. xi–xxx), a complete account of its sources (pp. xxx–xcviii), a detailed description of the manuscripts (pp. xcix–cxxxviii), and a statement on establishment of the text (pp. cxxxviii–cxlii).   Vol. II presents the third, fourth, and fifth parts of text (pp. 3–331) together with explanatory notes (pp. 333–65).   Vol. III comprises part six and portions of part seven of text (pp. 5–272), with explanatory notes (pp. 273–91).   Vol. IV consists of concluding section of the poem (pp. 1–80), explanatory notes (pp. 81–95), a commentary on fragment BN 14852 (pp. 97–99), a table of proper names (pp. 101–85), a glossary (pp. 186–251), and a table of contents (pp. 253–63).   The edition is highly rated by critics.   CR's:
       SF, 13 (1961), 131–32
       LR, XVI (1962), 391–92

NOTES AND STUDIES:
See also Batard 167, Blanchard 454, Bornstein 637, pp. 11–28, Cropp 444, Fox 435, Gompertz 169, Joukovsky-Micha 425, Kemp-Welch 582, Meiss 480, Mühlethaler 543, Muir 453, Willard 442.

176   Patch, Howard Rollin.   "Fortuna in Old French Literature."   Smith College Studies in Modern Languages, IV (1923), 1–32.
       Situates the Mutacion within pagan tradition of the Roman de la Rose and Boethius's Consolatio, basing his study primarily on Koch's summary of this work in 382.

177   _____.   The Goddess Fortuna in Mediaeval Literature.   1927: rpt. New York: Octagon Books, 1967.   CdP: notes p. 42, 48, 51, 52, 56, 60, 61, 64, 67, 68, 70, 71, 84, 91, 94, 96, 101, 102, 104, 105, 114, 117–19, 144.
       The numerous references to CH in the Notes deal with her portrayal of Fortuna in the Mutacion and Chemin de long estude.

178 Flutre, L.-M. "Eustache Deschamps et Christine de Pisan ont-
      ils utilisé les Faits de Romanes?" CN, XIII (1953), 229-40.
      Believes CH and Deschamps (804) were probably both ac-
      quainted with the Faits but found no evidence linking Deschamps
      directly to it. CH, on the other hand, may have borrowed from
      it in the Mutacion, as demonstrated by the chapter (XLIII, Book
      6) printed here.

179 Solente, Suzanne. "Le Jeu des échecs moralisés source de la
      Mutacion de Fortune." In Recueil de travaux offerts à M.
      Clovis Brunel par ses amis, collègues et élèves. (Mémoires et
      Documents publiés par la Société de l'École des Chartes, XII).
      Paris: Société de l'École des Chartes, 1955. II, 556-65.
      Reveals that Pt. III of the Mutacion is based on Jeu, Jean de
      Vignai's translation of Jacques de Cessoles' Solatium ludi scac-
      chorum.

180 Cigada, Sergio. "Il tema arturiano del 'Château Tournant':
      Chaucer e Christine de Pisan." SM, serie terza, II (1961), 576-
      606.
      Discusses Arthurian theme of the "revolving castle" and ex-
      plains how it figures in CH's Mutacion and Chaucer's House of
      Fame.

181 Woledge, Brian. "Le théme de la pauvreté dans la Mutacion de
      Fortune de Christine de Pisan." In Fin du Moyen Âge et Ren-
      aissance: mélanges de philologie françaises offerts à Robert
      Guiette. Antwerp: De Nederlandsche Boekhandel, 1961. pp.
      97-106.
      This study on CH's attitude toward poverty suggests that
      her compassionate treatment of the poor in the Mutacion was
      well ahead of her times.

182 Iinuri, L. "La fortuna de Dante en France de Christine de
      Pisan à Saint-John Pére." BSED, XVI (1967), 35-45.
      Comments on how CH used Dante's image of Fortune.

183 Clark, Cecily. "Charles d'Orléans: Some English Perspectives."
      MAe, XL (1971), 254-61.
      Orleans's (800) concept of Fortune as a personal enemy was
      not new, "having been used both by Christine de Pisan [in the
      Mutacion] and by Alain Chartier," p. 258.

184 Margolis, Nadia. "The Poetics of History: An Analysis of
      Christine de Pizan's Livre de la mutacion de Fortune." Ph.D.
      Stanford 1977. DAI, XXXVIII (1977), 3544A.
      This unpublished dissertation examines the Mutacion from
      three different angles: (1) as a poetic autobiography; (2) as
      historiography; and (3) as literature. Margolis analyzes the
      poem's structure and imagery, devoting some sixty pages (out
      of three hundred) to CH's representation of Fortuna. She also

considers how CH approached the question of feminism and free
will.

185 LE DIT DE LA PASTOURE (May 1403)
     A narrative poem in the pastoral tradition. It tells the story
     of a simple shepherdess, Marotile, who, while tending sheep in
     the forest, meets and falls in love with a charming nobleman.
     Realizing that Marotile is courting disaster, her friend Lorète
     urges her to stick to her own kind. But Marotile, greatly en-
     amored of the knight, cannot give him up. She continues to
     wait for him in the forest and they spend happy hours together.
     Eventually, however, the knight's visits decrease. As his ab-
     sences grow longer and longer Marotile is filled with anguish.
     In the end she becomes despondent, noting ruefully that her
     beloved has now been gone for more than a year. The mood
     of the poem has changed from carefree joy to wistful regret.

     MANUSCRIPTS:
     Baltimore, Walters Art Gallery 316, 15 ff.
     Chantilly, Musée Condé 492, ff. 166^r-182^v.
     London, BL Harley 4431, ff. 221^r-236^r.
     _____, Westminster Abbey Library MS 21, ff. 65^a-75^b.
     Paris, Arsenal 3295, ff. 309^r-344^v.
     _____, BN f.fr. 836, ff. 48^r-62^v.
     _____, __ ____ 2184, 45 ff.
     _____, __ ____ 12779, ff. 157^r-174^v.

     EDITION:
     See Roy 702, II, pp. 223-94.

     NOTES AND STUDIES:
     See also Le Gentil 411, Reisch 588, Wolfzettel 544.

186 Huizinga, Johan. The Waning of the Middle Ages: A Study of
     the Forms of Life, Thought and Art in France and the Nether-
     lands in the XIVth and XVth Centuries. 1924; 2nd ed. Lon-
     don: Arnold, 1937. CdP: p. 38, 63, 102, 114, 121, 145, 250,
     274, 292, 301.
         Well-known medievalist discusses CH in various contexts,
     claiming (p. 121) that her Dit de la pastoure marks the tran-
     sition of the pastoral to a new genre.

187 Zink, Michael. La Pastourelle: Poésie et Folklore au Moyen
     Âge. Paris: Bordas, 1972.
         Discusses CH's Dit and the historical development of the
     genre.

188 Farquhar, James Douglas, and Eric Hicks. "Christine de Pizan's
     Dit de la Pastoure in Baltimore: Membra disjecta." Scriptorium,
     XXX (1976), 192-200.

Presents codicological evidence confirming Sister Towner's
observation that Baltimore Walters MS 316, which contains text
of the Dit, is "identical with the missing leaves of MS BN f.fr.
604..." (p. 194). CR: SF, 63 (1977), 519.

189 Willard, Charity Cannon. "Jean Bodel and Christine de Pizan,
Pastoral Poets." MR, XXX, 3-4 (1980), 293-300.
Explains how CH and Bodel both used pastoral themes (in
her Dit) to make social statements and expose the breakdown of
chivalric ideals. CR: SF, 85 (1985), 146.

190 Blanchard, Joël. La pastorale en France aux XIVe et XVe
siècles: recherches sur les structures de l'imaginaire médiévale. (Bibliothèque du XVe Siècle, XLV). Paris: Champion,
1983. CdP: p. 11, 49, 93-118, 139-40, 225, 350, 351, 353.
The section on "Pastorale et courtoisie, " pp. 93-118, includes detailed analysis of CH's Dit. CR: SF, 84 (1984),
536-38.

191 L'EPISTRE À EUSTACHE MOREL (10 February 1404)
CH's letter to the French poet and diplomat Eustache Deschamps (804), pseudonym of Eustache Morel, is written in rhymed
couplets. It contrasts the lack of morals in her own times
with the high ethical standards of the ancient world. At the
end of her letter, CH offers an apology to the elder poet for
voicing her feminine opinion on these matters.

MANUSCRIPTS:
London, BL Harley 4431, ff. 255^v-257^r.
Paris, BN f.fr. 605, ff. 2^v-3^v.

EDITION:
See Roy 702, II, pp. 295-301.

STUDY:
See Frappier 25.

192 LE LIVRE DES FAIS ET BONNES MEURS DU SAGE ROY CHARLES
V (1404)
This is the official biography of Charles V of France (798).
Written almost a quarter century after his death, between 30
January and 30 November 1404, it was commissioned by Philip
the Bold, duke of Burgundy (823) as a tribute to his late
brother. The book contains unique firsthand observations on
fourteenth- and fifteenth-century French society which makes
it historically valuable. Yet strictly speaking, CH's treatise is
neither an objective history nor a true biography. It is instead a humanistic and moral portrait of the king.
The text is divided into three parts. In the first (36 chaps.),

CH discusses Charles's "nobility of heart," his birth and youth, and his affairs of state. She also describes his physical appearance and comments on his well-disciplined way of life. The last chapters of Part I are devoted to the king's virtues: prudence, justice, clemency, benignity, liberality, chastity, sobriety, truth, charity, and devotion.

The second part (39 chaps.) opens with a prologue mourning the sudden death of Philip the Bold. This is followed by a long discussion on chivalry, the object of which is to demonstrate that Charles was truly a chivalrous king. CH lists four qualities defining chivalry. She then presents a series of portraits of members of the royal family including the dukes of Anjou, Bourbon, Berry (812), Burgundy (823), Orleans (815), and other nobles. Several chapters are on the warrior Bertrand Du Guesclin (805) and Charles's military triumphs.

The third part of Charles V (72 chaps.) is generally thought to be the most original part of the book. It deals with "wisdom." After defining the term CH shows how this virtue manifested in the late king. She speaks about Charles's intellectual achievements proclaiming him a true philosopher, astrologer, artist, bibliophile, and friend of the University (of Paris). Comments are also made about the visit of the Holy Roman Emperor (Charles IV of Bohemia), the death of the queen, and the schism of the Church. After some digressions CH recounts the death of Du Guesclin and, finally, that of the king himself. The last chapter is the conclusion.

SOURCES:

Oral:
Etienne de Castel, CH's husband
Gilles Malet, royal librarian
Guillaume de Tignonville, Provost of Paris
Jean de Castel, CH's son
Jean de Montagu; royal secretary, Overseer of Finance
Marguerite de la Rivière; widow of Bureau de la Rivière, royal
    chamberlain
Thomas de Pizan, CH's father

Written:
Avis sur le débat des papes baillé au roi par l'Université de
    Paris
Chronique normande du XIVe siècle
De regimine principum, Gilles of Rome (Egidio Colonna); Henri
    de Gauchi's translation of
Faits de Du Guesclin
Flores chronicorum, Anonymous; Bernard Gui's translation of
Les Grandes Chroniques de France
Manipulus florum, Thomas Hibernicus
Metaphysics, Aristotle; St. Thomas Aquinas's commentary of
Relation latine anonyme de la mort de Charles V

MANUSCRIPTS:
Modena, Biblioteca Estense $\propto$ .n. 8. 7., 106 ff.
Paris, BN f.fr. 2862, 206 ff.
_____, ___ _____ 5025, 99 ff.
_____, ___ _____ 10153, 107 ff.
Rome, Biblioteca Apostolica Vaticana Reg. lat. 920, 111 ff.
Private Collection: M. Thomas de Castelnau, 375 pp.

EDITIONS:

193 Choissy, l'abbé de (François-Timoléon). Histoire de Charles
    cinquième roi de France. Paris: Antoine Dezallier, 1689.
        Extracts from Charles V are scattered throughout this 456-
    page volume.

194 Daniel, Gabriel. Histoire de France depuis l'établissement de
    la monarchie françoise dans les Gaules, dédiée au roy. Paris:
    J.-B. Deléspine, 1713. II, cols. 727-28.
        Prints passages from Charles V based on the abbé de Choissy's
    (193) text.

195 Lebeuf, l'abbé. "Vie de Charles V dit le Sage, roy de France,
    écrite par Christine de Pisan, Dame qui vivoit de son temps."
    In Dissertations sur l'histoire ecclésiastique et civile de Paris
    suivies de plusieurs eclaircissemens sur l'histoire de France.
    Paris: Lambert & Durand, 1743. III, 83-484.
        Extracts from Charles V (from BN f.fr. 5025) are printed
    on pp. 103-389; preceded by a biographical introduction, pp.
    83-102; and followed by historical notes, pp. 390-484. See
    Solente's discussion in 201, I, p. "c" on how Lebeuf mutilated
    CH's text.

196 "Mémoires ou Livre des faits et bonnes moeurs du sage roi
    Charles V, fait et compilé par Christine de Pisan, damoiselle
    accompli." In Collection universelle des mémoires particuliers
    relatifs à l'histoire de France. London/Paris: Roucher &
    Perrin. V, 1785.
        Presents incomplete edition of CH's text, pp. 99-279; together
    with an Introduction, pp. 87-98; and commentary, pp. 280-91.
    List of chapter headings, pp. 292-304.

197 Petitot, Claude B. "Notice sur la Vie et sur les ouvrages de
    Christine de Pisan." "Le Livre des Fais et Bonnes Meurs du
    Sage Roy Charles V par Christine de Pisan." In Collection
    complète des mémoires relatifs à l'histoire de France. Paris:
    Foucault. V, 1824; VI, 1825.
        This is the first unabridged edition of CH's text based partly
    on Lebeuf, 195. Parts 1 and 2 are in Vol. V, pp. 245-436,
    preceded by a critical notice on pp. 200-44. Part 3 is in Vol.
    VI, pp. 1-146, followed by additional commentary. Solente, 201,
    considers this edition linguistically defective.

198   Michaud, J.-F., and J.-J.-F. Poujoulat. "Notes sur Christine
      de Pisan." "Livre des Fais et Bonnes Meurs du Sage Roy
      Charles V par Christine de Pisan." In Nouvelle collection des
      mémoires pour servir à l'histoire de France depuis la XIIIe
      siècle jusqu'à la fin du XVIIIe. Paris: Guyot, 1836-1839.
          Prints text in two different versions: Vol. I, 591-637, in
      the original French; Vol. II, 1-145, in Modern French. The
      Notes (I, 583-90) credit CH with revitalizing the French lan-
      guage. Another edition of this work was published in 1857.

199   Buchon, J.-A.-C. Choix de chroniques et mémoires sur
      l'histoire de France avec notes et notices. Paris: Auguste
      Desrez, 1838.
          Prints complete text of Charles V, pp. 210-322, but changes
      numbering of CH's chapters. A notice on the author appears
      on pp. xii-xiv. This work was reissued in Paris 1842 by Mairet
      and Fournier; in 1861 in the Panthéon Littéraire (Vol. XXXIV),
      and in 1875 by H. Herluision in Orleans.

200   Le livre des faits et bonnes moeurs du sage roi Charles V.
      Chroniques et mémoires. (Société de Saint Augustine). Bruges:
      Desclée, de Brouwer et Cie, 1892.
          Presents Modern French text of Charles V with survey on
      CH and a selection of her poetry, pp. 1-391. On this edition,
      see Solente 201, pp. ci-cii.

201   Solente, Suzanne, ed. 'Le Livre des fais et bonnes meurs du
      sage roy Charles V' par Christine de Pisan. (Société de
      l'Histoire de France). Paris: Champion, 1936-1940; rpt.
      Geneva: Slatkine, 1977.
          Two-volume edition complete with critical apparatus, docu-
      mentation, and background material. Vol. I contains the first
      two parts of the text (with variants, pp. 1-244) and a compre-
      hensive Introduction. It discusses the author of the work and
      her father, Thomas de Pizan (pp. i-xxvi); the date and plan
      of the work (pp. xxvi-xxxii); the sources, in great detail (pp.
      xxxii-lxxx); CH as an historian (pp. lxxx-lxxxv); the manu-
      scripts (pp. lxxxv-xcvii); establishment of the text (pp. xcvii-
      xcviii); and previous editions (pp. xcviii-cii). Has table of
      chapter headings and extensive notes. Vol. II contains the
      third part of text (pp. 1-194), twenty-eight appendices (pp.
      195-217), and an alphabetical table identifying names and places
      cited in the text or Introduction (pp. 219-77). This edition has
      been highly praised by critics. CR's: 780.

      NOTES AND STUDIES:
      See also Beltran 306; Boldingh-Goemans 407; Camus 459, 460;
      Cropp 444; Lenient 508; Mombello 553; Rickard 505.

202   Duchemin, Henri. "Les sources du Livre des fais et bonnes
      meurs du sage roy Charles V de Christine de Pisan." Thesis.
      École des Chartes, 1891.

Describes Charles V as a unique moral portrait of the king
but sees no literary or historical merit in it.

203 Dupré, Alexandre. "Histoire de Charles V par Christine de
Pisan." In Mélanges historiques et littéraires, la plupart con-
cernant le pays blésois. VI, n.d., 33-44.
Unpublished study preserved in a MS at the Municipal Library of Blois. (Source of Reference: Wisman 729, p. xxxvii).

204 Delisle, Léopold Victor. Recherches sur la librairie de Charles
V. 2 vols. Paris: Champion, 1907; rpt. G. Th. van Heusden,
1967. CdP: I, 2, 10, 83, 134, 400; II, 129, 246, 286-93.
Fundamental reference work with lengthy extracts from
Charles V in Vol. I and an "Inventaire des livres," from the
libraries of Charles V (798), Charles VI (799), and Jean of
Berry (812) in Vol. II. The latter includes listing for CH's
works.

205 Delachenal, Roland. Histoire de Charles V. 5 vols. Paris:
Alphonse Picard, 1909. CdP: I, viii, ix, x, xii, xviii.
Thinks CH's biography has no historical value.

206 Solente, Suzanne. "Introduction historique à l'édition du Livre
des fais et bonnes meurs du sage roy Charles V." Thesis.
École des Chartes, 1921.
Prolegomena to author's critical edition, 201.

207 Ward, Charles Frederick. "The Writings of a Fifteenth Century
French Patriot, Jean (II) Juvenal des Ursins." PQ, II (1923),
63-72.
Suggests that Ursins' Histoire de Charles VI is partly based
on CH's Charles V.

208 Evans, Joan. Life in Medieval France. 1925; rev. London:
Phaidon Press, 1957. CdP: p. 114, 238.
CH cited on Charles V's (798) erudition and book collection.
Plate 88 is illustration of the Epistre d'Othea.

209 Calmette, Joseph. Charles V. Paris: Fayard, 1945.
Offers lengthy discussion on CH's biography, with conclusion that it is pedantic and hard to read, pp. 190-208.

210 Schramm, Percy Ernst. Der König von Frankreich: das Wesen
der Monarchie vom 9. zum 16. Jahrhundert. Band I: Text.
Weimar: Hermann Böhlaus Nachf., 1960.
Suggests that in Charles V, CH carefully avoided making
unflattering statements about the king, pp. 245-46.

211 Sherman, Claire Richter. The Portraits of Charles V of France
(1338-1380). (Monographs on Archeology and the Fine Arts
sponsored by the Archeological Institute of America and the

College Art Association of America, XX). New York: New
York Univ. Press, 1969.
   Considers CH's Charles V the "most complete and revealing"
source on the king's life, p. 9.

212 Spencer, Eleanor P. "The First Patron of the Très Belles
Heures de Notre-Dame." Scriptorium, XXIII (1969), 145–49.
   Cites CH on Charles V's (798) participation in Feast of Epi-
phany in January 1378.

213 Sherman, Claire Richter. "Representations of Charles V of
France (1338-1380) as a Wise Ruler." M & H, n.s. II (1971),
83–96.
   Explores CH's definition of the wise ruler as reflected in
Charles V.

214 Contamine, Philippe. Guerre, état et société à la fin du Moyen
Âge: études sur les armées des rois de France, 1337-1494.
Paris: Mouton, 1972. CdP: p. 137, 143, 156, 174, 175, 232,
576, 612, 651.
   CH's Charles V, Corps de policie, Livre de la paix used as
historical sources in discussion of medieval warfare and the
French royal army.

215 Bottineau, Yves. "L'Architecture des premiers Valois." GBA,
LXXXII (1973), 237–62.
   Includes references to CH and her impressions of Charles
V (798).

216 Contamine, Philippe. La Vie quotidienne pendant la guerre de
Cent Ans: France et Angleterre (XIVe Siècle). Paris: Hachette, 1976. CdP: p. 70, 162, 165.
   Cites Charles V on how the king used the Seine and Loire
as supply routes during the Hundred Years' War.

217 Rouy, François. L'Esthétique du traité moral d'après les oeuvres
d'Alain Chartier. Geneva: Droz, 1980. CdP: p. 36, 40, 78,
140n., 303-05, 309–11, 324n., 330n.
   Using CH's Charles V, makes comparison between the moralizing style of CH and Chartier (801).

218 Henneman, John Bell. "The Age of Charles V." In Froissart:
Historian. Ed. J. N. Palmer. Totowa, NJ: Rowman & Little-
field, 1981. pp. 36–49.
   In his discussion of Charles V (798), the author cautions
historians against being excessively influenced by "the tradition of Christine de Pisan," p. 49.

219 Combettes, Bernard. "Une Notion stylistique et ses rapports
avec la syntaxe: narration et description chez Christine de
Pisan." In La Génie de la Forme, mélanges de langue et

littérature offerts à Jean Mourot. Nancy: Presses universitaires de Nancy, 1982. pp. 51-58.
   Analyzes the narrative and descriptive elements in Charles
V in order to determine which one contributes most significantly
to the syntax.

220   De Winter, Patrick M. "The Grandes Heures of Philip the Bold,
      Duke of Burgundy: The Copyist Jean L'Avenant and His Pa-
      trons at the French Court." Speculum, LVIII (1982), 786-842.
         Prints excerpt from Charles V (Solente 201, II, 42) and cites
      CH on p. 811.

221   Sherman, Claire Richter. "Taking a Second Look: Observations
      on the Iconography of a French Queen, Jeanne de Bourbon
      (1338-1378)." In Feminism and Art History: Questioning the
      Litany. Ed. Norma Broude and Mary G. Garrard. New York:
      Harper & Row, 1982. pp. 101-16.
         Sees CH's eyewitness reports in Charles V as valuable testi-
      mony to the public life of Jeanne de Bourbon and her relation-
      ship with the king.

222   Willard, Charity Cannon. "Christine de Pizan, biographer of
      Charles V." Paper presented at the MLAA Centennial Conven-
      tion, Sheraton Centre, New York City, December 1983. 14 pp.
         A reevaluation of Charles V in light of recent (1981-1982)
      Paris exhibition devoted to this French monarch.

223   Quillet, Jeannine. Charles V roi lettré: essai sur la pensée
      politique d'un règne. (Presence de l'histoire. Collection His-
      torique). Paris: Académique Perrin, 1984. CdP: p. 12, 25,
      35, 37, 44, 46, 50-53, 55-57, 60-63, 79, 103, 105, 106, 138,
      140, 144, 163-66, 183, 184, 195, 204, 219, 225-32, 237, 266,
      270, 316, 318, 333, 335, 339, 347-49; Thomas de Pizan: pp.
      105-07.
         CH seen as important firsthand witness to Charles V (798)
      and his reign. Makes frequent reference to her anecdotes and
      opinions about him. See especially pp. 50-53 and pp. 225-32,
      "Christine de Pisan et la symbolique du corps social." Includes
      chronology, pp. 351-52, and bibliography, pp. 353-67.

224   LE LIVRE DU DUC DES VRAIS AMANS (1404-1405)
      A courtly romance based on a story allegedly confided to CH
      by a young nobleman who wished only to be known as "The
      Duke of True Lovers." The tale is narrated by the Duke. It
      chronicles his ten-year love affair with his married cousin, who
      is a princess. Having been kept away from her by a suspicious
      husband, he becomes ill with grief. Although the lovers ex-
      change letters they are unable to meet because the princess's
      confidante has gone away. To overcome this problem she turns
      to a former governess for help, inviting her for a visit.

However, the governess does not accept the invitation. Instead,
she sends her friend a letter warning of the endless difficulties
such extramarital affairs invariably create. The princess there-
upon breaks off the relationship only to resume it again later.
For the next two years the lovers continue to see each other
but, harassed by gossipers, are eventually forced to part. At
last the Duke goes abroad, joining an expedition to Spain. During this self-imposed exile they exchange love-letters in the
form of ballades. These are incorporated into the story via an
epilogue. In an inconclusive ending the Duke laments that
slanderers have forced him to abandon the fellowship of her to
whom he had made a promise of his whole love.

MANUSCRIPTS:
London, BL Harley 4431, ff. 143^r-177^v.
Paris, BN f.fr. 836, ff. 65^r-98^r.

EDITION:
See Roy 702, III, pp. 59-208.

TRANSLATION:

225   Kemp-Welch, Alice, trans. The Book of the Duke of True
      Lovers, now first translated from the Middle French of Christine
      de Pisan ... The Ballads rendered into the original metres by
      Laurence Binyon and Eric D. Maclagan. (The Medieval Library).
      London: Chatto & Windus, 1908; rpt. New York: Cooper
      Square, 1966.
          A prose translation with verse ballades. The edition con-
      tains a note by the translator (pp. ix-xv) claiming that CH's
      love story was based on an actual incident involving the Houses
      of Berry and Bourbon. Text, pp. 3-137. Includes six photo-
      gravure plates after illuminations in the original manuscript.

      STUDY:
      See also Dow 594, Kemp-Welch 586, Le Gentil 411, Painter 560,
      Riesch 588, Wolfzettel 544.

226   Dulac, Liliane. "Christine de Pisan et le malheur des Vrais
      amans." In Mélanges de langue et de littérature médiévales of-
      ferts à Pierre Le Gentil. Paris: SEDES, 1973. pp. 223-33.
          Uses Amans to analyze CH's attitude toward courtly love,
      with conclusion that she was ambivalent toward it and tried to
      reconcile her own personal ethics with those of her culture.

227   LE LIVRE DE LA CITÉ DES DAMES (1405)
      A didactic allegory inspired by Boccaccio's De claris mulieribus
      and St. Augustine's City of God. It was written as a rebuttal
      to such misogynic authors as Theophrastus, Matheolus, and Jean
      de Meun. One of CH's best-known and most explicit feminist

works, it narrates the lives of famous women from history, legend, and the Bible who have made special contributions to the world. The symbolic construction of the city serves as a framework for the book while the various exempla from the Mulieribus, reorganized and reinterpreted by CH, form its subject-matter.

The opening scene shows CH in her study wondering why it is that so many great philosophers, poets, and orators have consistently maligned the feminine sex. She decides that God made a vile creature when he created woman and laments the fact that she was not born into the world a man. While engrossed in these disturbing thoughts she has a vision. A ray of light falls upon her lap and as she lifts her head to see where it is coming from there appear before her three celestial queens: Reason, Rectitude, and Justice. They commission CH to build a "City of Ladies" where women could find refuge from abuse and slander. During the building of the figurative city, CH and the three queens have a debate about women. In the process they not only reveal the true nature of women but establish that women are basically virtuous and endowed by the Creator with the same intellectual and moral capacities as men.

The arguments offered on women's behalf constitute a systematic defense as well as an history of women. In Part I (48 chaps.) CH tells for what purpose this book was written and how, under Reason's command, she began to excavate the earth and lay the foundation for the City (Richards 234, I.8.1-10). After explaining why women do not sit on legal councils (I.11.1) she presents a series of sketches on exceptional women beginning with the empress of Ethiopia (I.12.1) and ending with Lavinia (I.41.1). Additional vignettes of women are given in Part II (69 chaps.). Here CH also raises the question of women's education, having Rectitude argue "Against those men who claim it is not good for women to be educated" (II.36.1-4). When most of the City's buildings are in place Rectitude is ready to select tenants for them. Among those chosen are the French queen Isabeau (811); the duchesses of Berry, Burgundy, Bourbon, and Orleans (825); and others of high rank (II.68.1-7). To these names are then added maidens from the bourgeoisie and virtuous women from all classes--past, present, and future. In Part III (19 chaps.) Lady Justice brings the Virgin Mary and her noble entourage to the City to live and preside over it (III.1.3). At the end of the book CH addresses the entire City of Ladies.

TEXTUAL SOURCES:
Decameron, Boccaccio (793)
De claris mulieribus ("Concerning Famous Women"), Boccacio
Golden Legend, Jacobus de Voragine
Speculum historiale, Vincent de Beauvais

MANUSCRIPTS:

Brussels, BR 9235, ff. 1^a-133^a

_____, ____ 9393, ff. 2^a-87^d.

Chantilly, Musée Condé 856, ff. 1^a-30^a.

Geneva, Bibliothèque Publique et Universitaire fr. 180, ff. 2^a-130^d.

Leiden, Bibliothek der Rijksuniversiteit Ltk 1819, 1.f.

Lille, Bibliothèque Municipale 390, ff. 1^r-277^v.

London, LB Harley 4431, ff. 288^c-374^a.

_____, ____ Royal 19. A. XIX, ff. 2^a-172^d.

Munich, Bayerische Staatsbibliothek Cod. gall 8, ff. 2^a-106^d.

New Haven, Yale Univ., Beinecke Library 318, 209ff.

Paris, Arsenal 2686, ff. 1-140^d.

_____, _____ 3182, 100 ff.

_____, BN f.fr. 607, ff. 1^a-79^b.

_____, ____ ____ 608, ff. 1^a-144^b.

_____, ____ ____ 609, ff. 1^a-152^d.

_____, ____ ____ 826, ff. 1^a-84^r.

_____, ____ ____ 1177, ff. 2^a-112^d.

_____, ____ ____ 1178, ff. 2^a-159^c.

_____, ____ ____ 1179, ff. 1^a-134^b.

_____, ____ ____ 1182, ff. 173^r-254^r.

_____, ____ ____ 24292, ff. 7^r-100^r.

_____, ____ ____ 24293, ff. 5^a-158^a.

_____, ____ ____ 24294, ff. 1^r-110^r.

Privas, Archives Départementales de l'Ardèche 7 cote I 6, ff. 25^r-189.

Rome, Biblioteca Apostolica Vaticana Palat. lat 1966, ff. 1^a-186^a.

_____, _____ _____ _____ Reg. lat 918, ff. 71^r-132^r.

Vienna, Osterreichische Nationalbibliothek Vindob. 2605, ff. 1^r-172^r.

EDITIONS:

228   Lange, Monika. "Livre de la cité des dames: Kritische Text-
      edition auf Grund der sieben überlieferten 'manuscrits originaux'
      des Textes." Ph.D. Hamburg 1974.

229   Curnow, Maureen Cheney, ed. "The Livre de la cité des dames
      of Christine de Pisan: A Critical Edition." Ph.D. Vanderbilt
      1975. DAI, XXXVI (1976), 4536-37A.
          Scholarly, two-volume edition made up of nine preliminary
      chapters, pp. 1-595, and the hitherto unedited (except for
      228) French text of the Cité, pp. 597-1036. Based on Paris,
      BN f.fr. 607, Curnow uses Harley 4431 as the major control
      manuscript and Brussels, BR 9393 as the secondary control.
      Includes notes, pp. 1037-1127; a glossary, pp. 1128-43; a list
      of proper names, pp. 1144-1219; and a list of works consulted,
      pp. 1220-45.

TRANSLATIONS:

230 Stede der Vrouwen. 1475.
This is a Flemish translation executed at the command of
Jan de Baenst, a Bruges government official under Philippe the
Good. Text is extant in only one manuscript, London, BL Add.
20698, 333 ff.--listed as Lof der Vrouwen. Maureen Curnow
discusses this translation in 229 (pp. 300-21) and 243 (p. 118).
See also Lievens, 240.

231 The Boke of the Cyte of Ladyes. London: H. Pepwell, 1521.
Early English translation printed in 190 folios by Henry Pepwell. The original translation, made between 1509 and 1521 by
Brian Anslay, is no longer extant but Pepwell's printed text
survives. One complete copy and a two-page fragment are preserved at the British Library, London. Another copy is at the
Corpus Christi College Library, Oxford University. Reprinted
in 233.

232 Dibdin, Thomas Frognall. Typographical Antiquities. London:
W. Miller, 1810-1819.
Contains extract from first chapter of Brian Anslay's transla-
tion, 231.

233 Bornstein, Diane, ed. Distaves and Dames: Renaissance Trea-
tises For and About Women. Delmar, NY: Scholars' Facsimiles
and Reprints, 1978.
Third treatise in this collection is facsimile reproduction of
Anslay's sixteenth-century English translation, the Boke of the
Cyte of Ladyes, 231.

234 Richards, Earl Jeffrey, trans. The Book of the City of Ladies.
New York: Persea, 1982.
First new translation of this text and the only one in Modern
English prose since 1521. Translated from a photocopy of Harley 4431 and utilizing both the Anslay (231) and Curnow (229)
editions, it includes a foreword by Marina Warner (pp. xii-xvii),
the text (pp. 3-257), notes on the text (pp. 259-71), an index
of proper names (pp. 273-81), four illustrations from the Harley
MS, and an excellent Introduction (pp. xix-li). In the Introduc-
tion, Richards makes a survey of CH's life and works, assesses
CH as a writer, discusses the significance of the Cité in her
thought, deals with the crucial question of her feminism (see
642), and offers an explanation as to how she modified Boccac-
cio's Mulieribus. CR's: 778. See also:
Publishers Weekly, CCXXI (26 March 1982), 60.
Booklist, LXXVIII (1 May 1982), 1134.
Library Journal, CVII (1 May 1982), 887.
New York Times, CXXXI (5 July 1982), 15.
Book World, XII (8 August 1982), 9.
Los Angeles Times Book Review (22 August 1982), 8.
Harper's Magazine, CCLXI (September 1982), 74.
Choice, XX (October 1982), 260.

Nation, CCXXXV (6 November 1982), 473.
MS Magazine, VII (December 1982), 36.
Nation (25 December 1982), 696.
Publishers Weekly, CCXXIV (20 October 1983), 68.
Punch, CCLXXXV (21 December 1983), 56.
NYTBR, LXXXIX (1 January 1984), 32.
Observer, London (22 January 1984), 53.
Punch, CCLXXXVI (8 February 1984), 57.
New Statesman, CVII (17 February 1984), 25.
Times Educational Supplement (17 February 1984), 27.
Biography, VII (Summer 1984), 266.
Women's Review of Books, III (January 1986), 14.

235 Hicks, Eric, and Thérèse Moreau, trans. Le Livre de la cité
     des Dames. (Série Moyen Âge). Paris: Stock, 1986.
         This is the first publication of the Cité des dames in Modern
     French. The 292-page paperback (with a colorful reproduction
     of CH and the Cité on its cover) consists of an Introduction
     (pp. 13-24), an analysis of the work (pp. 25-28), a chronology
     of CH's writings (pp. 29-34), the text (pp. 35-278), and a
     table of chapter headings (pp. 279-91). The Introduction com-
     ments on how astonishingly modern the Cité really is.

236 Zimmerman, Margarete, trans. Das Buch von der Stadt der
     Frauen. Aus dem Mittelfranzösischen übersetzt und mit einem
     Kommentar und einer Einleitung. Berlin: Orlanda-Frauenverlag,
     1986.
         A 312-page German translation with an Introduction and
     Notes.

     NOTES AND STUDIES:
     See also Bornstein 279, Delany 659, Margolis 530, Melegari 587,
     Muir 453, Rigaud 585, Tupper 29, Willard 278.

237 Jeanroy, Alfred. "Boccacce et Christine de Pisan: le De claris
     mulieribus principale source du Livre de la cité des dames."
     Romania, XLVIII (1922), 93-105.
         Identifies the Mulieribus as chief source for the Cité and
     prints passages from both to show how CH handled Boccaccio's
     text. On the question of whether she used Boccaccio's original
     Latin text or a French translation, see Curnow's Introduction
     to 229 and Bumgardner 488, p. 41.

238 Golenistcheff-Koutouzoff, Elie. L'Histoire de Griseldis en France
     au XIVe et XVe siècle. Paris: Droz, 1933; rpt. Geneva: Slat-
     kine, 1975.
         Evaluates success of Boccaccio's Griselda tale in terms of its
     reception in fourteenth- and fifteenth-century France; its Latin
     translation by Petrarch; its prose translation by Philippe de
     Mézières; and its use by CH in the Cité (Richards 234, II.11.2,
     II.50.1-4, II.51.1). Pages 153-248 present verse and prose ver-
     sions of Griselda in French.

239 Rice, John P. "A Note on Christine de Pisan and Cecco d'As-
     coli." _Italica_, XV (1938), 149-51.
        Reflects on CH's allusion in the _Cité_ to d'Ascoli's _Acerba_,
     calling attention to some "striking parallels" between her father's
     and Ascoli's careers.

240 Lievens, Robrecht. "Kerstine van Pizen." _Spiegel der Letteren_,
     III (1959), 1-16.
        Dutch scholar discusses the _Stede der Vrouwen_, a Flemish
     version of the _Cité_. CR: 768.

241 Bozzolo, Carla. "Il _Decameron_ come fonte del _Livre de la cité
     des dames_ di Christine de Pisan." In _Miscellanea di studi e
     ricerche sul Quattrocente francese_. Ed. Franco Simone. Turin:
     Giappichelli, 1967. pp. 3-24.
        Traces three tales in the _Cité_ directly to Boccaccio: the
     wife of Bernado, II.9; Ghismonda, IV.1; Lisabetta, IV.5. CH's
     interpretation of these tales suggests that she wanted to give the
     narrative her own moral vision. CR: 750.

242 Simone, Franco. "La présence de Boccacce dans la culture fran-
     çaise du XVe siècle." _JMRS_, I (1971), 17-32.
        Aside from using Boccaccio's (793) _De claris mulieribus_ and
     Decameron in the _Cité_, CH also borrowed from his _De casibus
     virorum illustrium_.

243 Curnow, Maureen Cheney. "The Boke of the Cyte of Ladyes,
     an English Translation of Christine de Pisan's _Le Livre de la
     cité des dames_." _BF_, III (Fall 1974), 116-37.
        Informative discussion on Brian Anslay's translation, 231.
     Deals with the content and influence of the original work; the
     Pepwell printing, 231; the various extant MSS and editions;
     date of the translation (between 1509 and 1521); and with the
     translation itself. Also analyzes the textual relationship between
     Anslay's translation and the French version, with conclusion
     that he probably used London, BL Royal 19.A.XIX or a now non-
     extant MS closely related to it. Includes text of Pepwell's pro-
     logue and colophon. See also author's critical ed. of _Cité_, 229.
     CR: _SF_, 57 (1975), 527.

244 Reno, Christine M. "Christine de Pisan's Use of the _Golden
     Legend_ in the _Cité des dames_." _BF_, III (Fall 1974), 89-99.
        Shows how CH adapted Jacobus de Voragine's _Golden Legend_
     to her own polemical purposes and suggests that her modifica-
     tions of the _Legend_ parallel significant developments in fifteenth-
     century prose style. The author subsequently changed CH's
     main source for the Saints (discussed here p. 91) from the
     Legend to the _Miroir historiale_--see p. 84 n.4 of her essay in
     IFW, 251. CR: _SF_, 57 (1975), 527.

245 David, Natalie Zemon. "'Women's History' in Transition: The

European Case." Feminist Studies, III (Spring-Summer 1976),
83-103.
   Foremost female historian sees the Cité as an "unbroken line"
in genre of women's history.

246 Tournoy, Gilbert, ed. Boccaccio in Europe: Proceedings of
the Boccaccio Conference, Louvain, December 1975. Louvain:
Louvain Univ. Press, 1977.
   CH mentioned in various contexts. See especially papers by
C. Bozzolo on the Quarrel, p. 20; and G. Delmarcel on Boc-
caccio and the Cité des dames, p. 68, 81-82.

247 Dulac, Liliane. "Un mythe didactique chez Christine de Pizan:
Sémiramis ou la veuve héroïque (Du De mulieribus claris de
Boccace à la Cité des dames." In Mélanges de philologie romane
offerts à Charles Camproux. Montpellier: Centre d'Études Oc-
citanes de l'Université Paul Valéry, 1978. pp. 314-43.
   Explains how and why CH made her Sémiramis figure in the
Cité more masculine than her counterpart in the Mulieribus.
Prints Boccaccio's Latin text and Middle French translation of
Sémiramis and the corresponding passage from the Cité, after
BN f.fr. 607. CR: 757.

248 McMillan, Ann Hunter. "Evere an hundred goode ageyn oon
badde": Catalogues of good women in medieval literature."
Ph.D. Indiana 1979. DAI, XL (1980), 5437A.
   Deals with medieval catalogs of noble pagan women like Ovid's
Heroïdes and Boccaccio's De claris mulieribus. Third chapter
shows how the Cité makes use of pagan women warriors.

249 Kristeller, Paul Oskar. "Learned Women of Early Modern Italy:
Humanists and University Scholars." In Beyond Their Sex:
Learned Women of the European Past. Ed. Patricia A. Labalme.
New York: New York Univ. Press, 1980. pp. 91-116.
   Brief references to the Cité des dames (p. 102) and CH as
one of the learned women of Middle Ages (p. 92).

250 Bornstein, Diane. "An Analogue to Chaucer's Clerk's Tale."
Chaucer Review, XV (1981), 322-31.
   The analogue is the Griselda tale in the Cité (Richards 234,
II.11.2; II.50.1-4; II. 51.1) printed here on pp. 325-30. Cites
CH's inclusion of Griselda (in Cité) as proof of her acceptance
of subordination of women.

251 Reno, Christine M. "Virginity as an Ideal in Christine de Pizan's
Cité des dames." In IFW (1981), 69-90.
   Finds that CH not only made the concept of chastity the
central theme of the Cité but she used it as vehicle of tran-
scendence for women. The Cité can also be read as feminist
response to Jean de Meun's part of the Roman de la Rose. Includes good notes; see especially n.4 p. 84 for Reno's revision
of a source in 244. CR: SF, 78 (1982), 529-30.

252 Delany, Sheila. "A City, a Room: the Scene of Writing in Christine de Pizan and Virginia Woolf." In Delany, Writing Woman: Women Writers and Women in Literature, Medieval to Modern. New York: Schocken, 1983. pp. 181-97, notes pp. 217-18.
     Many similarities found between "scene of writing" in CH's Cité and Woolf's A Room of One's Own: both use enclosed spaces as image of security and protection, bear similar architectural titles, and have comparable opening scenarios. Resemblances also noted in the two writers' personal backgrounds.

253 Hindman, Sandra L. "With Ink and Mortar: Christine de Pizan's Cité des dames (an Art Essay)." FS, X (1984), 457-77.
     Specialist on the Othea miniatures (84) turns her attention to the text and images in the Cité and discusses CH's collected works in Harley 4431. Article followed by six plates, pp. 478-83.

254 Liebertz-Grün, Ursula. "Marie de France, Christine de Pisan und die deutschsprächige Autorin im Mittelalter." Euphorion, LXXVII, heft 3 (1984), 219-36.
     Section on CH relatively short (pp. 233-36), but author credits the Cité with paving way for such German-speaking women writers as Elisabeth von Nassau-Saarbrücken and Eleonore von Österreich.

255 Ferguson, Margaret W., Maureen Quilligan, and Nancy J. Vickers, eds. Rewriting the Renaissance: The Discourses of Sexual Difference in Early Modern Europe. London/Chicago: Univ. of Chicago Press, 1986.
     This collection of 18 essays includes reprint by C. Jordan (576) on CH and the Cité des dames, pp. 242-58. Editors suggest (p. xxi) that feminists can challenge canonical tradition by recovering previously ignored cultural documents of the so-called "'minor figures'" like CH. See also p. 378 n.5 and p. 392 n.23.

256 Phillippy, Patricia. "Establishing Authority: Boccaccio's De Claris Mulieribus and Christine de Pisan's Livre de la Cité des Dames." RR, LXXVII (1986), 167-94.
     Discusses CH's ambivalence toward male literary tradition and explains how and why--to assert her own ideological independence--she revised Boccaccio's text.

257 Schulenburg, Jane Tibbetts. "The Heroics of Virginity: Brides of Christ and Sacrificial Mutilation." In Women in the Middle Ages and the Renaissance: Literary and Historical Perspectives. Ed. Mary Beth Rose. Syracuse, NY: Syracuse Univ. Press, 1986. pp. 29-72.
     Notes on p. 55 that useful models of virginal defense can be found in Chap. XLVI (Pt. 2) of the Cité. See also p. xiii of Introduction.

258   Stuard, Susan Mosher, ed. Women in Medieval History and His-
      toriography. Philadelphia: Univ. of Pennsylvania Press, 1987.
      CdP: p. xiii, 27, 62, 167, 168.
          Thinks the Cité des dames (cited on p. 62 as the "Citie des
      Femmes") serves the cause of iconography rather than narrative
      history. CR: Choice (November 1987), 533.

259   LE LIVRE DES TROIS VERTUS (Le trésor de la cité des dames)
      1405
      A book of etiquette and moral instruction aimed at women of
      all ages and walks of life. It gives a detailed picture of the
      manners and customs of CH's day thereby recreating for modern
      readers domestic life as it was lived in fifteenth-century France.
      Composed as a sequel to the Cité des dames (227), this didactic
      treatise provides a complete blueprint for a feminine education
      defining women's roles in contemporary society and outlining their
      duties and responsibilities. At the same time it tries to foster
      a sense of dignity and self-confidence in women.
          In the prologue CH is again visited by the Three Virtues,
      Reason, Rectitude, and Justice, who urge her to continue with
      the important work begun in the Cité. The Virtues, together
      with a fourth allegorical figure called Worldly Prudence, have
      been appointed to prepare women for admission to the utopian
      City of Ladies. They are about to deliver a "leçon de sapience"
      on correct feminine behavior which CH has been asked to tran-
      scribe. Although their lectures also offer psychological advice,
      the Virtues' main concern is to help women solve the problems
      of everyday life.
          The treatise is divided into three parts. In the first (26
      chaps.), the teachings are directed at queens, princesses, and
      women from the nobility. In the second (13 chaps.), at ladies
      of the Court and noblewomen of lesser rank. In the third (13
      chaps.), at women from the bourgeosie. The advice given is
      consistent with the social position, marital status, and lifestyle
      of each group addressed. High-born ladies are thus instructed
      in the handling of servants and in the running of a husband's
      estate during his absence. Ladies-in-waiting and others employed
      in the household of a princess are urged to be loyal to their
      mistresses, avoid scandal, and eschew envious thoughts. Dames
      and damoiselles are told not to wear conspicuous dress or indulge
      in arrogance or pride. Women of the bourgeoisie are exhorted
      to love their spouses, run their homes properly, and exercise
      discretion so as not to bring disgrace upon themselves. In-
      structions in proper conduct are also offered to wives of mer-
      chants, tradesmen, laborers, servants, chambermaids, widows,
      the elderly, the poor, nuns, and even to femmes de folle vie.
      Upon concluding their dictation the Virtues vanish, leaving CH
      tired but eager to pass these valuable lessons along to women
      of all classes throughout the world.

TEXTUAL SOURCES:
De dictis e factis memorabilibus, Valerius Maximus
Politics, Aristotle

MANUSCRIPTS:
Boston, Public Library 1528, 98 ff.
Brussels, BR 9236, ff. 134^r-224^r.
_____, ___ 9551-9552, ff. 1-87.
_____, ___ 10973, 90 ff.
_____, ___ 10974, 92 ff.
Dresden, Sächsische Landesbibliothek Oc. 55, 151 ff. (MS lost
    as of 1938-1945).
Lille, Bibliothèque Municipale fonds Godefroy 152, ff. 18-109.
London, BL Add. 15641, 176 ff.
_____, ___ ____ 31841, 71 ff.
New Haven, Yale Univ., Beinecke Library 427, 95 ff.
Oxford, Bodley D5, 208 ff.
Paris, Arsenal 3356, ff. 129-264.
_____, BN f.fr. 452, 93 ff.
_____, ___ ____ 1091, ff. 15^v-101.
_____, ___ ____ 1177, ff. 113-207.
_____, ___ ____ 1180, 114 ff.
_____, ___ ____ 22937, 89 ff.
_____, ___ ____ 25294, 194 ff.
Saint Omer, Bibliothèque Municipale 127, ff. 1-104.
The Hague, Koninklijke Bibliotheek 131.C.26.
Vienna, Österreichische Nationalbibliothek Cod. Vindob. 2604,
    93 ff.

EDITIONS--Note: a modern edition has been prepared by C. C.
Willard for the Bibliothèque du XVe Siècle.

260 Le trésor de la cité des dames. Paris: Antoine Vérard, 1497.
     Early printed edition.

261 Le trésor de la cité des dames. Paris: Michel Le Noir, 1503.
     Early printed edition.

262 Le trésor de la cité des dames. Paris: Denis Janot et Jehan
     André, 1536.
         The misspelling of CH's surname (Pisan instead of Pizan)
     can be traced to the title page of this early printed edition.

263 Debower, Lore Loftfield. "Le Livre des trois vertus of Chris-
     tine de Pisan." Ph.D. Massachusetts 1979. DAI, XL (1979),
     1454-55A.
         Unpublished, modern edition based on the Boston Public Li-
     brary manuscript. The text (pp. 118-411) is preceded by intro-
     ductory chapters dealing with women's roles in the Middle Ages
     (pp. 1-7), the life of CdP (pp. 8-23), her works (pp. 26-44),
     her reputation and literary influences (pp. 48-68), her audience
     (pp. 73-88), the style of Vertus (pp. 89-105), and its manuscripts

(pp. 106-16). Includes a bibliography (pp. 412-19), an Index
Nominum, an index with the dedicatory epistle to Marguerite
of Nevers, and a table showing the chronological printings of
CH's work. Has no glossary.

TRANSLATIONS (see also entry no. 826):

264 O Espelho de Christina. Lisbon: Hernão de Campos, 1518.
A Portuguese translation.

265 Carstens-Grokenberger, Dorothee, ed. Christine de Pisan:
'Buch von den drei Tugenden' in portugiesicher Übersetzung.
(Portugiesische Forschungen der Görresgesellschaft, hgg. von
Hans Flasche, zweite Reihe, Band I). Münster, Westfalen: As-
chendorffsche Verlagsbuchhandlung, 1961.
   An edition of the Portuguese translation, O Livre das tres
vertudes, based on Madrid Biblioteca Nacional MS 11515 (manuscript lacks subtitle and dedications). Besides the text, pp.
38-152, the edition contains an Introduction, a short glossary,
an index of names, plates of the manuscript's title page, and
plates of the colophon of the printed Lisbon edition. This edition has been both praised and attacked by critics. CR's:
754. See also:
   Broteria, LXXV (1962), 491-93
   Revista Portuguesa de Filologia, XII (1962-1963), 757, and
      XIII (1964-1965), 362-64

266 Lawson, Sarah, trans. 'The Treasure of the City of Ladies,'
or 'The Book of the Three Virtues.' Middlesex, U.K./New York:
Penguin Books, 1985.
   This is the first translation of Trois vertus into English.
The text, pp. 31-180, is preceded by an Introduction, pp. 15-
27. Has no notes, glossary, bibliography, or other scholarly
apparatus. CR: 767. See also:
   Times Educational Supplement (5 April 1985), 23
   Los Angeles Times Book Review (21 July 1985), 8
   Booklist, LXXXI (August 1985), 1622
   Women's Review of Books, III (January 1986), 14

NOTES AND STUDIES:
See also Dow 594, Favier 423, Kemp-Welch 586, Margolis 530,
Melegari 587, Rigaud 585, Willard 567.

267 Laigle, Mathilde. 'Le Livre des trois vertus' de Christine de
Pisan et son milieu historique et littéraire. (Bibliothèque du
XVe Siècle, XVI). Paris: Champion, 1912.
   Important 375-page study which discusses Vertus' theme and
examines CH's educational ideas and views on women. Also
deals with the work's title, date, and composition. CR: 766.

268 Willard, Charity Cannon. "The Three Virtues of Christine de
Pisan." Boston Public Library Quarterly, II (1950), 291-305.

Describes Boston Public Library MS 1528 containing <u>Vertus</u>
as "the only book by Christine in America in its original form"
(p. 304), and discusses this text's importance and influence.

269 Kelso, Ruth. <u>Doctrine for the Lady of the Renaissance</u>. Urbana: Univ. of Illinois Press, 1956. CdP: p. 5, 6, 8, 13, 19,
26, 27, 29, 30, 32, 85, 87, 121, 127, 128, 210, 230–63, 281–84,
291, 301–03.
Significant references to CH in opening pages and throughout
the book. See especially Chap. VII where author discusses
<u>Vertus</u> and CH's ideas on women at court.

270 Figueiredo, A. J. de. "Espelho de Cristina." <u>Revista Brasileira
de Filologia</u>, III (1957), 117–19.
Deals with the two Portuguese translations of <u>Vertus</u> in Madrid, Biblioteca Nacional MS 11515 and in Lisbon Biblioteca Nacional. For more on these translations, see Willard 271 and
Bernard in 827.

271 Willard, Charity Cannon. "A Portuguese Translation of Christine de Pisan's <u>Livre des trois vertus</u>." <u>PMLA</u>, LXXVIII (1963),
459–64.
Indicates that the Portuguese translation in Madrid, Biblioteca Nacional, MS 11515, was made at request of queen Isabel
of Portugal between 1447 and 1455 and printed in Lisbon in
1518.

272 Acworth, Evelyn. <u>The New Matriarchy</u>. London: Victor Gol-
lancz, 1965.
In section on the "Social and Economic Life in the Middle
Ages" author quotes from <u>Vertus</u>.

273 Willard, Charity Cannon. "The Manuscript Tradition of the
<u>Livre des trois vertus</u> and Christine de Pizan's audience." <u>JHI</u>,
XXVII (1966), 433–44.
Traces <u>Vertus</u>' manuscript tradition to the French nobility
but shows that by the end of Middle Ages CH's audience also
included bourgeois and educated townspeople.

274 Bell, Susan Groag, ed. <u>Women: From the Greeks to the French
Revolution</u>. A Historical <u>Anthology</u>. Belmont, CA: Wadsworth
Publishing, 1973. CdP: p. 6, 163, 165, 169, 171, 174, 180.
Various comments concerning CH's views on women in society
with special reference to <u>Trois vertus</u>.

275 Willard, Charity Cannon. "A Fifteenth-Century View of Women's
Role in Medieval Society: Christine de Pizan's <u>Livre des trois
vertus</u>." In <u>The Role of Women in the Middle Ages: Papers
of the Sixth Annual Conference of the Center for Medieval and
Early Renaissance Studies, State Univ. of New York at Bingham-
ton. 6–7 May 1972</u>. Ed. Rosemarie Thee Morewedge. Albany:
State Univ. of New York, 1975. pp. 90–120.

A critical discussion of the feminist and humanist attitudes
in Trois vertus. Attributes the didactic tone of this treatise
to CH's belief that "women had a serious role to play in society"
(p. 100). However, Willard advises latter-day feminists not to
read more into the work than is actually there. CR: 785.

276 Dulac, Liliane. "Inspiration mystique et savoir politique: les
conseils aux veuves chez Francesco da Barberino et chez Christine de Pizan." In Mélanges à la mémoire de Franco Simone:
France et Italie dans la culture européenne, I: Moyen Age et
Renaissance. (Bibliothèque Franco Simone, IV). Geneva:
Slatkine, 1980. pp. 113-14.
Comparative study of the widowhood theme in Vertus (1405)
and Barberino's Del Reggimento e Costumi di Donna (Bologna,
1875). Dulac was unable to demonstrate direct borrowing by
Barberino from Vertus but found striking similarities between
the two works, most notably in their advice to widows. CR:
SF, 75 (1981), 532.

277 Bornstein, Diane. "The Ideal of the Lady of the Manor as Reflected in Christine de Pizan's Livre des trois vertus." In IFW
(1981), 117-28.
Tries to show that CH's portrayal of the "Lady of the Manor"
in Vertus was not just a theoretical construct but a reflection
of the realities of fifteenth-century life. CF: SF, 78 (1982),
530.

278 Willard, Charity Cannon. "Christine de Pizan's Livre des Trois
Vertus: Feminine Ideal or Practical Advice?" In IFW (1981),
91-116.
The latter. Vertus deals with the everyday problems of real
women whereas the Cité des dames (227) focuses on the achievements of legendary women. This seems to account for the difference in tone between the two works.

279 Bornstein, Diane. The Lady in the Tower: Medieval Courtesy
Literature for Women. Hamden, CT: Archon Books, 1983. CdP:
on the Livre des trois vertus, p. 44, 67-70, 71, 75, 82-93, 103,
105-12, 120; on the Cité des dames, p. 12, 27-28, 30, 70, 71,
83, 87-93, 101; on the Avision, p. 27; on Charles V, p. 82;
on Fais d'armes et de chevalerie, p. 92.
A survey of didactic writings for and about women that discusses CH's contributions to medieval courtesy literature, with
special reference to the above works. CR: 748.

280 EPISTRE À LA REINE (Epistre à la Royne de France; Epistre
à Isabeau de Bavière; Lettre à Isabeau de Bavière) 1405
A petition for peace composed on 5 October 1405 when civil war
in France seemed imminent. Though officially addressed to the
French queen, Isabeau of Bavaria (811), this epistle was probably

also meant for her brother-in-law, Louis of Orleans (815), who
had become her constant companion after the onset of Charles
VI's (799) mental illness.   Through the Queen, Louis tried to
gain control over the dauphin and the French regency but his
political ambitions led to a fierce power-struggle with his cousin,
John the Fearless of Burgundy (814).   Having political ambitions
of his own, Burgundy was determined to undermine his rival's
influence at the royal court.   The Burgundian-Orleanist conflict (see 792, 814, 815) came to a head in August 1405 when
John discovered that Louis and Isabeau had conspired to trans-
fer the dauphin from Paris to the Château of Melun.   The inci-
dent turned into a political crisis that prompted both sides to
mobilize their troops.

It was during this crucial period that CH drafted her letter
to the Queen.   In it she implores Isabeau to become the peacemaker between the two factions in order to spare the nation
from civil war.   Not only does her timely epistle evoke the ter-
rors of war but in suggesting that France might be dishonored
by a great army it actually anticipated Agincourt which was
only a decade away.   After describing the devastation a civil
war would bring, CH beseeches the Queen to give her request
serious consideration.   To this letter she added a postscript in
form of a rondeau, which she placed after her signature.   It
is not clear for whom it was intended, but presumably she wrote
it for Louis of Orleans or John the Fearless.

MANUSCRIPTS:
Brussels, BR IV 1176, 8 ff.
Chantilly, Musée Condé 493, ff. 427^V-29^V.
Oxford, All Souls 182, ff. 230^d-32^d.
Paris, BN f.fr. 580, ff. 53^r-54^V.
_____, ___ _____ 604, ff. 314^r-314^V.
_____, ___ _____ 605, ff. 1-2^V.

EDITIONS:
See also Wisman 729, pp. 70-83.

281   Mirot, Léon.   "L'enlèvement du Dauphin et le premier conflit
entre Jean san Peur et Louis d'Orléans."   RQH, XCVI (1914),
415-19.
      Prints text of the Epistre.

282   Legge, Mary Dominica, ed.   "Christine de Pisan to Isabelle of
Bavaria, Paris, October 5, 1405."   No. 99 of the Anglo-Norman
Letters and Petitions from All Sould MS 182.   (Anglo-Norman
Text Society, III).   Oxford: Blackwell, 1941; rpt. 1971.
      Legge's critical edition is based on All Souls MS 182, with
variants from the three Parisian manuscripts, BN f.fr. 580, 605,
604.   The text, pp. 144-50, is preceded by a history of All
Souls.   Replaces Thomassy, 701.

NOTE:
See also Lenient 508, Reno 486, Thomassy 701, Willard 472.

283   Verdon, Jean. _Isabeau de Bavière_. Paris: Tallandier, 1981.
       Pages 142-43 contain references to CH and the _Epistre_. In-
       cludes reproduction of frontispiece from Harley 4431.

284   L'AVISION-CHRISTINE (1405)
       This is a dream-vision in which CH explores three different
       realms: the material, the intellectual, the spiritual. It is also
       in part an autobiographical account of her life written at age
       forty when she thought she had passed the midpoint of her
       "pilgrimage."
       Following her usual tripartite format, she devotes the first
       part of the treatise (ff. 1-24) to a figurative description of her
       birth and meeting with the Crowned Lady who symbolizes France.
       The latter narrates a condensed version of French history in-
       volving a mythical garden and Golden Bough from Troy. The
       Lady describes for CH how a shoot from the Bough was tran-
       planted into the soil of Gaul, where it took root and flourished.
       The plants growing in the garden signified newly acquired
       French territories; the weeds, foreign invaders; the gardeners
       tending the vegetation, France's good and bad rulers. The
       Golden Bough had been on the verge of extinction but was saved
       by the dawn of a new age. Tracing the rise and fall of the
       French kingdom, the Crowned Lady recalls the Merovingian kings,
       Childeric, the early Capetian dynasty, St. Louis, and other
       historical personages. When she reaches CH's own era she
       makes a diagnosis of the country's ills, analyzing the moral de-
       ficiencies of France's contemporary rulers. The inept Charles
       VI (799) is alluded to as a butterfly and noble bird of prey.
       While lamenting the nation's decline under his rule the Crowned
       Lady glances backward to the glorious reign of Charles V (798).
       The second part of the book (ff. 25-48) continues the uni-
       versal history begun in the _Mutacion_ (174). Taking place in
       Paris, the "second Athens," it ranges over a wide variety of
       subjects from cosmology and science to politics, philosophy, and
       religion. Here we see CH visit the University of Paris where
       she engages in a dialogue with a shadowy figure later identified
       as Dame Opinion. Claiming to be the daughter of Ignorance and
       of the desire for knowledge, Opinion expounds on her role in
       human affairs. Though it is her mission to inspire people to
       seek the truth, she is unable to lead them to it as Opinion and
       Truth are incompatible. It is suggested that no mortal, however
       wise, can escape her influence. CH too is reminded by Opinion
       of her part in the debate over the _Roman de la Rose_. In this
       section Opinion discusses CH's writing. She urges her to con-
       tinue with it and predicts that after her death a valiant prince
       would come who, hearing of her work, will wish to have known
       her. After having demonstrated Dame Opinion's sway over

humankind, CH concludes that the world is governed more often by opinion than knowledge.

In the third part of the book (ff. 49-79) she tells how Philosophy brings her consolation at last. In a talk with this Boethian figure CH reveals the story of her life. Personal losses and other past misfortunes are recounted. After airing her private grievances and grappling with unresolved psychological conflicts, she learns from Philosophy that suffering is part of the divine plan and that true happiness can only be found in God.

TEXTUAL SOURCES:
De Consolatione Philosophiae, Boethius
Divine Comedy, Dante
Grandes Chroniques de France
Metaphysics, Aristotle; St. Thomas Aquinas's commentary of

MANUSCRIPTS:
Brussels, BR 10309, 79 ff.
Paris, BN f.fr. 1176, 81 ff.
Private Collection, ex-Phillipps 128.

EDITIONS:
Note: Christine M. Reno is presently preparing a new edition of this text.

285 Babcock, Earl Brownell. "A Critical Edition of the Vision of Christine de Pizan, Part III." Ph.D. Chicago 1915.

286 Towner, Sister Mary Louise, ed. Lavision-Christine: Introduction and Text. (The Catholic Univ. of America Studies in Romance Languages and Literatures, VI). Washington, DC: The Catholic Univ. of America, 1932; rpt. New York: AMS Press, 1969.

This edition is based on the Brussels MS with variants from Paris 1176. The Introduction offers a biographical summary of the author (pp. 1-13), an analysis of the text (pp. 14-54), and a discussion of the manuscripts and present edition (pp. 55-70). Text (pp. 73-193) is followed by notes clarifying complicated passages (pp. 195-205), a bibliography (pp. 207-209), an index of proper names (pp. 211-17), and an index rerum (pp. 218-20).

NOTE AND STUDIES:
See also Blanchard 454; Bornstein 279, 637; Cropp 444; Fantuzzi 376; Friedman 77; Koch 382; Muir 453; Wieland 375; Willard 442.

287 Reno, Christine M. "Self and Society in L'Avision-Christine of Christine de Pizan." Ph.D. Yale 1972. DAI, XXXIV (1972), 1292A.

Explores the dialectical unity of the Avision and CH's attempt to resolve the "tension" between herself and society. The study

(I) surveys CH's life and works, (II) deals with the dialectic
of the Avision, (III) considers the dialectic vis-a-vis CH as a
woman and widow, (IV) discusses the unfolding dialectic and
rejection of Dame Opinion, and (V) analyzes the third part of
the work. Appendix I treats the Avision and CH's later writings. Appendix II provides a short summary of the Avision.
Reno is now in process of preparing new critical ed. of this
text.

288 Sotheby & Co. Bibliotheca Phillippica. Medieval Manuscripts.
     n.s. Pt. VII. London: Sotheby, 1972.
        Sotheby's 1972 Sales Catalog states on p. 61 that the author
     of the Avision's preliminary gloss in Phillips MS 128 is unknown.
     Since then a study by Ouy and Reno has identified the author
     of this gloss. It is CH. For a full account of this important
     codicological discovery see 289 below.

289 Ouy, Gilbert, and Christine M. Reno. "Identification des auto-
     graphes de Christine de Pizan." Scriptorium, XXXIV (1980),
     221-38.
        Important manuscript study that led to identification of CH's
     handwriting. Investigation centered on little-known text of the
     Avision in ex-Phillipps MS 128 (now in private collection) of
     which a codicological description is given in Appendix II. In-
     cludes specimen pages of the three Avision MSS.

290 Durley, Maureen Slattery. "The Crowned Dame, Dame Opinion,
     and Dame Philosophy: The Female Characteristics of Three
     Ideals in Christine de Pizan's Lavision-Christine." In IFW,
     (1981), 29-50.
        Probes the psychological meaning of the three allegorical
     figures in the Avision and explains what their progression from
     the material to the immaterial life symbolizes. CR: SF, 78
     (1982), 529.

291 LE LIVRE DE PRUDENCE (Le Livre de prudence a l'enseignement
     de bien vivre) c. 1405-1406
     This work is a translation, with gloss, of the Pseudo-Seneca's
     (Martin de Braga) De Quattuor Virtutibus. It deals with virtues
     presumably leading to wisdom: Prudence, Fortitude, Temperance,
     Justice.

     TEXTUAL SOURCES:
     Bible
     Church Fathers
     Pseudo-Seneca (Martin de Braga)
     (selected) Philosophers

     MANUSCRIPTS:
     Brussels, BR 11065-11073, ff. 236^r-72^r.

_____, ___ 11074-11078, ff. 72^r-115^r.
London, BL Harley 4431, ff. 268^a-287^c.
Paris, BN f.fr. 605, ff. 5^v-22^r.
_____, __ _____ 2240, ff. 1-36^v.
_____, __ _____ 5037, ff. 182-221.
Rome, Biblioteca Apostolica Vaticana Reg. lat. 1238, ff. 1^r-46^r.

EDITION:
No modern edition exists.

NOTE AND STUDY:
See Picherit 294, Tuve 471.

292 LE LIVRE DE LA PROD'HOMMIE DE L'HOMME (c. 1405-1406)
This is a revision of 291, dedicated to Louis of Orleans (815).
No modern edition exists of this work.

NOTE AND STUDY:

293 Solente, Suzanne. "Date de deux ouvrages de Christine de
Pisan." BEC, XCIV (1933), 422.
    Reconsiders date of two works discussed in review article
(775a) with conclusion that Prod'hommie was written before the
Livre du corps de policie.

294 Picherit, Jean-Louis. "Le Livre de la Prod'hommie de l'homme
et le Livre de Prudence de Christine de Pisan: chronologie,
structure et composition." MA, XCI (1985), 381-413.
    Deals with CH's use of the Pseudo-Seneca's (Martin de Braga)
De Quattuor Virtutibus in Prod'hommie and the Livre de prudence. Picherit attributes the translation of de Braga's Latin
text to someone other than CH but feels the prologue and glos-
ses are definitely hers. He offers interesting explanation as
to how CH's two versions of Virtutibus came to be written and
reexamines their structure and chronology. CR: SF, 92 (1987),
271.

295 LE LIVRE DU CORPS DE POLICIE (1406-1407)
A "mirror" for the prince written for the French dauphin, Louis
of Guyenne. It attempts to create a harmonious society by pre-
scribing specific roles for each of the three estates: princes,
nobles, the people. The general plan for the work comes from
the Policraticus (1159) of John of Salisbury, as does the meta-
phor of a "body politic" composed of a head, trunk, arms and
legs. However, Policie is neither a translation of that text nor
an exposition of it; rather, it is a collection of facts gathered
from various sources, primarily from Valerius Maximus. Its
most immediate source though may have been Jean Gerson's sermon "Vivat Rex" to which CH's treatise has been compared (see
Willard, 450, p. 178).

Being analogous to the human body, the Body Politic is divided into three parts each corresponding to a different part
of the human anatomy. Part I (33 chaps.) is addressed to the
prince or head of the body. It deals with the prince's education and recommends that he be taught moral values as well as
practical skills. Discipline, humanistic learning, and early ex-
posure to the workings of government are stressed.

Part II (20 chaps.) is addressed to knights or the arms and
hands of the body. Dealing with the attributes of knighthood,
it lists six qualities considered essential for good knights.
They include devotion to arms, bravery in combat, a sense of
honor, the lending of mutual support, keeping one's word, and
knowledge of military matters and of one's enemy.

Part III (10 chaps.) is addressed to the "université de tout
le peuple" or the trunk and legs of the body. It concerns the
common people and defines their place in the body politic.

Although CH was not unsympathetic to the masses she strongly
opposed popular rule. She believed in hereditary monarchy and
remained a divine-right monarchist to the end, as Chaps. XXIV
and XXV clearly demonstrate. Her ideal monarch was Charles
V (798), whom she holds up here and elsewhere as a model for
all future French rulers to emulate.

TEXTUAL SOURCES:
Bible
Church Fathers
De dictis et factis memorabilibus, Valerius Maximus; Simon de
    Hesdin and Nicholas Gonesse's French translation of
De officiis, Cicero
De regimine principum, Egidio Colonna (Gilles of Rome)
De re militari, Vegetius
De Senectute
Ethics, Aristotle; Nicole Oresme's French translation of
Policraticus, John of Salisbury
Rhetoric, Aristotle

MANUSCRIPTS:
Besançon, Bibliothèque Publique 423, 81 ff.
Brussels, BR 10440, 59 ff.
Chantilly, Musée Condé 294, 100 ff.
London, BL Harley 4410, 72 ff.
New York, Public Library, Spencer Collection 17, ff. 127-86.
Paris, Arsenal 2681, 94 ff.
_____, BN f.fr. 1197, 106 ff.
_____, __ _____ 1198, 62 ff.
_____, __ _____ 1199, 58 ff.
_____, __ _____ 12439, ff. 46^V-225.

EDITION:

296 Lucas, Robert Harold, ed. 'Le Livre du corps de policie' of

Christine de Pisan: A Critical Edition. (Textes littéraires français, CXLV). Geneva: Droz, 1967.

Edition is based on BN f.fr. 12439. The text, pp. 1-205, is preceded by a 49-page Introduction which deals with the sources, manuscripts, previous editions, date of composition, establishment of text, and the text itself. It also gives the historical background for the work and comments on CH's political thought. Includes a bibliography, pp. 207-11, and an appendix with the variants from the English manuscript and printed edition. Lacks index of names and glossary for obscure passages. Edition has been cited for misprints and faulty punctuation. CR's: 769. See also:

SF, 34 (1968), 125
EHR, LXXXIV (April 1969), 386
BHR, XXXII (1970), 228-31

TRANSLATIONS:

297 The Body of Polycye. London: John Skot, 1521.
A Middle English translation.

298 The Body of Polycye. (The English Experience, CCCIV). Amsterdam/New York: Da Capo Press, Theatrvm Orbis Terrarvm Ltd., 1971.

Facsimile, unpaged and with illustrations, of the Skot edition printed in London in 1521 from copies preserved at John Rylands (shelfmark 15056) and Cambridge Univ. (Sel. 4.38) libraries. Head of title reads: "Du Castel."

299 Bornstein, Diane, ed. The Middle English Translation of Christine de Pisan's 'Livre du corps de policie' edited from MS C.U.L. Kk. 1.5. (Middle English Texts, VII). Heidelberg: Carl Winter, 1977.

This edition was transcribed from the unique manuscript at Cambridge Univ. Library with variants from Skot's 1521 (297) printed edition and the French original. It consists of the text of the Body of Polycye (p. 39-193), notes (pp. 194-213), a glossary (pp. 214-20), a bibliography (pp. 221-24), and an introductory chapter containing the critical apparatus (pp. 8-38). The editor presents evidence here, on which she elaborates in 305, suggesting that the translator of this work may have been Anthony Woodville (97). She also discusses the "style clergial" used in the translation and supplies full citations to CH's sources in the notes. Includes facsimiles of MS C.U.L. Kk. 1.5 (p. 20) and of the title page of the Skot edition (p. 21). CR: 747. See also Speculum, LIII (1978), 433.

NOTES AND STUDIES:
See also Contamine 214, Joukovsky-Micha 425, Mombello 553, Solente 293, Willard 442.

300 Bennett, Henry S. Chaucer and the Fifteenth Century. 1947;

2nd ed. Oxford: Clarendon Press, 1965.
Reveals (p. 303) that John Skot's sixteenth-century translation, The Body Polycye (297), is not the same work as the Body
of Polocye. The latter seems to be an anonymous translation
of the Corps de policie dating from c. 1470.

301   Bell, Dora M. L'Idéal éthique de la royauté en France au Moyen
Âge d'après quelques moralistes du temps. Geneva: Droz;
Paris: Minard, 1962.
Includes a critique of Policie and the Livre de la paix, pp.
105-31.

302   Bornstein, Diane. "Humanism in Christine de Pisan's Livre du
corps de policie." BF, III (Fall 1974), 100-15.
Gives reasons why Policie should be viewed as a humanistic
document rather than as a conservative piece of chivalric idealism. CR: SF, 57 (1975), 527.

303   _____. "Reflections of Political Theory and Political Fact in
Fifteenth-Century Mirrors for the Prince." In Medieval Studies
in Honor of Lilliane Herlands Hornstein. Ed. Jess B. Bessinger,
Jr., and Robert R. Raymo. New York: New York Univ. Press,
1976. pp. 77-85.
Discusses Policie in terms of its humanistic influences and as
mirror of the political struggles of the day.

304   _____. "French Influence on Fifteenth-Century English Prose
as Exemplified by the Translation of Christine de Pisan's Livre
du corps de policie." MS, XXXIX (1977), 369-86.
Shows how CH's "style clergial" influenced both the English
translation of Policie and Caxton's translation of the Livre des
fais d'armes et de chevalerie. On CH's style clergial, see also
Burnley 507 and Ferrier 716.

305   _____. "Sir Anthony Woodville as the Translator of Christine
de Pisan's Livre du corps de policie." FCS, II (1979), 9-19.
Uses internal and external evidence to demonstrate that Woodville translated this work. Similarities in style, language, and
translational procedures between the Body of Polycye and Woodville's other translations are noted. Discusses Woodville also in
299, pp. 31-36. CR: SF, 77 (1982), 322.

306   Beltran, Evencio. "Christine de Pizan, Jacques Legrand et la
Communiloquium de Jean de Galles." Romania, CIV (1983), 208-
28.
Identifies the Communiloquium (c. 1304) as important but
hitherto unrecognized source for Legrand's Sophilogium and CH's
Corps de policie and Long estude, and calls attention to the
stylistic similarities between it and CH's Charles V. Extracts
from above texts on pp. 215-22 demonstrate the extent of Legrand's and CH's borrowings. CR: SF, 86 (1985), 360.

307 COMPLAINTES AMOUREUSES (1407)
     CH composed two complaintes. The first consists of 240 lines,
     the second of 192. Both deal with the pursuit of love. Allu-
     sions are made to Pygmalion, the history of Deucalion and Pyrrha,
     and to the punishment of Anaxarete.

     MANUSCRIPTS:
     Chantilly, Musée Condé 492, ff. 35^r-36^v.
     London, BL Harley 4431, ff. 48^r-49^v, 56^v-58^r.
     Paris, Arsenal 3295, ff. 69^r-72^v.
     _____, BN f.fr. 604, ff. 27^r-28^v.
     _____, __ _____ 835, ff. 50^r-51^v.
     _____, __ _____ 12779, ff. 33^r-34^v.
     _____, __ Moreau 1686, ff. 67^r-70^v.

     EDITION:
     See Roy 702, I, pp. 281-95.

308 ENCORE AUTRES BALLADES (1409-1410)
     To the Autres ballades (171) CH appended nine more poems en-
     titled Encore autres ballades and a ballade cycle called Cent
     ballades d'amant et de dames (309).

     MANUSCRIPT:
     London, BL Harley 4431, ff. 49^v-51^r.

     EDITION:
     See Roy 702, I, pp. 271-79.

309 CENT BALLADES D'AMANT ET DE DAME (1409-1410)
     A cycle of one hundred short lyrics presented in dialogue form.
     They chronicle a love affair between a Lover and his Lady that
     ends in bitter disappointment for the Lady. Bereft and ill in
     bed with a fever, she gives voice to her regrets in a "Lay de
     Dame" at the conclusion of the cycle.

     MANUSCRIPT:
     London, BL Harley 4431, ff. 376^r-98^r.

     EDITIONS:
     See Roy 702, III, pp. 209-317.

310 Cerquiglini, Jacqueline, ed. Christine de Pizan: Cent Ballades
     d'Amant et de Dame. (Collection 10/18, Bibliothèque Médiévale,
     No. 1529). Paris: Union Générale d'Éditions, 1982.
         An update of Roy, 702, III, pp. 209-317. The text (pp. 31-
     140) is preceded by an Introduction (pp. 7-24), a statement on
     the establishment of the text (pp. 25-27), and a bibliography
     (pp. 28-30). It is followed by notes (pp. 141-44), a glossary

(pp. 145-55), and a table of proper names for characters ap-
pearing in text (pp. 157-58). CR's:
  Rapports, LIII (1983), 183-84
  RLR, XLVII (1983), 259-60
  FCS, VII (1983), 345-47
  Romania, CIV (1983), 155-56
  MF (1983), 112
  SF, 83 (1984), 334-35
  MA, XC (1984), 317-20
  RPh, XXXVIII (1984-1985), 103-04

STUDY:
See also Du Bos 704, Willard 539, Wolfzettel 544.

311 Willard, Charity Cannon. "Christine de Pizan's Cent ballades
     d'amant et de dame: Criticism of Courtly Love." In Court and
     Poet: Selected Proceedings of the Third Congress of the Inter-
     national Courtly Literature Society, Liverpool, 1980. (ARCA,
     Classical and Medieval Texts, Papers and Monographs, V). Liver-
     pool: Francis Cairns, 1981. pp. 357-64.
       Suggests that the above ballades (a) reveal CH's misgivings
     about courtly love; (b) attempt to persuade women to deal with
     the realities of life instead of perpetuating illusions from the
     past; and (c) reflect CH's mature understanding of both poetic
     form and human experience.

312 LES SEPT PSAUMES ALLEGORISÉS (1409-1410)
     A lengthy prayer based on the seven penitential psalms. It
     was written between 26 June 1409 and 1 January 1410 at the
     request of Charles the Noble, king of Navarre. The psalms are
     "allegorized," or, figuratively interpreted. To each verset of the
     seven psalms (nos. 6, 31, 37, 51, 101, 129, 142) there is at-
     tached a prose meditation and petition. In these CH makes
     reference to familiar figures of her age: her patron Charles
     the Noble, king Charles VI (799), queen Isabeau (811), the
     French princes. Also, to the students of the University of
     Paris, the Church, the Popes, and to her own parents, friends,
     and benefactors.

     MANUSCRIPTS:
     Brussels, BR 19087, 87 ff.
     _____, ___ IV 1093, 97 ff.
     Paris, BN nouv. acq. fr. 4792, ff. 1^r-88^r.
     Private Collection: MS formerly in the collection of the Earl of
        Ashburnham.

     EDITION:

313 Rains, Ruth Ringland, ed. 'Les sept psaumes allegorisés' of
     Christine de Pisan: A Critical Edition from the Brussels and

Paris MSS. Washington, DC: The Catholic Univ. of America
Press, 1965.
    This is the first transcription of the Psaumes. The text
(pp. 84-158) is preceded by six preliminary chapters covering
the Psalms (pp. 1-23); The Penitential Psalms, The Number
Seven and Catechism (pp. 24-36); Allegory and Les sept psaumes
(pp. 37-50); The Author (pp. 51-63); The Historical Background (pp. 63-73); and The Origin of Medieval Libraries and
Manuscripts of the Psalms (pp. 74-83). The introductory chapters also deal with the meaning of the word allegorisés (a figurative method of interpretation using rhetoric) and the present
Psalter. The Latin text is given for comparison. Notes identifying Biblical and traditional elements appear at the end of each
Psalm. A glossary (pp. 159-69), a bibliography (pp. 170-79)
and a genealogical table of the House of Valois (p. 180) follow
the text. CR's: 776. See also:
    MA, LXXIII (1967), 171-73
    MAe, XXXVI (1967), 199-202
    RR, LIX (1968), 214-15

STUDY:

314 Delisle, Léopold Victor. "Notice sur Les sept psaumes alle-
    gorisés de Christine de Pisan." Notices et extraits des manu-
    scrits de la Bibliothèque Nationale et autres bibliothèques.
    XXXV, 2e partie (1896), 551-59.
        Basic study of the Psaumes and two of its manuscripts, MS
    Ashburnham and Paris, BN nouv. acq. fr. 4792.

315 LE LIVRE DES FAIS D'ARMES ET DE CHEVALERIE (1410)
    A manual on the art of warfare compiled from ancient and medi-
    eval sources. It contains information for knights about weap-
    onry, defense, military strategy, and rules concerning the wag-
    ing of war. According to those rules war is lawful when under-
    taken for "justice," that is, against usurpation and oppression.
    It is unlawful when waged for revenge or aggression. CH tried
    to make her rules for warfare as humane and civilized as pos-
    sible, basing them on Christian law and ethics. She outlawed
    the use of poisoned missiles, excessive ransom, plundering,
    and other barbaric practices. Her ideas are said to have con-
    tributed to the concept of international law but, according to
    her biographer, her motive for writing the treatise was to fos-
    ter discipline and loyalty in the French army (Willard, 450, p.
    186).
        Although this book is a compilation of Latin and French texts
    rather than an original work, CH used her sources with skill
    and imagination. Her invocation to the Roman goddess Minerva
    (at the beginning) is original, as is the idea of adapting Roman
    army codes to contemporary circumstances and conditions. The
    manual is divided into four books each focusing on some aspect
    of warfare.

Book I (29 chaps.) was inspired by Vegetius. It states
Fais' basic premise: that God permits the waging of war for
"just" causes. After apologizing in the prologue for daring to
speak on such an important subject CH presents a discussion on
the causes of and justification for war. She gives reasons why
kings should not personally engage in battle (except in civil
war) and talks about the selection of leaders, fortifications,
campsites, supplies, and the qualities of a good constable.

Book II (38 chaps.) makes extensive use of Frontinus's
Stratagemata. Here CH deals with methods of defense, military
equipment, weapons used in naval warfare, and the strategies
employed by great generals.

Book III (27 chaps.) considers the legalistic side of warfare.
It is constituted of questions and answers which form a dialogue
between CH and her master Honoré Bouvet (Bonet 795), on
whose L'Arbre des batailles (c. 1387) the last two books of
this treatise are based.

Book IV (17 chaps.) discusses regulations applying to military
and civilian populations. It examines such issues as legalized
reprisals, safe-conduct, treaties, and judicial duels and combats.
The last chapter, on armorial insignia, looks at the question of
who should be permitted to have a coat of arms.

TEXTUAL SOURCES:
Arbre des batailles, L'; Honoré Bouvet (Bonet 795)
Bible
Church Fathers
De dictis et factis memorabilibus, Valerius Maximus
Epitoma rei militaris, Vegetius; Jean de Vignai's translation of
    (most important source)
Stratagemata, Frontinus

MANUSCRIPTS:
Bordeaux, Bibliothèque Municipale 815, ff. 1-156^V.
Brussels, BR 9009-90011, ff. 117-226^V.
_____, ___ 10205, 162 ff.
_____, ___ 10476, 132 ff.
Cambridge, Fitzwilliam Museum Add. no. 48 CFM21, 108 ff.
Cambridge, MA, Harvard Univ., Houghton Library 169, 254 ff.
Leningrad, Bibliothèque Saltykov Chtchédrine, F.II. 96, 82 ff.
London, BL Harley 4605, 116 ff.
_____, ___ Royal 15. E. VI, ff. 405-38.
_____, ___ _____ 19. B. XVIII, 99 ff.
Oxford, Bodley 824, 143 ff.
Paris, BN f.fr. 585, 132 ff.
_____, ___ _____ 603, ff. 1-80.
_____, ___ _____ 1183, 222 ff.
_____, ___ _____ 1241, ff. 1-83^r.
_____, ___ _____ 1242, 166 ff.
_____, ___ _____ 1243, 134 ff.
_____, ___ _____ 23997, 154 ff.

_____, ___ Duchesne 65, ff. 79-82.

Turin, Archivio di Stato J. b. II. 15, 96 ff.

_____, Biblioteca Reale, Raccolta di Saluzzo 17, 242 ff.

_____, _____ _____, _____ ___ _____ 328, 317 ff.

EDITIONS:

316 L'Art de chevalerie selon Végèce suivi du livre des faits d'armes
     et de chevalerie. Paris: Antoine Vérard, 1488.
        Early printed edition published in finely executed folio. Ver-
     ard's text is said to depart considerably from the original. He
     modified CH's title, omits her name as author, changes the sex
     of the narrator from female to male, drops the invocation to
     Minerva and, in Book III, replaces CH and Bouvet (Bonet 795)
     with "L'Aucteur" and "Le Disciple."

317 L'Arbre des batailles et fleur de chevalerie selon Végèce, avec-
     ques plusieurs hystoires et utilles remonstrances du fait de
     guerre par luy extraictes de Frontin, Valere et de plusieurs
     aultres aucteurs comme pourrez veoir cy apres. Paris: Philippe
     Le Noir, 1527.
        This is a rare early printed edition based on Vérard. CH's
     name has again been omitted and further editorial changes have
     been made in the text. On a recently discovered copy of this
     edition, see Wareham 333.

TRANSLATIONS:

318 Caxton, William, trans. The Boke of the Fayt of Armes and of
     Chyualrye. Westminster: W. Caxton, 1489 or 1490.
        Early printed edition by Caxton made at request of Henry
     VII of England. On the date of publication, see Byles 319, pp.
     xxix-xxx.

319 Byles, A. T. P., ed. The Book of Fayttes of Armes and of
     Chyualrye: translated and printed by William Caxton from the
     French original by Christine de Pisan. (EETS, o.s., CLXXXIX)
     1932; reissued with corrections London: Oxford Univ. Press,
     1937; rpt. Millwood, NY: Kraus, 1985.
        This is the first new edition of Fayttes to appear in nearly
     500 years. No Modern French text has ever been published.
     Byles's Introduction discusses the author of the treatise (pp.
     xi-xiv); the manuscripts (pp. xiv-xxvi); the printers Vérard,
     Le Noir, Caxton (pp. xxvi-xxxvi); the sources (pp. xxxvi-li);
     Caxton as translator (pp. li-lv); and the principle of editing
     (p. lvi). Latin citations in the margins of text show how CH
     compiled her information on military organization. The text (pp.
     1-292) is followed by an appendix giving the "Contents of Vege-
     tius' Epitoma rei militaris" (pp. 293-97) and by a second appen-
     dix showing the extent of CH's textual borrowings from the
     Arbre des batailles of Honoré Bouvet--Bonet 795--(pp. 298-99).

Includes index of persons and places (pp. 301-04), a glossary
of obsolete words (pp. 305-15) and three plates. CR's: 752.

320 The Fayt of Armes and of Chyualrye. (The English Experience,
     XIII). Amsterdam/New York: Da Capo Press, Theatrvm Orbis
     Terrarvm Ltd., 1968.
         Facsimile of Caxton's 1489 translation, 318.

     NOTES AND STUDIES:
     See also Blake 105, Bornstein 297.

321 Blades, William. The Biography and Typography of William
     Caxton, England's First Printer.   1877; rpt. with new Intro-
     duction by James Moran. London: Frederick Muller, 1971.
         Blades was the editor of CH's Moral Proverbs (101) and one
     of England's first bibliographers. Here he discusses her Book
     of Fayttes as an illustration of Caxton's typography, pp. 332-
     34.

322 Nys, Ernest. Études de droit international et de droit politique.
     Paris: Fointemoing, 1896.
         Noted Belgian jurist traces the influence of Bouvet's (Bonet)
     Arbre des batailles (see 795) on CH's Fais d'armes. Also ex-
     plains why Fais came to occupy the important place it did in the
     later Middle Ages. (The chapter on CH and Bouvet was re-
     printed from the Revue de Droit International et de Législation
     Comparée, 14e année and appeared as a 25-page off-print under
     the title "Honoré Bonet et Christine de Pisan," Brussels: C.
     Muquart, 1882). See also Nys 546.

323 Bühler, Curt Ferdinand. Caxton Studies ... 8[pp.] illus.
     (facsim.) [Mainz, 1940].
         Used Pierpont Morgan Library copies of CH's Book of Fayttes,
     the Golden Legend, and the book called Caton to investigate
     Caxton's printing techniques.

324 Coopland, George William, ed. The Tree of Battles of Honoré
     Bonet: An English Version with an Introduction. Liverpool,
     U.K./Cambridge, MA: Harvard Univ. Press, 1949. CdP: p.
     11, 12, 22, 24, 25, 32, 34, 40, 45, 47, 48.
         In the Introduction attempts to clarify the connection between
     Bouvet (Bonet 795), CH, and Fais d'armes. Coopland thinks
     the master-disciple relationship CH alludes to in Fais may actually
     have existed.

325 _____. "Le Jouvencel (Re-Visited)." Symposium, V (1951),
     137-86.
         After making a detailed study of Jean de Bueil's Jouvencel,
     Coopland comes to conclusion that Chaps. XIV and XVII (in Pt.
     2) were copied from CH's Fais d'armes.

326 Aurner, Nellie Slayton. Caxton: Mirrour of Fifteenth-Century

Letters. A Study of the Literature of the First English Press.
New York: Russell & Russell, 1965. CdP: p. 82, 92, 186,
187.
     Draws attention to Caxton's epilogue in The Boke of the Fayt
(318) in which he acknowledges CH's authorship.

327 Coopland, George William, ed. Philippe de Mézières. Le Songe
     du Vieil Pelerin. 2 vols. Cambridge, U.K.: Cambridge Univ.
     Press, 1969.
          Vol. I, 19, notes that entire passages of Jean de Bueil's Le
     Jouvencel were lifted from CH's Fais d'armes--as discussed in
     greater detail in Coopland 325. A reference to CH also in Vol.
     II, n. 12.

328 Barber, Richard. The Knight and Chivalry. New York:
     Charles Scribners', 1970. CdP: p. 139, 336.
          Comments on Fais d'armes and CH's attitude toward knights.

329 Willard, Charity Cannon. "Christine de Pizan's Treatise on the
     Art of Medieval Warfare." In Essays in Honor of Louis Francis
     Solano. Ed. Raymond J. Cormier and Urban T. Holmes. (Univ.
     of North Carolina Studies in the Romance Languages and Litera-
     tures, XCII). Chapel Hill: Univ. of North Carolina Press,
     1970. pp. 179-91.
          Gives description of Harvard, Houghton Library MS 168 con-
     taining text of the Livre des Fais d'armes et de chevalerie and
     speculates on CH's motives for writing it. Willard thinks the
     real inspiration behind this treatise may have been Petrarch
     rather than Vegetius.

330 Bornstein, Diane. Mirrors of Courtesy. Hamden, CT; Archon
     Books, 1975. CdP: pp. 39-44, 61.
          Suggests that the rules for armed conflict as outlined in
     Fais d'armes influenced not only medieval warfare but such
     special courts as the High Court of Chivalry in England.

331 Wisman, Josette A. "L'Epitoma rei militaris de Végèce et sa
     fortune au Moyen Âge." MA, LXXXV (1979), 13-31.
          Discusses Vegetius's influence on Fais d'armes, showing that
     CH sometimes translated the author directly whereas at other
     times she merely transposed his ideas. Includes chapter head-
     ings from Fais and the Epitoma to demonstrate the order and
     extent of CH's borrowings.

332 Contamine, Philippe. La Guerre au Moyen Âge. (Nouvelle Clio.
     L'Histoire et ses Problèmes). Paris: Presses Universitaires de
     France, 1980. CdP: p. 233, 263, 272, 284, 352, 439, 453,
     455, 464.
          Repeatedly cites Fais d'armes and the Livre de la paix on
     questions of French military history.

333 Wareham, T. E. "Christine de Pisan's Livre des Faits d'Armes
     et de Chevalerie and its fate in the sixteenth century." In
     SMSRQF (1981), 135–42.
         Describes how this work was mutilated at the hands of its
     first two editors (Vérard 316, and Le Noir 317) and calls atten-
     tion to a hitherto unknown (second) copy of Le Noir's in the
     Municipal Library of Nancy. CR:
         SF, 79 (1983), 125
         Speculum, LX (1985), 230

334 LA LAMENTACION SUR LES MAUX DE LA FRANCE (La Lamenta-
     cion sur les maux de la guerre civile du 23 août 1410) 1410
     A plea for peace addressed to the French princes, the queen,
     the royal council, and all the French people. The petition was
     drafted after failure of the Peace of Chartres (1409) when
     France was once again on the brink of civil war. Like CH's
     earlier letter to the Queen (280), of which it is reminiscent,
     this personal and moving document tries to warn the nation of
     the impending disaster. It implores the princes to do every-
     thing in their power to head off the approaching calamity. CH
     addresses her Lament most especially to Jean of Berry (812),
     to whom she now makes this final appeal: "Oh, Duke of Berry,
     Noble Prince ..." she cries, "How is it possible that your ten-
     der heart can bear to see you ... assembled ... to bear painful
     arms against your nephews?" (Wisman 729, p. 91). Unfortu-
     nately for all concerned, CH's letter came too late. For the
     truce that was signed at Bicêtre on 2 November 1410 collapsed,
     and civil war broke out the following year when the Armagnacs
     marched on Paris and the Burgundians intercepted them there
     in September 1411--see 792.

     MANUSCRIPT:
     Paris, BN f.fr. 24864, ff. 14^r-18^r.

     EDITION:
     See also Thomassy 701, pp. 141-49; Wisman 729, pp. 84-95.

335 Kennedy, Angus J. "La lamentacion sur les maux de la France
     de Christine de Pisan." In Mélanges de langue et littérature
     françaises du Moyen Âge et de la Renaissance offerts à Charles
     Foulon. Rennes: Institut de Français, Univ. de Haute-Bretagne,
     I, 1980. pp. 177-85.
         First new edition since Thomassy's nineteenth-century Essai
     (701), with corrections of the latter's text. CR: SF, 74 (1981),
     333.

336 LE LIVRE DE LA PAIX (1412-1413)
     A treatise on the education of princes dedicated to Louis of
     Guyenne. It attempts to teach the French dauphin how to

become a responsible and successful ruler and to instill in him
high moral principles. Having been inspired by the French
civil war and a popular uprising known as the Cabochian Revolt (796), this treatise also serves as a platform for CH's political ideas. The first chapters were written in September 1412
following the Treaty of Auxerre (August 1412). The second
part was drafted a year later after the signing of the Treaty
of Pointoise, in September 1413.

Divided into three parts, Paix deals with Prudence in Part
I (15 chaps.); with the virtues necessary for knights and princes
in Part II (18 chaps.); and with governing the nation or "la
chose publique" in Part III (48 chaps.). In various parts of
the book CH praises Louis of Guyenne for his peace efforts and
urges him to do all he can to preserve the peace. Citing examples from the life of the dauphin's grandfather, Charles V
(798), she suggests that a good ruler should cultivate in addition to prudence and justice the virtues of magnanimity, benignity, liberality, force (i.e., strength of character) and truth,
as outlined in her Livre des fais et bonnes meurs du sage roy
Charles V (192). In the third part of the book she alludes to
the recent Cabochian reign of terror and cautions the French
princes against granting the "diabolical common people" too
much authority. Yet even as she denounces popular rule, CH
was genuinely concerned about the welfare of the masses and
did not hesitate to remind the self-indulgent prince of his duty
to the nation and the people.

TEXTUAL SOURCES:
Book of Proverbs
Elenchiis, Aristotle
Ethics, Aristotle
Dits moreaux des philosophes, a translation by Guillaume de
    Tignonville of John of Procida's Dicta Philosophorum
Livre des fais et bonnes meurs du sage roy Charles V, CdP
Livre du trésor, Brunetto Latini
Paradiso (Parts III-V), Dante
Politics, Aristotle
Psalms, The
Rhetoric, Aristotle
Also: Boethius, Cicero, Gautier de Chatillon, Guido Fava, Ovid,
    Valerius Maximus, John of Salisbury, Seneca, Vegetius.

MANUSCRIPTS:
Brussels, BR 10366, ff. 1-108.
Paris, BN f.fr. 1182, ff. 1-128^V.

EDITION:

337 Willard, Charity Cannon, ed. The 'Livre de la Paix' of Chris-
    tine de Pisan: A Critical Edition with Introduction and Notes.
    's-Gravenhage: Mouton, 1958.

First modern edition of Paix based on Brussels, BR 10366
with the better-known Paris MS 1182 serving as the secondary
manuscript. The Introduction (pp. 9-54) deals with the text,
sources, manuscripts, and style and language of the work. It
also gives a complete account of the historical circumstances
surrounding the treatise and offers a discussion on CH and the
young duke of Guyenne. A final evaluation of the book is made
in the concluding section of the Introduction. Following the
text (pp. 55-181) there are notes (pp. 183-214) and a bibliography (pp. 215-19). This edition has been put on microfilm
as part of the MLAA Collection of Photographic Facsimiles, No.
480 F, Univ. of California Library, Berkeley. CR's: 784. See
also:
> Speculum, XXXIV (1959), 147-49
> RpH, XIII (1959-1960), 101-02
> LR, XV (1961), 171-73

NOTES AND STUDIES:
See also Batany 501; Bell 301; Contamine 214, 332; Cropp 444;
Favier 423; Mombello 553; Muir 453; Sneyders de Vogel 343;
Willard 487.

338 Viollet, Paul. "Quelques textes pour servir à l'histoire politique
des Parisiens au XVe siècle." Mémoires de la Société de l'Histoire de Paris. IV (1877), 155-82.
> One of the texts discussed is the Livre de la paix, pp. 168-
72.

339 Temple, Maud Elizabeth. "Paraphrasing in the Livre de la paix
of Christine de Pisan of the Paradiso, III-V." PMLA, XXXVII
(1922), 182-86.
> Tries to demonstrate Dante's influence in Paix by tracing
certain lines to his Divine Comedy.

340 Bartsch, Karl. Chrestomathie de l'ancien français (VIIIe-XVe
siècles). 12th ed. Leipzig: F. C. W. Vogel, 1927. CdP: pp.
284-86 and no. 89.
> French grammar prints extracts from Paix, the Enseignemens
moraux, and four of CH's poems.

341 Vale, Malcolm Graham Allan. War and Chivalry: Warfare and
Aristocratic Culture in England, France and Burgundy at the
End of the Middle Ages. London: Duckworth, 1981. CdP:
p. 10, 63, 64, 66, 68, 145.
> Discusses Paix and CH's view on military matters.

342 L'AVISION DU COQ (1413)
This work is no longer extant, but CH mentions it by name in
third part of the Livre de la paix, BN f.fr. 1182, f. 102^r.

STUDY:

343 Sneyders de Vogel, K. "Une oeuvre inconnue de Christine de
   Pisan." In Mélanges de philologie romane et de littérature médiévale offerts à Ernest Hoepffner. Paris: Les Belles Lettres,
   1949. pp. 369-70.
       The unknown work, L'Avision du coq, is no longer extant.
   CH refers to it in third part of her Livre de la paix--see above.
   Solente had already cited this text in 206, p. 3, a quarter of
   a century earlier.

344 L'EPISTRE DE LA PRISON DE VIE HUMAINE (L'Epistre de la
   prison de vie humaine et d'avoir reconfort de mort d'amis et
   patience en adversité) 1414-1418
   A consolatory letter addressed to Marie of Berry, duchess of
   Bourbon, and to all Frenchwomen having lost loved ones through
   war or other causes. It comprises twelve sections and a conclusion. The first acknowledges Marie's past kindnesses to CH
   and extends sympathies to her for the heavy losses she suffered
   at Agincourt (1415) and elsewhere. The title for this meditative
   work comes from St. Bernard, who likened human existence to
   a prison from which mortals could escape only through death.
   The epistle reminds readers of their mortality, provides examples
   of how the persecutors of humanity are punished, and gives
   reasons why CH's compatriots should bear their misfortunes with
   patience and fortitude. CH tells them, after Aristotle, that
   death is a natural process for all, not to be feared by the
   righteous. The compensation for dying young is avoiding the
   miseries and infirmities of old age. At the end, she describes
   how God bestows the joys of Paradise upon those who die with
   grace.

   TEXTUAL SOURCES:
   Aristotle
   Consolatio pro morte amici, possibly Vincent of Beauvais
   De arte moriendi, Albert Magnus
   De Consolatione Philosophiae, Boethius
   De dictis et factis memorabilibus, Valerius Maximus
   De remediis fortuitorum, Pseudo-Seneca
   Dits moreaux des philosophes, a translation by Guillaume de
       Tignonville of John of Procida's Dicta Philosophorum
   Doctors of the Church
   Florus
   Lactantius
   Macrobius, from the Commentary on the Dream of Scipio
   Maximianus, from the Elegiae
   Ovid
   Phaedo, Plato
   Prosper, from the Epigrammatum liber
   Quintillian
   Scriptures

Secundus
Speculum historiale, Vincent of Beauvais
Theodolus, from the Ecologa
(for additional sources, see Wisman 729, pp. xxviii-xxx)

MANUSCRIPT:
Paris, BN f.fr. 24786, ff. 36^r-97^r.

EDITIONS:
See also Wisman 729, pp. 1-69.

345 Kennedy, Angus J., ed. Epistre de la prison de vie humaine.
     Glasgow: Univ. of Glasgow, 1984 (Distrib. London: Grant &
     Cutler, Ltd., 11 Buckingham St., London W.C. 2).
        First complete edition, with glossary and index, of previously
     unedited text. Clarifies difficult passages and identifies CH's
     sources--on latter, see also Kennedy 349. Another edition of
     this work was put out simultaneously by Wisman, see note above.
     CR's: 765. Speculum, LXII (1987), 770-71.

     NOTE AND STUDY:
     See also Cropp 444, Margolis 530.

346 Solente, Suzanne. "Un traité inédit de Christine de Pisan:
     L'Epistre de la Prison de Vie Humaine." BEC, LXXXV (1924),
     263-301.
        Describes discovery of two previously unknown texts, Vie
     humaine, in BN f.fr. 24786 (of which partial edition is given
     here), and the Heures de contemplation sur la Passion de Nostre
     Seigneur, in BN nouv. acq. fr. 10059.

347 Kennedy, Angus J. "Christine de Pizan and Maximianus." MAe,
     LIV (1985), 282-83.
        Identifies source of a Latin quotation in Vie humaine (ll.
     380-81, Kennedy 345) as the Elegiae of Maximianus but was un-
     able to trace the other two Latin quotations in lines 335-37 and
     344-49.

348 LES HEURES DE CONTEMPLATION SUR LA PASSION DE NOSTRE
     SEIGNEUR (1420-1424)
     A short religious piece intended for all women stricken by loss
     or other misfortune. Presented in form of the Book of Hours,
     this translation of the Passion offers topics for reflection and
     meditation. It was written after the signing of the infamous
     Treaty of Troyes (1420) but may have been inspired by a more
     personal tragedy: the death of CH's son Jean de Castel (on
     this question, see Willard 728, p. 339, and 450, p. 203).

     MANUSCRIPTS:
     Paris, BN nouv. acq. fr. 10059, ff. 114^r-44^r.
     The Hague, Koninklijke Bibliotheek MS 73 J 55.

EDITION:
Unedited.

STUDY:
See Solente 346.

349 LE DITIÉ DE JEHANNE D'ARC (1429)
A poetic tribute to Joan of Arc (813). It commemorates her
heroic victory at Orleans, celebrates the subsequent coronation
at Reims of Charles VII, and gives thanks to God for his divine
guidance. Composed on 31 July 1429, right after these historic
events occurred, this rousing poem is thought to have been the
first long literary work to honor Joan during her lifetime. Its
sixty-one stanzas express strong patriotic and religious senti-
ments, as well as a profound personal pride in the feminine sex.
Besides rejoicing in the liberation of Orleans and Château-Thierry,
the Ditié predicts harmony in Christendom, forecasts a Crusade
to the Holy Land, and makes a final plea for peace and unity
under France's newly crowned ruler.

MANUSCRIPTS:
Berne, Bibliotheca Bongarsiana 205, ff. 62^r-68^r.
Carpentras, Bibliothèque Inguimbertine 390, ff. 81^r-90^v.
Grenoble, Bibliothèque Municipale U. 909. Rés., ff. 98^r-102^r.

EDITIONS:
See also Wisman 572.

350 Jubinal, Achille. "Ung Beau Ditié fait par Christine de Pisan
à la louange de Jeanne d'Arc." In Rapport à M. le Ministre de
l'Instruction publique, suivi de quelques pièces inédites tirées
des manuscrits de la Bibliothèque de Berne. Paris: Librairie
Spéciale des Sociétés Savantes, 1838. pp. 75-88.
     First transcription of all sixty-one huitains of CH's poem
from the Berne MS. Text is known to contain errors.

351 Buchon, J.-A.-C. "Documents divers sur Jeanne d'Arc." In
Choix de chroniques et mémoires sur l'histoire de France avec
notes et notices. Paris: Auguste Desrez, 1838. pp. 540-43.
     A transcription of the Grenoble fragment. Text considered
inaccurate.

352 Quicherat, Jules. "Christine de Pisan." In Procès de condamnation et de réhabilitation de Jeanne d'Arc dite la Pucelle d'Orléans.
(Société de l'Histoire de France). Paris: Renouard, V, 1849.
pp. 3-21.
     Prints all sixty-one strophes from the Berne manuscript but
provides no critical apparatus. Scholars consider this transcription unreliable.

353 Herluison, H. Jeanne d'Arc: chronique rimée par Christine
     de Pisan. Orleans: Herluison, 1865.
     A 41-page edition of all sixty-one stanzas, after Quicherat
     352.

354 Le Roux de Lincy, Antoine Jean Victor, and L. M. Tisserand.
     "Apostrophe de Christine de Pisan aux Parisiens dans 'Ung Beau
     Ditié fait l'an M.CCCC.XXIX à louange de Jeanne d'Arc.'" In
     Paris et ses historiens au XIVe et XVe siècles. Paris: Impri-
     merie Impériale, 1867. pp. 420-27.
     An incomplete edition containing thirty-nine huitains: I-VI,
     XIII-XIV, XXI-XXV, XXVII-XXX, XXXIII-XXXVI, XXXIX-XLV,
     XLVIII-LI, LIII-LVI, LX-LXI. No critical apparatus.

355 Fabre, Joseph-Amant. "Stances de Christine de Pisan sur
     Jeanne d'Arc." In Procès de réhabilitation de Jeanne d'Arc.
     Paris: Hachette, 1913. II, 307-30.
     Fabre's edition is based on Quicherat, 352.

356 Roche, Ch. de., and G. Wissler. "Documents relatifs à Jeanne
     d'Arc et à son époque extraits d'un manuscript du XVe siècle
     de la Bibliothèque de la ville de Berne." In Festschrift Louis
     Gauchat. Aarau: Sauerlander, 1926. pp. 329-52.
     Text is based on all three manuscripts. Variants given at
     bottom of the page. The editors provide a full description of
     Berne but only a brief account of the Carpentras and Grenoble
     manuscripts. Edition known to contain errors.

357 Kennedy, Angus J., and Kenneth Varty, eds. "Christine de
     Pisan's Ditié de Jehanne d'Arc." NMS, XVIII (1974), 29-55;
     XIX (1975), 53-76.
     This two part study-edition was issued as separate monograph
     in 1977 (see 358 below). It includes photographic reproductions
     of Berne 205 showing the complete text and plates of both Car-
     pentras 390 and Grenoble U 909 Rés. with extracts of text.
     CR: 763.

358 Kennedy, Angus J., and Kenneth Varty, eds. Ditié de Jehanne
     d'Arc: Christine de Pisan. (Medium Aevum Monographs, n.s.,
     IX). Oxford: Society for the Study of Mediaeval Languages
     and Literature, 1977.
     Highly praised critical edition based on 357. It contains the
     French text of the poem (pp. 28-40), a Modern English prose
     translation of it (pp. 41-50), and an excellent Introduction.
     The latter discusses the date and place of composition, manu-
     scripts, previous editions and the present edition. Also, the
     structure, themes, style, and versification of the poem. As in
     357, a complete set of photographic plates of the base manu-
     script (Berne 205) and two plates with specimens of the second-
     ary manuscripts (Carpentras and Grenoble) are again provided.
     Has table of events with historical background (p. 24); a list

of CdP's main works (pp. 25-26); variants and rejected readings
(pp. 51-59); literary, historical, and linguistic notes (pp. 60-
74); a bibliography (pp. 75-80); a glossary (pp. 81-101); and
a list of proper names (pp. 102-03). CR's: 764. See also:
   Romania, XCVII (1976), 142-43
   EHR, XCV (October 1980), 897
   SF, 73 (1981), 131

NOTES AND STUDIES:
See also Lenient 508, Lownsberry 404.

359 France, Anatole. Vie de Jeanne d'Arc. 2 vols. Paris: Calman-
     Lévy, 1908. I, 28-37.
     Thinks CH's Ditié strongly resembles a treatise written by
    the Archbishop (Gelu) of Embrum. A more recent study by
    Fraioli, 368, confirms this.

360 Jan, Eduard Feodor von. Das literarische Bild der Jeanne d'Arc
     (1429-1926). Halle (Saale): Max Niemeyer, 1928; rpt. in ZRP,
    Beihefte, Heft 74-76 (1923-1928), 1-193. CdP: pp. 5-11, 14,
    20, 21, 38, 52, 159, 174, 183, 188.
     Gives lengthy analysis of the Ditié and prints several stanzas
    from it, pp. 5-11.

361 Fernand-Demeure. "Christine de Pisan première poète de
     Jeanne d'Arc." RM, CXCIX (1930), 78-88.
     Sees the Ditié as an enthusiastic but straightforward account
    of Joan's march on Orleans.

362 Bastaire, Jean. "De Christine de Pisan à Jean Anouilh: Jeanne
     d'Arc à travers la littérature." RLM, LXXI-LXXIII (1962), 11-
    31.
     This literary survey of Joan of Arc (813) argues against rec-
    ognizing CH as first writer to eulogize Joan, citing an anonymous
    poet who allegedly wrote about her prior to the Ditié.

363 Kennedy, Angus J., and Kenneth Varty. "Vernage: two cor-
     rections to Godefroy." MAe, XLIV (1975), 162-63.
     Authors show that the word "vernage," which appears in
    Godefroy's printed text of the Ditié, is based on a misreading
    of yvernage in Berne MS 205. See p. 162 for the corrections.

364 Wisman, Josette A. "L'éveil du sentiment national au Moyen
     Âge: la pensée politique de Christine de Pisan." RH, CCLVII
    (1977), 289-97.
     Cites CH's political thinking in Ditié as evidence of a rising
    French nationalism and identifies elements in her work expressing
    a national consciousness. CR: 789.

365 Lynn, Thérèse Ballet. "The Ditié de Jeanne d'Arc: Its Politi-
     cal, Feminist and Aesthetic Significance." FCS, I (1978), 149-55.

Ditié seen as important socio-politico-feminist statement but
as insignificant from artistic standpoint. The author differs
with Kennedy and Varty (357) on poem's religious aspect. She
feels CH's feminism reflects same ambivalence as her political
views. CR: 770.

366 Dulac, Liliane. "Un écrit militant de Christine de Pizan: Le
Ditié de Jehanne d'Arc." In Aspects of Female Existence: Proceedings from the St. Gertrud Symposium 'Women in the Middle
Ages,' Copenhagen, September 1978. Ed. Birte Carlé, Nanna
Damsholt, Karen Glente, Eva Trein Nielsen. Copenhagen: Gyl-
dendalske Boghandel Nordisk Forlag, 1980. pp. 115-34.
     Suggests that the Ditié was politically motivated and should
be viewed as a militant piece of work. Also, that CH was more
interested in influencing than in recording the events of 1429.
CR: 758.

367 Fraioli, Deborah Ann. "The Image of Joan of Arc in Fifteenth
Century French Literature." Ph.D. Syracuse 1981. DAI, XLII
(1981), 2124A.
     A survey on how Joan of Arc's (813) contemporaries saw her,
with special reference to the Ditié, O insigne lilium, and the
Latin poem Virgo puellares. See also Fraioli 368, 371.

368 _____. "The Literary Image of Joan of Arc: Prior Influences."
Speculum, LVI (1981), 811-30.
     Gerson's De quadam puella, De mirabili victoria, and a treatise
by the Archbishop Jacques Gelu which Anatole France mentions
in 359 are the prior influences. Author explains here why CH's
portrayal of Joan (in Ditié) as a virgin warrior and nurturing
mother was unique.

369 Pernoud, Régine. Jeanne d'Arc. Paris: Seuil, 1981.
     Mentions CH in connection with the Ditié and prints several
lines from it, p. 23.

370 Warner, Marina. Joan of Arc: The Image of French Heroism.
New York: Alfred A. Knopf, 1981. CdP: p. 25, 63, 165, 169,
171, 177, 180, 181, 199, 206, 219, 220.
     Repeatedly cites CH on Joan of Arc (813) and presents ex-
cerpts from the Ditié, based on Kennedy-Varty 358, but fails
to mention that this poem was CH's last-known work.

371 Fraioli, Deborah Ann. "L'image de Jeanne d'Arc: que doit-
elle au milieu littéraire et religieux de son temps?" In Jeanne
d'Arc, une époque, un rayonnement. Colloque d'histoire médiévale Orléans. Octobre 1979. Paris: CNRS, 1982. pp. 191-
96.
     Discusses the biblical, prophetic, and patriotic elements in
the Ditié and shows how literary tradition shaped Joan of Arc's
(813) image.

372 Sarde, Michèle. <u>Regard sur les Françaises Xe siècle-XXe siècle</u>.
     Paris: Stock, 1983.
          Places CH in tradition of Joan of Arc (813), Agnes Sorel,
     Liane de Pougy, and Simone de Beauvoir. The <u>Ditié</u> is discussed
     (pp. 339-43) in terms of the political situation of 1429. See also
     p. 10 and pp. 331-33.

BIO-LITERARY MATERIAL AND
GENERAL CRITICISM

373 Boivin le Cadet (Jean Boivin de Villeneuve). "Vie de Christine de Pisan et de Thomas de Pisan son pere." Mémoires de Littérature, tirez des Registres de l'Academie Royale des Inscriptions et Belles Lettres. Paris: Imprimerie Royale, 1736. II, 704-14.

First basic study to deal with CdP and her works. Contains lengthy extracts from the texts; an account of Thomas de Pizan; a description of a miniature from the Cité de dames; and a partial listing of the writings.

374 Marchand, Prosper. Dictionnaire historique ou mémoires critiques et littéraire. The Hague: P. de Hondt, 1758-1759. II, 146-50.

This general survey of CH has a page-long footnote (p. 147) reproducing part of the "Catalogue des Écrits de Christine de Pizan, Tiré de l'Inventaire des livres de Jean de France, Duc de Berri."

375 Wieland, Christoph Martin. "Über Christine von Pisan und ihre Schriften." Der Teutsche Merkur, I (1781), 200-29.

Little-known essay dealing with CH's writings and influence on her contemporaries. Discusses the Dit de Poissy, the Enseignemens moraux, Avision, Chemin de long estude, and other works.

376 Fantuzzi, Giovanni. Notizie degli scrittori bolognesi. VII. Bologna: Stampa di San Tommaso d'Aquino, 1789.

Traces CH's genealogy through the Avision and other sources to show that the Pizans came from Pizzano not Pisa. This is relevant for correct spelling of CH's family name.

377 Gautier, A.-F. Notice sur Christine de Pisan. Bordeaux: Henry Faye, 1844.

About one third of this 31-page offprint (from the Actes de l'Académie des Sciences, Belles Lettres et Arts de Bordeaux, c. 1843, V, 555-83) is devoted to a patriotic account of France; the rest is a survey of CH's life and works.

378 Pizzano, Biago da. Le Chiese parrocchiali della diocesi di Bo-
     logna. II. Bologna, 1847.
         Includes discussion on CH's surname and ancestry. On this
     subject, see also Beck 443, Fantuzzi 376, Nicolini 405.

379 Lacroix, Paul. Science and Literature in the Middle Ages and
     the Renaissance. 1878; reissued New York: Frederick Ungar,
     1964.
         Brief reference to CH as poet, philosopher, historian, and
     author of Charles V. Figs. 371 and 372 show miniatures from
     Livre des fais d'armes et de chevalerie.

380 Robineau, E. M. D. Christine de Pisan, sa vie, ses oeuvres.
     Saint Omer: Fleury-Lemaire, 1882.
         Originally published as separate articles in local journals,
     this 400-page volume was the first general study of CH to ap-
     pear since Thomassy's 1838 Essai, 701. Closely follows Boivin,
     373.

381 Aubertin, Charles. Histoire de la langue et de la littérature
     française au Moyen Âge. 2nd ed. Paris: Belin, 1883. CdP:
     II, 100-03, 109.
         General survey comparing CH with Deschamps (804) and
     Froissart (806).

382 Koch, Friedrich. Leben und Werke der Christine de Pizan.
     Goslar a. Harz: Ludwig Koch, 1885.
         Part I of this Leipzig dissertation gives general overview of
     CH based on the Avision. A disproportionate number of pages
     (forty-two) are devoted to the years up to 1405, when that
     work was written, and relatively few (nine) to the remainder
     of CH's life. Part II provides a classified list of the manu-
     scripts and writings, bibliographical notes, and citations to
     eighteenth- and nineteenth-century sources containing bio-
     graphical material on CH.

383 Stein, H. "Christine de Pisan en Gâtinais." Annales de la
     Société Historique et Archéologique du Gâtinais. XI (1893),
     163-65.
         On Thomas and Christine de Pizan's visit to Gâtinais in 1372.

384 Petit de Julleville, Louis. Histoire de la langue et de la littéra-
     ture française des origines à 1900. II. Moyen Âge. Paris:
     Colin, 1896. CdP: p. 152, 357-66.
         Critical examination of CH as poet, scholar, humanist, moral-
     ist and historian.

385 Gröber, Gustav, ed. Grundriss der Romanischen Philologie.
     Strassburg: Trübner, 1902.
         Vol. II includes survey of CH's major works with an analy-
     sis of her method of composition.

386   Henry, Frederick P. "Christine de Pisan: Her Life and Writing
      Catholic World, LXXVIII (1904), 647-61.
           General survey which also compares CH with Froissart (806)
      and speculates on the monetary value of her writings.

387   Paris, Gaston. Esquisse historique de la littérature française
      au Moyen Âge depuis les origines jusqu'à la fin du XVe siècle.
      Paris: Armand Colin, 1907. CdP: p. 200, 220, 222, 226-27,
      252.
           Well-known early twentieth-century French scholar discusses
      CH's works and places her among foremost medieval lyric poets
      in France.

388   Doutrepont, Georges. La Littérature française à la cour des
      ducs de Bourgogne. (Bibliothèque du XVe Siècle). Paris,
      1909; rpt. Geneva: Slatkine, 1970. CdP: pp. xiii-xvi, xx-xxi,
      li, 87, 97, 143, 189, 203, 231, 274-78, 280, 287, 292-93, 301,
      372-73, 376-77, 408, 475, 477, 479, 492, 502, 510-11, 520.
           Many significant references to CH and her association with
      the Burgundian Court and library.

389   Faguet, Emile. Histoire de la littérature française depuis les
      origines jusqu'à la fin du XVIe siècle. 16th ed. Paris: Plon-
      Nourit, 1910.
           General survey with unfavorable comparison of CH with Frois-
      sart (806), pp. 126-28.

390   Lanson, Gustave. Histoire de la littérature française. 1912;
      rpt. Paris: Hachette, 1952. CdP: p. 139, 157, 166-68, 172.
           See p. 167 for Lanson's famous put-down of CH as an "in-
      sufferable bluestocking."

391   Paris, Gaston. Mélanges de littérature française du Moyen Âge.
      Publié par Mario Roques. 1912; rpt. New York: Lenox Hill,
      1971. CdP: p. 61, 62, 491.
           Speculates as to whose side CH was on during Burgundian-
      Orleanist conflict in French civil war--see 792, 814, 815.

392   Wright, C. H. C. A History of French Literature. (Oxford
      French Series). 1912; 2nd ed. New York: Oxford Univ. Press,
      1925. CdP: p. 59, 116-20, 213.
           This general survey of CH points out that she had great in-
      fluence on her age.

393   Longnon, Jean. "Une Femme de lettres au XVe siècle: Chris-
      tine de Pisan." Revue Critique des Idées et des Livres, XXI
      (1913), 431-42.
           Critical discussion with focus on CH's development as a
      writer.

394   Tilley, Arthur Augustus. The Dawn of the French Renaissance.
      1918; reissued New York: Russell & Russell, 1968.

In his discussion of CH the author wrongly states, p. 72, that she "wrote nothing after 1413". He seems to overlook her Epistre de la prison de vie humaine (1414-1418), the Heures de contemplation sur la Passion (1420-1424), and the Ditié de Jehanne d'Arc (1429).

395   Mignon, Maurice. "La Culture Dantesque en France: De Christine de Pisan à Lamennais." In Mignon, Les Affinités intellectuelles de l'Italie et de la France. Paris: Librairie Hachette, 1923. pp. 208-55.
       Traces the Dantean tradition from CdP and Marguerite of Navarre to the writers Rivarol, Fauriel, Lamennais, and Ozanam. Also refers to the poets Alain Chartier (801) and Martin Le Franc (817) but fails to mention Philippe de Mézières (819) who has been credited, by G. di Stefano in 168 (pp. 159-61), with being first French writer to cite Dante.

396   Jeanroy, Alfred. "Christine de Pisan et Dante." In Mélanges sur Dante. Ed. Maurice Mignon. Rome: n.pub., 1924. pp. 352-65.

397   Campbell, P. G. C. (Percy Gerald Cadogan). "Christine de Pisan en Angleterre." RLC, V (1925), 659-70.
       Traces CH's success in fourteenth- and fifteenth-century England--as measured by her influence on various British writers; by how many of her MSS were copied there; and by the number of works that were translated into English language.

398   Pinet, Marie-Josèphe. Christine de Pisan 1364-1430: étude biographique et littéraire. (Bibliothèque du XVe Siècle, XXXV). Paris: Champion, 1927; rpt. Geneva: Slatkine, 1974.
       Important pioneering study still not out of date. The 463-page biography is packed with bibliographical and literary information. Is divided into two parts the first giving an account of CH's life and works, the second making a survey of the writings. Covers such topics as CH's sources, influences, themes, literary development and didactic method. Book includes partial listing of the MSS and editions but errors in citation and chronology have been found. Pinet also suffers from awkward format and needless repetition. CR's: 775. See also:
       Romania, LIV (1928), 319-20
       GSLI, XCII (1928), 133-39
       MP, XXVI (1928-1929), 373-74
       Revue Critique, n.s. XCVI (1929), 58-60

399   Cartellieri, Otto. The Court of Burgundy: Studies in the History of Civilisation. Trans. Malcolm Letts. London: Kegan Paul, Trench, Trubner: New York: Knopf, 1929; rpt. 1970. CdP: p. 8, 18, 25, 88, 97, 105, 110, 114, 117, 118, 165, 174, 184.

Numerous references to CH with discussion of Philip of Burgundy's (823) patronage and the artists who illustrated her
manuscripts.

400   Bossuat, Robert. Histoire de la littérature française. Le Moyen
      Âge. I. Publié sous le direction de J. Calvet. 1931 De Gegord;
      reissued Paris: Del Ducca, 1962. CdP: p. 201, 209, 228,
      243-46, 254, 275.
      Unfavorable judgment of CH in the survey of CH's life and
      works on pp. 243-46. Compare Bossuat's ideas on her "lack
      of originality" with more recent criticism by Richards 234 (p.
      xxxi) and Quilligan 641.

401   Voretzsch, Karl. Introduction to the Study of Old French
      Literature. Trans. Francis M. Du Mont. New York: Stech-
      ert, 1931.
      The English edition of this now-dated German work has var-
      ious critical references to CH, placing her in the transitional
      period between Middle Ages and Renaissance, p. 487.

402   Solente, Suzanne.   "Deux chapitres de l'influence littéraire de
      Christine de Pisan." BEC, XCIV (1933), 27-45.
      Finds evidence of CH's influence in Pierre de Lesnauderie's
      Louenge de mariage and in a fifteenth-century text, the En-
      seignements que une dame laisse a ses deulx filz en forme de
      testament (BN f.fr. 11919).

403   Du Castel, Françoise. Ma grand-mère Christine de Pizan. Paris:
      Hachette, 1936.
      Good introduction for general reader by one of CH's descen-
      dants. Includes lengthy excerpts from the writings and hand-
      some plates. CR: RH, CLXXXIV (1938), 397.

404   Lownsberry, Eloise. Saints and Rebels. New York: Longmans,
      Green, 1937.
      CH is one of twelve humanitarians whose contributions to so-
      ciety are examined here, pp. 294-316.   Prints excerpts, in Eng-
      lish, from the Ditié and Proverbes moraux.

405   Nicolini, Elena. "Cristina da Pizzano (L'origine e il nome)."
      CN, I (1941), 143-50.
      Argues, on basis of family's origin from village of Pizzano,
      that CH's surname should be spelled Pizan, not Pisan.   This
      opinion also expressed by Beck 443, Fantuzzi 376, and Pizzano
      378.

406   Rosier, Madeleine Fernande (Sister Marie, O.S.U.) "Christine
      de Pisan as a Moralist." Ph.D. Toronto 1945.

407   Boldingh-Goemans, W. L. Christine de Pizan 1364-1430: haar
      tijd, haar leven, haar werken. Rotterdam: Nijgh & van Ditmar,
      1948.

Bio-literary portrait of CdP and her times. In fifteen chapters covers CH's background, role in Rose affair, biography of Charles V, feminist writings, French civil war and other relevant topics. Leans heavily on Pinet, 398.

408 Bailly, Renée. "La Bonne Dame de Pisan." Mercure de France, CCCV (1949), 563-70.
General overview with comments on CH's dits, Livre des trois jugemens, and Débat de deux amans. Also assesses political situation of 1418.

409 Abry, E., J. Bernès, P. Crouzet, and J. Léger. Les Grands Écrivains de France illustrés. Paris: Marcel Didier, 1950. 604 illus.
Vol. I, 84-85, includes two paragraphs on CH together with text of "Seulete suy" and reproductions from a Bibliothèque de l'Arsenal manuscript.

410 Cohen, Gustave. Tableau de la littérature française médiévale: idées et sensibilités. Paris: Richard-Masse, 1950. CdP: p. 56, 108, 122, 123, 132.
Scattered references to CH with brief overview on p. 132. Plate IX is a picture of the author.

411 Le Gentil, Pierre. "Christine de Pisan, poète méconnu." In Mélanges d'histoire littéraire offerts à Daniel Mornet. Paris: Nizet, 1951. pp. 1-10.
Sees CH as gifted but neglected poet. Discussion covers such works as the Cent ballades, Dit de la pastoure, and Livre du duc des vrais amans.

412 Solente, Suzanne. "Christine de Pisan (1365-1430?)." In Dictionnaire des lettres françaises. I. Le Moyen Âge. Publié sous la direction du Cardinal Georges Grente. Paris: Arthème Fayard, 1951-1964. pp. 183-87.
This general survey includes listings of CH's writings, critical editions, and bio-literary bibliographies.

413 Wilson, Margaret S. "A Revaluation of Christine de Pisan as a Literary Figure." Ph.D. Stanford 1952.

414 Steinberg, S. H., ed. Cassell's Encyclopaedia of World Literature. 2 vols. New York: Funk & Wagnalls, 1953.
Entry for CH in Vol. I, 775, describes her as the "first woman humanist in France." Also comments on her efforts to achieve technical perfection and greater realism in treatment of courtly love.

415 Cohen, J. M. A History of Western Literature. 1956; rev. Chicago: Aldine Publishing, 1963.
Is of opinion that CH was the only French poet of her time to be aware of the new Petrarchan style, p. 71.

416   Calmette, Joseph. The Golden Age of Burgundy: The Magni-
       ficent Dukes and their Courts. Trans. Doreen Weightman. New
       York: Norton, 1963.
              Includes casual references to CH on the Duke of Burgundy's
       (823) patronage, her remarks about him, and her glorification
       of the female sex, pp. 226-27.

417   Schmidt, Albert-Marie. XIVe et XVe siècle français: les sources
       de l'humanisme. Paris: Seghers, 1964. CdP: p. 78, 115,
       185-88.
              Contains biographical sketch of CH as first woman of letters
       in France. Two reproductions.

418   Tilley, Arthur Augustus. Medieval France: A Companion to
       French Studies. New York: Hafner, 1964.
              Unfavorable comparison of CH with Machaut (816) and Des-
       champs (804), p. 314. See also pp. 272 and 318.

419   Le Gentil, Pierre. La littérature française du Moyen Âge. (Col-
       lection Armand Colin, CCCLXIX. Section de Langues et Littéra-
       ture). 2nd ed. Paris: Armand Colin, 1966. CdP: p. 154,
       164-66.
              Includes a review of CH and her writings. Feels the didactic
       works deserve greater attention than they have thus far re-
       ceived.

420   Schmidt, Albert-Marie. "Christine de Pisan." RSH, CXXII-
       III (1966), 159-74.
              This article was supposed to have been the first chapter of
       a book on CH but author's death intervened. Reprinted in
       Favier, 423.

421   Vaughn, Richard. John the Fearless: The Growth of Burgun-
       dian Power. New York: Barnes & Noble, 1966.
              CH considered central link between John the Fearless (814)
       and the fifteenth-century literary world. Page 235 has reprint
       of Burgundian inventory listing items for CH.

422   Becker, Philippe Auguste. Zur romanischen Literaturgeschichte:
       ausgewählte Studien und Aufsätze. Munich: Francke, 1967.
              Pages 511-40 are reprint of Becker's 1931 review article of
       Pinet (in ZFSL, 775c) in which he makes complete survey of CH
       and her works. Is still valid.

423   Favier. Marguérite. Christine de Pisan: muse des cours sou-
       veraines. (Collection: Ces femmes qui ont fait l'histoire, n.s.).
       Paris/Lausanne: Recontre, 1967.
              Full-length, 223-page portrait aimed at general reader. Is
       written in style that blends CH's words (in italics) with those
       of the author. In the section "Formation d'une femme de let-
       tres," Favier discusses CH's literary models naming writers whom

she read and was fond of quoting. First chapter is a reprint
of 420; the last, a review of the Livre de la paix, Trois vertus,
and Dit de Poissy. Includes chronology; some errors.

424 Guth, Paul. Histoire de la littérature française. I. Des ori-
     gines époques au siècle des lumières. Paris: Arthème Fayard,
     1967.
     A general survey of CH, pp. 38-40, describes her as a har-
     binger of women's liberation and symbol of heroic womanhood.

425 Joukovsky-Micha, Françoise. "La notion de vain gloire de Simund
     de Freine à Martin Le France." Romania, LXXXIX (1968), 1-
     30, 210-39.
     Shows (with examples drawn from the Mutacion, Long estude,
     Corps de policie and other works) how the concept of "la gloire"
     developed in CH's writings, pp. 210-17.

426 Badel, Pierre-Yves. Introduction à la vie littéraire du Moyen
     Âge. (Collection Études Supérieures). Paris: Bordas, 1969.
     CdP: p. 42, 107, 162-63.
     Brief comments on CH's place in medieval literature.

427 Le Louet, Jean. "Christine de Pisan ou le haut bréviaire de la
     monarchie." Médicine de France, CCI (1969), 43-50.
     General overview of CH's life and works.

428 Meckenstock, Ingeborg. "Formen der Einsamkeitserfahrung bei
     Christine de Pisan und Charles d'Orléans." Ph.D. Bonn 1969.

429 Solente, Suzanne. "Christine de Pisan." In Histoire littéraire
     de la France. XL. Paris: Imprimerie Nationale, 1974, pp.
     335-422; first pub. Imprimerie Nationale & C. Klincksieck, 1969.
     Straightforward, factual account by late Pizan scholar. Con-
     tains 13-page biographical introduction, "Sa Vie," and a 62-
     page survey of the writings, "Ses Écrits." In the latter Solente
     gives a summary of each of CH's works, discussing format, dedi-
     cations, sources, etc. She also lists and gives pertinent in-
     formation about the manuscripts with bibliographical citations to
     editions and studies. Includes section on works wrongly attri-
     buted to CH and an analysis of her style and language. Con-
     cluding section deals with CH's contributions, literary reputation,
     and influence. CR's:
     SF, 41 (1970), 324-25
     BHR, XXXIII (1971), 471-72

430 Bumgardner, George Haagen, Jr. "Tradition and Modernity
     from 1380-1405: Christine de Pizan." Ph.D. Yale 1970. DAI,
     XXXI (1971), 6593A.
     Uses CH's writings to show that French traditionalism could
     assimilate modern trends.

431 Malignon, Jean. Dictionnaire des écrivains français. Paris:
     Seuil, 1971.
       Entry for CH, pp. 121-22.

432 Poirion, Daniel. Littérature française. II. Le Moyen Âge 1300-
     1480. Paris: Arthaud, 1971. CdP: pp. 203-10, 264-65, 312.
       Makes survey of CH's writings in Chap. III, 203-10. The
     medievalist considers CH's works important both from a literary
     and ideological standpoint. Includes chronology.

433 Du Castel, Françoise. Damoiselle Christine de Pizan, veuve de
     Me Etienne de Castel 1364-1431. Paris: A. & J. Picard, 1972.
       Expanded version of Du Castel 403, based on CH's published
     works and manuscripts. The spectacular set of plates (126 as
     opposed to the 24 in previous edition) come primarily from the
     manuscript collection of the Bibliothèque Nationale, Paris. CR:
     756. See also:
       BTAM, XI (1972-1975), 542-43
       SF, 49 (1973), 115

434 Mombello, Gianni. "J.-M.-L. Coupé e H. Walpole: Gli amori
     di Christine de Pizan." SF, 46 (1972), 5-25.
       Thinks it was Coupé rather than Horace Walpole who spread
     the rumor about CH's alleged romance with the Earl of Salis-
     bury. On the problematic date of their first meeting, see also
     Laidlaw 445.

435 Fox, John. A Literary History of France: The Middle Ages.
     New York: Barnes & Noble, 1974. CdP: pp. 271-73, 274,
     276, 277, 296, 302-03, 325, 326, 338.
       Includes good, critical discussions on CH's didactic works,
     pp. 271-73, and poetry, pp. 302-03. Author feels the Mutacion
     could have been a great work but ultimately failed to rise above
     "the sum of its disparate parts."

436 McLeod, Enid. The Order of the Rose: The Life and Ideas of
     Christine de Pizan. London: Chatto & Windus; Totowa, NJ:
     Roman & Littlefield, 1976.
       First full-length biography of CH in English. Aimed at a
     general audience, it reconstructs CH's life and milieu in four-
     teen chapters, 185 pages, with an Appendix or final chapter on
     the author's fortunes in England. Though absorbing and emi-
     nently readable, this work has been cited for inaccuracies and
     use of dated material. Its greatest weakness perhaps is the
     inadequate bibliography on pp. 178-82. CR's: 771. See also:
       RJ, XXVII (1976), 240-43
       New Statesman, XCI (11 June 1976), 784
       Choice, XIII (July-August 1976), 670

437 Lough, John. Writer and Public in France, from the Middle
     Ages to the Present Day. Oxford: Clarendon Press, 1978.
     CdP: p. 14, 15, 19, 21, 23-26, 29.

Discusses CH's income, suggesting that her earnings must have come from sources other than her writings. Lough maintains that France had no real professional writers, male or female, until the eighteenth century.

438 Margolis, Nadia. "Christine de Pizan's Use of Sources." Ninety-Third Annual Convention of the MLAA, Americana Hotel, New York City, December 1978.
Deals with CH as reader of Petrarch's Trionfi and Boccaccio's Amorosa Visione.

439 Tuchman, Barbara W. A Distant Mirror: The Calamitous 14th Century. New York: Alfred A. Knopf, 1978.
General overview of CH, pp. 217–19. Also discusses CH, Gerson (807), and the Roman de la Rose, pp. 480–81; CH's feminism, p. 209; her eulogy of Du Guesclin (805) and Charles V (798), p. 268; and her views on the failures of chivalry, p. 509. Historian Tuchman calls Charles V an "important and original work" p. 218.

440 McMillan, Ann Hunter. "Men's Weapons, Women's War: The Nine Female Worthies, 1400–1640." Mediaevalia, V (1979), 113–39.
Discusses Deschamps' (804) and Boccaccio's (793) influence on CH and explains how she diverged from her models.

441 Grabois, Aryeh. The Illustrated Encyclopedia of Medieval Civilization. New York: Mayflower Books, 1980.
CH described as "one of the most important intellectuals" during times of Charles VI (799) and Charles VII, p. 207.

442 Willard, Charity Cannon. "Christine de Pizan: the Astrologer's Daughter." In Mélanges à la mémoire de Franco Simone: France et Italie dans la culture européenne. I. Moyen Age et Renaissance. (Bibliothèque Franco Simone, IV). Geneva: Slatkine, 1980. pp. 95–111.
Shows how Thomas de Pizan's profession influenced CH's writings and career as reflected in her choice of scientific sources, affinity for Dante, and use of astrological images--in such works as the Othea, Mutacion, Avision, Long estude, and Corps de policie. CR: SF, 75 (1981), 532.

443 Beck, Jonathan, and Gianni Membello, eds. Seconda Miscellanea di Studi e Ricerche sul Quattrocento Francese. Chambéry/Turin: Centre d'Études Franco-Italien, 1981.
Contains studies by Bumgardner 488, Françon 537, Hicks 141, Reno 638, Wareham 333, and Willard 37. Also, interesting footnote by Beck, pp. xiv–xix, on CH's surname. CR: 746.

444 Cropp, Glynnis M. "Boèce et Christine de Pizan." MAe, LXXXVII (1981), 387–417.

Sees CH as important transmitter of the Consolatio and Boethian tradition. Cropp found evidence of his influence in six of CH's works including the Mutacion, Long estude, Charles V, Avision, Paix, and Vie humaine. Latter is mistakenly cited, on p. 411, as "la dernière des oeuvres de Christine, dont nous avons une édition." This overlooks the Ditié. CR: 755.

445   Laidlaw, J. C. "Christine de Pizan, the Earl of Salisbury and Henry IV." FS, XXXVI (1982), 129-43.
      Changes date of first meeting between CH and Earl of Salisbury from 4 November 1396 to toward end of 1398 (p. 134). Henry IV received copies of CH's works after Salisbury's execution on 7 January 1400. CR: SF, 83 (1984), 335.

446   Lalande, Denis. "Quelques premières attestations dans le vocabulaire du Livre des fais de Jehan le Maingre, dit Bouciquaut." Romania, CIII (1982), 332-36.
      Unlike Picherit in 448, does not attribute Bouciquaut to CdP.

447   Pernoud, Régine. Christine de Pisan. Paris: Calmann-Lévy, 1982. ("Livre de poche," 1985).
      Good introduction to CH for general reader. Provides no scholarly apparatus other than two-page bibliography but is strong on historical background. 222 pages. CR's: 774. See also SF, 86 (1985), 359-60.

448   Picherit, Jean-Louis. "Christine de Pisan et le Livre des Faicts du bon Messire Jean le Maingre, Dit Boucicaut Mareschal de France et Gouverneur de Gennes." Romania, CIII (1982), 299-331.
      Picherit attempts to attribute this work to CH, stating that "nous amènent à envisager l'attribution de la biographie de Boucicaut à Christine de Pisan" p. 331. CR: SF, 86 (1985), 360.

449   _____. "De Philippe de Mézières à Christine de Pisan." MF, XIII (1983), 20-36.
      De Mézières may have been possible influence on CH. Discusses their biographical links and mutual interest in social, political, and religious themes. CR: SF, 94 (1988), 132.

450   Willard, Charity Cannon. Christine de Pizan: Her Life and Works. New York: Persea, 1984.
      First-rate literary biography by foremost scholar in the field. Superseding McLeod (436) and other biographical works now in print (423, 433, 447), this is best single source on CdP and her age to date. The 266-page, eleven-chapter study uses a chronological approach, covering all major phases of CH's life and literary career. The writings are discussed at length and illuminated by the author's unique insights as well as by a wealth of pertinent historical and literary detail. Includes pas-

sages from CH's works, some never before translated into Modern English. Also, documentation and explanatory notes (pp. 224-42); an up-to-date, classified bibliography (pp. 243-54); an index (pp. 255-66); and 22 black-and-white illustrations. A highly praised and indispensable work. CR's: 788. See also:
   Publisher's Weekly, CCXXVI (12 October 1984), 42
   Library Journal, CIX (1 November 1984), 2062
   Booklist, LXXXI (1 December 1984), 477
   MS Magazine, XIII (December 1984), 40
   Book World, XV (10 February 1985), 4
   Los Angeles Times Book Review (14 April 1985), 10
   New Directions for Women, XIV (May 1985), 18
   Wilson Library Bulletin, LIX (May 1985), 631
   Virginia Quarterly Review, LXI (Summer 1985), 79
   Women's Review of Books, III (January 1986), 14
   RQ, XXXIX (Spring 1986), 69

451 Stuip, R. E. V., and C. Vellekoop, eds. Middeleeuwers over vrouwen. Utrecht: HES, 1984-1985.
   Offers general survey of CH's life and works, pp. 81-93.

452 Lalande, Denis, ed. Le Livre des fais du bon messire Jehan le Maingre, dit Bouciquaut, Mareschal de France et Gouverneur de Jennes. (Textes Littéraires Français, CCCXXXI). Paris/ Geneva: Droz, 1985.
   The editor of this definitive edition establishes here that Bouciquaut was not written by CH--even though the fourth book deals with "vertus et bonnes meurs" and resembles her Charles V. Cf. Picherit 448. CR's:
   SF, 86 (1985), 360
   MAe, LVI (1987), 340

453 Muir, Lynette R. Literature and Society in Medieval France: The Mirror and the Image, 1100-1500. New York: St. Martin's Press, 1985.
   Pages 225-44 provide good summary of CH for general reader. Among works discussed are the Cité des dames, L'Avision, the Mutacion de Fortune, and Livre de la paix.

454 Blanchard, Joël. "Christine de Pizan: les raisons de l'histoire." MA, XLII (1986), 417-36.
   Insightful study of CH's quest for "truth" and spiritual unity in the Mutacion, Long estude, and Avision.

455 Margolis, Nadia. "Christine de Pizan: The Poetess as Historian." JHI, XLVII (1986), 361-75.
   Deals with CH's emergence as an historical writer. Margolis traces her development from the lyric poetry to her more impersonal political treatises, demonstrating that historiography was an important form of expression for CH.

456   Noakes, Susan.   "From Boccaccio to Christine de Pizan: Read-
      ing the Corpus."   In Noakes, Timely Reading: Between Exe-
      gesis and Interpretation.   London/Ithaca: Cornell Univ. Press,
      1988.   Chap. IV, pp. 98-134.
          Dante and CH shown as figures who develop models of read-
      ing which integrate exegesis and interpretation.   Demonstrates
      through CH that these two elements are symbiotically connected
      rather than being mutually competitive.

• III •

SPECIAL TOPICS

(a)   Manuscripts and Manuscript Illumination

See also Bühler 67; Delisle 314; Farquhar 188; Hicks 141; Hindman 84, 253; Ignatius 80; Meyer in 702, pp. xxi-xxiv; Mombello 75; Ouy and Reno 289; Sallier 58; Walton 103; Willard 268, 271, 329.

457   Dibdin, Thomas Frognall. The Bibliographical Decameron, or Ten Days pleasant Discourse upon Illuminated Manuscripts.... London: W. Bulmer, Shakespeare Press, 1817. I, cxxxiv-vi.
     Contains a study of Harley 4431.

458   The Phillipps Manuscripts: Catalogus Librorum Manuscriptorum in Bibliotheca D. Thomae Phillipps, Bt. Impressum typis Medio-Montanis 1837-1871; rpt. London, 1971.
     The unique autograph copy of CH's Avision (ex-Phillipps MS 128) is listed on p. 2 of the Catalogus.

459   Camus, Giulio (Jiulio). I codici francesi della Regia Biblioteca Estense. Modena: Società Tipografica Antica Tipografia Soliani, 1889.
     Includes notice on Modena, Biblioteca Estense α n. 8.7 which contains the text of the Livre des fais et bonnes meurs du sage roy Charles V, p. 12.

460   _____. Notices et extraits des manuscrits français de Modène antérieurs au XVIe siècle. Modena: E. Sarasino, 1891.
     Page 9, 10 carries a less detailed notice on Charles V than the above, 459.

461   Champion, Pierre. La Librairie de Charles d'Orléans, avec un album de facsimiles. (Bibliothèque du XVe Siècle, II). Paris: Champion, 1910. CdP: pp. viii-ix, 31, 32.
     When Charles of Orleans (800) inherited his mother's (825) manuscript collection he came into possession of CH's works.

462   Van den Gheyn, J. Christine de Pisan: Epître d'Othéa, déesse

de la Prudence, à Hector, chef des Troyens. Reproduction des
100 miniatures du ms 9392 de Jean Miélot. Brussels: Vromant,
1913.
   Presents 100 black-and-white illustrations from Brussels, BR
9392 with famous Miélot rearrangement of the Othea miniatures.

463 Martin, Henry Marie Radegonde. La miniature française du
     XIIIe au XVe siècle. 2nd rev. ed. Paris: G. van Oest, 1924.
        This volume on the art of French miniatures was one of first
     studies to recognize the artistic significance of Harley 4431.

464 Chesney, Kathleen. "Two Manuscripts of Christine de Pisan."
     MAe, I (1932), 35-41.
        The two MSS, Bodleian 421 and Bodleian Laud 570, both con-
     tain the Epistre d'Othea but Laud 570 is the important one since
     it is believed to be the manuscript used by Stephen Scrope for
     his English translation.

465 Coville, Alfred. Recherches sur quelques écrivains du XIVe
     et du XVe siècle. Paris: Droz, 1935.
        The author reports finding Jean de Dervil's coat of arms on
     BN MS f.fr. 1187, a manuscript containing the text of the
     Epistre d'Othea (p. 167).

466 Schaefer, Lucie. "Die Illustrationen zu den Handschriften der
     Christine de Pizan." Marburger Jahrbuch für Kunstwissenchaft.
     X (1937), 119-208. Plates.
        Comprehensive iconographical survey with over thirty pages
     on Harley 4431. Identifies the six miniaturists who worked on
     the various manuscripts and analyzes each artist's style. In-
     cludes valuable indexes listing CH's illustrated manuscripts.

467 Porcher, Jean. Manuscrits à peintures en France du XIIIe au
     XVIe siècle. Paris: Bibliothèque Nationale, 1955.
        Includes comments on the illustrations in CH's manuscripts.

468 Meiss, Millard. "The Exhibition of French Manuscripts of the
     XIIIth-XVIth Centuries of the Bibliothèque Nationale." AB,
     XXXVIII (1956), 187-96. Plates.
        Informative article on the artists who illuminated CH's manu-
     scripts. Focus is on the "Luçon" or "Christine Master" whose
     work can be seen in Paris, BN f.fr. 606, 607, 603, 833-36;
     also, in London BL Harley 4431 and Brussels, BR 9392. Plate
     illustrating this artist's style precedes article.

469 Bühler, Curt Ferdinand. The Fifteenth-Century Book: The
     Scribes, The Printers, The Decorators. Philadelphia: Univ. of
     Pennsylvania Press, 1960.
        Cites French and English texts of the Epistre d'Othea as
     example of medieval manuscripts with identical illustrations, p.
     86.

470 Willard, Charity Cannon. "Christine de Pisan's Clock of Tem-
     perance." EC, II (Fall 1962), 149-54.
     Explains how CH turned "clocks" into moral symbol associated
     with the cardinal virtue of Temperance. The Clock of Temper-
     ance appears as an illustration in manuscripts of the Epistre
     d'Othea.

471 Tuve, Rosemond. "Notes on the Virtues and Vices." Journal
     of the Warburg and Courtauld Institutes (Univ. of London),
     XXVI (1963), 264-303; XXVII (1964), 42-72.
     Iconographical and textual study on the Virtues which throws
     light on CH as translator and glossator of classical texts.
     Focuses especially on the Othea in Bodleian Laud 570 and on
     the Livre des quatre Vertus Cardinaulx of which CH may have
     been the anonymous translator. A treatise added on to CH's
     Livre de prudence is identified as the translation of Alanus de
     Insulis's De virtutibus et de vitiis e de donis Spiritus Sancti.

472 Willard, Charity Cannon. "An Autograph Manuscript of Chris-
     tine de Pizan?" SF, 27 (1965), 452-57.
     Presents internal evidence showing that the rondeau added
     on to the Epistre à la reine (in BN f.fr. 580, f. 54v⁰) as a
     postscript was written by CH herself. This study cited by Ouy
     and Reno in their investigation of CH's autograph manuscripts,
     see 289.

473 Bühler, Curt Ferdinand. "The Morgan Manuscript (M 39) of
     Le Livre de Melibee et de Prudence." In Studies in Language
     and Literature in Honor of Margaret Schlauch. Ed. Mieczyslaw
     Brahmer, Stanislaw Helsztyński, and Julian Kryżanowski. War-
     saw: Polish Scientific Publishers [1966]. pp. 49-54.
     Reveals that Melibee is a translation of Renaud de Louhans
     which has been wrongly attributed to CH--some authorities have
     ascribed it to Jean de Meun. The original Latin text, Liber
     consolationis et consilii, is by Albertanus Causidicus Brixiensis
     (c. 1190-c. 1250).

474 Meiss, Millard. French Painting in the Time of Jean de Berry:
     The Late XIVth Century and the Patronage of the Duke. 2
     vols. London: Phaidon, 1967.
     Vol. I of this outstanding set discusses CH's manuscripts
     and illustrators, notably the "Master of the Cité des Dames" and
     "Master of the Epître d'Othéa." Vol. II, the Plate volume, con-
     tains the actual reproductions with additional notes on the ar-
     tists and paintings.

475 Mombello, Gianni. "Notizia su due manoscritti contenenti L'Epi-
     stre Othea di Christine de Pizan ed altre opere non identificate
     (Paris, BN Nlles. Acq. Fr. 6458, Oxford Bodleian Library, MS.
     Laud. misc. 570)." SF, 31 (1967), 1-23.
     Detailed analysis of the manuscripts cited above. See also
     Mombello 75.

476 Pickering, F. P. Literature and Art in the Middle Ages. (also
     pub. under title, Literatur und darstellende Kunst im Mittelalter).
     Coral Gables, FL: Univ. of Miami Press, 1970.
         This iconographical survey cites the Epistre d'Othea as ex-
     ample of late medieval text generously illustrated with Fortune
     pictures, p. 216.

477 Meiss, Millard, and Sharon Off. "The Bookkeeping of Robert
     d'Estampes and the Chronology of Jean de Berry's Manuscripts."
     AB, LIII (1971), 225-35.
         Discusses dates and sequence of events relating to item No.
     959 of d'Estampes' 1413 Inventory and to Jean of Berry's manu-
     script collection of CH's works in BN f.fr. 835, 606, 836.

478 _____. "Atropos-Mors: Observations on a Rare Early Human-
     ist Image." In Florilegium Historiale: Essays Presented to Wal-
     lace K. Ferguson. Ed. J. G. Rowe and W. H. Stockdale: Tor-
     onto: Univ. of Toronto Press with the Univ. of Western Ontario,
     1971. pp. 152-59.
         Deals with the illustration of death in BN f.fr. 606, f. 17,
     containing the Epistre d'Othea. Includes Plates.

479 Bozzolo, Carla. Manuscrits des traductions françaises d'oeuvres
     de Boccace, XVe siècle. (Medioevo e Umanesimo, XV). Padua:
     Antenore, 1973. CdP: p. 43 n.1, 95, 98, 99.
         Discovered three of CH's manuscripts among Boccaccio's tran-
     slated works: (a) BN f.fr. 5037 containing text of Prod'hommie
     de l'homme; (b) Phillipps 3648 containing the Cité des dames;
     (c) Chantilly MS 856 (562) containing incomplete text of the
     Cité.

480 Meiss, Millard. French Painting in the Time of Jean de Berry:
     The Limbourgs and their Contemporaries. 2 vols. London:
     Thames & Hudson, 1974; New York: George Braziller, 1975.
         Vol. I is a lavish, oversize text-volume with over ninety
     references to CH. It contains a great deal of information on
     CH's manuscripts, miniatures, and illustrators, as well as a
     learned discussion on her unique role in the history of manu-
     script illumination. See especially Meiss's comments on the Muta-
     cion, Cité, and Othea whose pictures are said to constitute an
     important cycle in Western iconography, p. 37. The plates,
     catalogs, appendices, bibliographical citations in back of book
     have additional references to CH and her manuscripts.

481 Hicks, Eric. "The Second 'Autograph' Edition of Christine de
     Pizan's Lesser Poetical Works." Paper presented at the Second
     St. Louis Conference on Manuscript Studies; St. Louis, MO,
     1975. An abstract of this paper published in Manuscripta, XX
     (March 1976), 14-15.
         The autograph manuscripts are identified as Paris, BN f.fr.
     835 and 12779; London BL Harley 4431; and the manuscript de-
     scribed by Willard in 472, BN f.fr. 580.

482 (New York City) Metropolitan Museum of Art. The Secular
     Spirit: Life and Art at the End of the Middle Ages. New York:
     E. P. Dutton in association with the Metropolitan Museum of
     Art, 1975.
         Cloisters' Exhibition Catalog contains a facsimile manuscript
     illustration of the Livre des trois vertus from Yale, Beinecke
     Library MS 427 together with commentary, p. 161. Also, illus-
     tration of the Roman de la Rose from Pierpont Morgan Library
     MS 48, with a reference to the Epistre au dieu d'Amours, p.
     159.

483 Wilkins, David. "Woman as Artist and Patron in the Middle
     Ages and the Renaissance." In The Roles and Images of Women
     in the Middle Ages and Renaissance. Ed. Douglas Radcliff-
     Umstead. (Univ. of Pittsburgh Publications on the Middle Ages
     and Renaissance, III). Pittsburgh: Center for Medieval and
     Renaissance Studies, 1975. pp. 107-31.
         Includes discussion of CH as important patron of manuscript
     illustration, pp. 116-17.

484 Hindman, Sandra L., and James Douglas Farquhar. Pen to
     Press: Illustrated Manuscripts and Printed Books in the First
     Century of Printing. [College Park, MD] Art Dept., Univ. of
     Maryland [with] Dept. of the History of Art, Johns Hopkins
     Univ. [Baltimore] 1977. CdP: p. 65, 67, 178; Epistre d'Othea,
     48, 49, 160, 167-69, fig. 67.
         Discusses two sets of rubrics ornamenting the Epistre d'Othea
     in Harley 4431 and BN f.fr. 606, and uses Erlangen, Universi-
     tätsbibliotek MS 2361 containing text of the Othea for studying
     different ruling techniques in manuscripts.

485 Wisman, Josette A. "Manuscrits et éditions des oeuvres de
     Christine de Pisan." Manuscripta, XXI (1977), 144-53.
         Useful chronological listing (incomplete) of CH's MSS, edi-
     tions, and translations with critiques on all modern editions.
     CR: 790.

486 Reno, Christine M. "The Cursive and Calligraphic Scripts of
     Christine de Pizan." Ball State Univ. Forum, XIX, 3 (1978),
     3-20.
         Deals with author's research on one of CH's autograph manu-
     scripts. Through codicological evidence uncovered in ex-Phillipps
     MS 128, Reno was able to identify CH's scribal hand and thus
     prove Willard's hypothesis (472) re rondeau at conclusion of the
     Epistre à la reine correct.

487 Willard, Charity Cannon. "An Unknown Manuscript of Christine
     de Pizan's Livre de la paix." SF, 64 (1978), 90-97.
         The manuscript under discussion originally belonged to Jean
     V of Créquy and was more recently sold (1976) at Drouot-Rive-
     Gauche, Paris. The significance of this unknown Paix MS is

that it became direct link between early fifteenth-century humanism and the later Court of Burgundy.

488   Bumgardner, George Haagen, Jr.   "Christine de Pizan and the
       Atelier of the Master of the Coronation." In SMSRQF, (1981),
       32-52.
           Explains how the collaboration of fifteenth-century miniaturists
       and writers (like CH) brought about a creative interaction be-
       tween medieval art and literature. Also speculates on how CH's
       association with the Coronation Master may have encouraged the
       manuscript production of Boccaccio's (793) works. CR's:
           SF, 79 (1983), 124
           Speculum, LX (1985), 229

489   Hindman, Sandra L.   "The Iconography of Queen Isabeau de
       Bavière: A Frontispiece to Christine de Pizan's Collected Works."
       Paper presented at College Art Association Meeting, 27 February
       1981.
           This study has been incorporated in Hindman's new book,
       84.

490   Willard, Charity Cannon.   "The Duke of Berry's Multiple Copies
       of the Fleur des Histoires d'Orient." In From Linguistics to
       Literature: Romance Studies Offered to Francis M. Rogers.
       Ed. Bernard H. Bichakjian.   Amsterdam: John Benjamins B.V.,
       1981. pp. 281-91.
           Calls attention to marked resemblance between London, BL
       MS Cotton Otho D II containing text of Fleur and early copies
       of the Mutacion, the similarity being attributed to fact that same
       artist probably illustrated both works.

491   De Winter, Patrick M.   "Christine de Pizan, ses enlumineurs et
       ses rapports avec le milieu bourguinon." Actes du 104ᵉ Con-
       grès National des Sociétés Savantes, Bordeaux, 1979.   Paris:
       Bibliothèque Nationale, 1982.   pp. 335-76.
           Discusses CH's dealings with the Burgundian Court and con-
       siders her role as copyist-editor of her own books, with special
       attention to the manuscripts produced in her atelier and the minia-
       turists who worked on them: the Maitre du Roman de la Rose
       Valencia, the Maître de l'Epistre d'Othea, the Maitre de la Cité
       des dames, and the Maître des Heures Egerton 1070. CR: SF,
       86 (1985), 360.

492   Hindman, Sandra L.   "The Composition of the Manuscript of
       Christine de Pizan's Collected Works in the British Library:
       A Reassessment." British Library Journal, IX (August 1983),
       93-123.
           Meticulous study of Harley 4431, the co-called Queen's MS.
       Deals with both format and contents giving a full account of
       Harley's manuscript tradition, art and artists, literary signifi-
       cance (it's an autograph), and codicological structure. Also

describes how talented craftsmen in CH's atelier assembled independent and disparate sections of the codex to produce one
seamless masterpiece. Includes ten plates and a five-page table
on quires, signatures, artists, and decorators.

493   _____. "The Iconography of Queen Isabeau de Bavière (1410-
1415): An Essay in Method." GBA, CII (October 1983), 102-
10.
Detailed analysis of the style and imagery of frontispiece in
Harley 4431. Cites paleographical evidence indicating that the
entire MS is an autograph--as suggested in Hindman 492 above
and Hicks 481. Author tries to determine here whether the
frontispiece's stylistic realism is based on actual fact or CH's
imagination. Includes Plate.

494 Laidlaw, J. C. "Christine de Pizan--An Author's Progress."
MLR, LXXVIII (1983), 532-50.
Discusses CH's manuscripts and traces the successive re-
visions she made in her ballades, rondeaux, and larger works.
Laidlaw urges editors to base their critical editions on Harley
4431 since that was the last collection prepared by CH herself.

495 Ouy, Gilbert. "Une énigme codilogique. Les signatures des
cahiers dans les manuscrits autographes et originaux de Christine de Pizan." In Calames et Cahiers. Mélanges de codicologie
et de paléographie offerts à Léon Gilissen. Sous la direction
scientifique de Jacques Lemaire et Émile Van Balberghe. Brussels: Centre d'Études des manuscrits, 1985. VIII, pp. 119-31.
On CH's relationship to the production of her MSS.

496 Laidlaw, J. C. "Christine de Pizan--A Publisher's Progress."
MLR, LXXXII (1987), 35-75.
In this sequel to 494 Laidlaw charts CH's progress as a publisher, focusing on the MSS produced between 1399 and the end
of 1404. Deals also with the duke of Berry's (812) 1408 collection and that of Queen Isabeau (811) dating from 1410 or 1411.
Includes five Tables: I. Contents and Decorations of the "Livre
de Christine," pp. 68-70; II. Collation and Signatures of the
Duke's MS, p. 70; III. Contents and Decorations of the Duke's
MS, pp. 71-73; IV. Collation and Signatures of the Queen's MS,
p. 73; V. Contents and Decorations of the Queen's MS, pp. 74-
75.

(b) Style and Language

See also Binais 90, Bornstein 299, Ferrier 716.

497 Müller, Ernst. Zur Syntax der Christine de Pisan. Greifswald:
Julius Abel, 1886.

Linguistic analysis with focus on CH's use of pronouns, definite and indefinite articles, gender, the partitive genitive, and the subjective.

498 Aust, Rudolph. Beiträge zur französischen Laut- und Formen-lehre nach den Dichtungen des Guillaume de Machault, Eustache Deschamps und der Christine de Pisan. I. Der Vocalismus. Breslau: Buchdruckerei zum Gutenberg Anton Schreiber, 1889. Breslau dissertation.

499 Gay, Lucy M. "On the Language of Christine de Pisan." MP, VI (1908), 69-96.
     Compares CH's language with that of her predecessors, contemporaries, successors, using the "tableau de la langue" in Darmsteter and Hatzfeld's Le seizième siècle en France. Editions studied include the Oeuvres poétiques (Roy 702), Long estude (Püschel 156), and Charles V (Michaud and Poujoulat 198).

500 Bruins, Jan Gerard. Observations sur la langue d'Eustache Deschamps et de Christine de Pisan. Amsterdam/Dordrecht: De Dordrechtsche Drukkerij, 1925.
     Linguistic comparison which focuses on grammar rather than style. Thinks CH's language is more "modern" and elegant than Deschamps' (804).

501 Batany, Jean. Français médiéval. Paris: Bordas, 1972.
     Presents excerpts from the Livre de la paix together with a "Questionnaire Linguistique" and seven pages of analysis of Paix's vocabulary, grammar, and syntax, as exercise for university students, pp. 260-67.

502 Mombello, Gianni. "Note sur deux acceptions curieuses et rares de talent au Moyen Âge." In Études de langue et de littérature du Moyen Âge offerts à Félix Lecoy. Paris: Champion, 1973. pp. 433-43.
     Discusses the word talent which appears in the Epistre d'Othea.

503 Zumthor, Paul. "Autobiography in the Middle Ages?" Genre, VI (1973), 29-48.
     Explains how the referential pronoun "I" came to be identified in the fifteenth century with the person of the author and suggests that it was used in this sense by CH, Deschamps (804), and Charles of Orleans (800), p. 45.

504 _____. Langue, texte, ~enigme. Paris: Seuil, 1975.
     The chapter on "Autographie au Moyen Âge" considers how Machaut (816), Deschamps (804), and CH contributed to the development of autobiographical writing.

505 Rickard, Peter. Chrestomathie de la langue française au quin-zième siècle. Cambridge: Cambridge Univ. Press, 1976.

Uses CH's texts and those of her contemporaries to illustrate
High Medieval style. Extracts from Charles V are on pp. 58-
62; notes on CH, pp. 297-300. Includes useful glossary.

506 Houston, John Porter. The Traditions of French Prose Style:
A Rhetorical Study. Baton Rouge: Louisiana State Univ. Press,
1981. CdP: pp. 3-5, 8, 11, 141, 142.
Evaluates CH as expository writer and discusses her contributions to the Middle French prose style. Houston likens her
attempt at "logical movement" to the scholastic outlines of the
Summa Theologica, p. 8.

507 Burnley, J. D. "Christine de Pizan and the So-Called Style
Clergial." MLR, LXXX (1986), 1-6.
Argues that CH's prose works were not written in the style
clergial at all but in the "curial" style used by the French
chancellories.

(c) Poetics

508 Lenient, C. La Poésie patriotique en France au Moyen Âge.
1891; rpt. (Research and Source Works Series, DCCC). New
York: Burt Franklin, 1971. CdP: p. 345, 371-83.
Gives critique of CH on basis of her patriotism and contributions to France. The Ditié, Charles V, and her letter to
queen Isabeau are all discussed in those terms.

509 Champion, Pierre. Histoire poétique du XVe siècle. (Bibliothèque du XVe Siècle, XXVII-XXVIII). 2 vols. Paris: Champion, 1923. CdP: I, vii, 8, 68, 69, 73-76, 175, 228; II, 3,
21, 33, 42, 102.
Scattered references to CH in both volumes with critique of
the poetry in I, 73-76. Singles out the Débat de deux amans
and Dit de la Rose for grudging praise but generally considers
CH's poetry prosaic.

510 Tiffen, W. J. "Trois poèmes de Christine de Pisan." M.A.
Leeds 1929.
Deals with the Epistre au dieu d'Amours, Dit de la Rose,
and the Débat de deux amans.

511 Chamard, Henri. Les origines de la poésie française de la
Renaissance. Paris: Ancienne Librairie Fontemoing, 1932.
General discussion of CH's poetry on pp. 74-75 (with some
condescending remarks).

512 Siciliano, Italo. François Villon et les thèmes poétiques du Moyen
Âge. Paris: Armand Colin, 1934; rpt. A.-G. Nizet, 1979.
CdP (1934 ed.): footnotes p. 3, 33, 106, 166, 174, 176, 180,

195, 213, 215, 251, 254, 257, 261, 286, 288, 300, 302, 323, 327, 328, 329, 332, 334, 364, 369, 371, 411, 412, 413, 415, 432, 437, 557.

Well over thirty references to CH in the notes but rarely mentioned in text.

513 Patterson, Warner Forrest. Three Centuries of French Poetic Theory: A Critical History of the Chief Arts of Poetry in France (1328-1630). 2 vols. Ann Arbor: Univ. of Michigan Press, 1935; rpt. 3 vols. New York: Russell & Russell, 1966. CdP: I and II, p. 74, 98-101, 115, 126, 127, 173, 222, 497, 819, 938; III, pp. 67-68, 77, 86-90, 125, 130-31, 166-70.

CH repeatedly cited in all three volumes. See especially "Anthology A" in Vol. III which uses her poems to illustrate development of Middle French verse.

514 Van Tieghem, Philippe. Histoire de la littérature française. Paris: Arthème Fayard, 1949.

Suggests that CH's "feminine lyricism" lacks style and should not be regarded as poetry, p. 50.

515 Cohen, Gustave. La Poésie en France au Moyen Âge. (Bibliothèque d'Études Historiques). Paris: Richard-Masse, 1952. CdP: pp. 113-18, 130, 134, 154.

Assessment of CH as eloquent but flawed lyric poet. Prints three of her poems and the ballade Deschamps (804) wrote to her, pp. 113-14.

516 Cohen, Robert Greer. The Writer's Way in France. Philadelphia: Univ. of Pennsylvania Press, 1960.

Cites CH's ballades as illustration of highly emotional poetry.

517 Fox, John. The Poetry of Villon. London: Thomas Nelson, 1962.

Classes CH with writers who took up poetry through force of circumstance, p. 142.

518 Poirion, Daniel. Le Poète et le prince: l'évolution du lyrisme courtois de Guillaume de Machaut à Charles d'Orléans. (Univ. de Grenoble, Publications de la Faculté des Lettres et Science Humaines, XXXV). Paris: Presses Universitaires de France, 1965. CdP: pp. 237-54, 333-48, 374-91, 407-22, 428-56, 458-76, 487-505, 517-43, 548-69, 577-78, 580-611.

A classic work with many significant references to CH and discerning observations on her merits as a writer. Sees her not only as an influence on Charles of Orleans (800) but as an important poet in her own right--see also Poirion 7.

519 Wilkins, Nigel. "The Structure of Ballades, Rondeaux and Virelais in Froissart and Christine de Pisan." FS, XXIII (1969), 337-48.

Discusses the influence of musical patterns on above poets, noting that editors sometimes overlook the musical structure upon which formes-fixes verse is based.   CR: 783.

520   Françon, Marcel.   "Sur les rondeaux de Christine de Pisan."
SF, 46 (1972), 68-70.
Thinks the reason CH's rondeaux appear shortened is because copyists working on Harley 4431 only transcribed part of the refrain.

521   Zumthor, Paul.   Essai de poétique médiévale.   Paris: Seuil, 1972.   CdP: p. 25, 66, 67, 133, 135, 266, 269, 271, 272, 274, 276, 306.
Various comments on CH and her lyric poetry.   Notes that in her writings CH often referred to herself as "il."

522   Françon, Marcel.   "On the Rondeaux of Christine de Pisan."
HLB, XXI (1973), 380-81.
Reproduces one of CH's rondeaux from BN f.fr. 835 and suggests that editors Roy (702), Varty (715) and Wilkins (721) should have used eight lines in triolet instead of seven.

523   Jodogne, Omer.   "Le Rondeau du XVe siècle mal compris."   In Mélanges de langue et de littérature médiévales offerts à Pierre Le Gentil.   Paris: SEDES et CDU, 1973.   pp. 399-408.
Brief comments (p. 402) on CH's rondeaux, notably those in BN f.fr. 835, 606, 836 and 605.

524   Sasu, Voichita.   "Christine de Pisan."   Studia Universitatis Babeş-Bolyai.   Series Philologia.   I (1973), 109-17.
Deals with CH's love poems.

525   Françon, Marcel.   "La Structure du rondeau."   MAe, XLIV (1975), 54-59.
Makes the point that neither CH nor Charles of Orleans (800) handled the refrain differently than their contemporaries.

526   Sabatier, Robert.   La Poésie du Moyen Âge.   (Histoire de la Poésie Française).   Paris: Albin Michel, 1975.   CdP: p. 214, 238, 272, 313, 323-27, 328, 329, 332, 340-41, 346, 348.
Various observations and critical comments on CH and her poetry.   See especially pp. 323-27.

527   Bloch, R. Howard.   Medieval French Literature and Law.   Berkeley: Univ. of California Press, 1977.
Contains references to the ballades dialoguées of CdP, Eustache Deschamps (804), Jean Régnier, Charles of Orleans (800), and François Villon, p. 167.

528   Kelly, F. Douglas.   Medieval Imagination: Rhetoric and the Poetry of Courtly Love.   Madison: Univ. of Wisconsin Press,

1978. CdP: p. 5, 6, 79, 106, 108, 109, 110, 146, 177, 195,
199, 227, 232, 233.
    Repeated references to CH as part of the late medieval liter-
ary tradition. Discusses her lyric cycles and individual poems
noting that such themes as infidelity, old age, war, and death
tend to recur in her works as well as in those of Alain Chartier
(801) and Charles of Orleans (800). CR: SF, 74 (1981), 280-
85.

529 Lacy, Norris J. "Villon in his Work: the Testament and the
     Problem of Personal Poetry." EC, XVIII (Spring 1978), 60-69.
        Explains why readers perceive Villon and CH as "personal"
     poets with distinct poetic personae. CH's is that of the "loving
     mother ... bereaved widow and frequent polemicist" (p. 68).

530 Margolis, Nadia. "The Human Prison: The Metamorphoses of
     Misery in the Poetry of Christine de Pizan, Charles d'Orléans,
     and François Villon." FCS, I (1978), 185-92.
        Penetrating psychological and literary study on three late
     medieval poets who used imprisonment theme to express per-
     sonal anguish. Identifies various prison images in CH's prose
     and poetry with special reference to the Epistre de la prison de
     vie humaine, the Cité des dames, and Trois vertus. CR: SF,
     77 (1982), 322.

531 Garey, Howard B. "The Fifteenth-Century Rondeau as Alea-
     tory Polytext." Musique naturelle et musique artificielle. In
     Memorium Gustav Rees. MF, V (1979), 193-236.
        Structural analysis of the rondeau with observations on CH,
     Chartier (801), and Charles of Orleans (800).

532 Kemp, Walter H. "'Dueil angoisseus' and 'Dulongesux.'" Early
     Music, VII 4 (1979), 520-21.
        Discusses Gilles Binchois' musical setting of CH's ballade
     "Dueil angoisseus" and comments on its subsequent adaptation
     for Nos. 59 and 60 of the Buxheimer Orgelbuch.

533 Price, Paola Malpezzi. "The Topos of the Eyes and of Vision
     in the Love Poetry of Christine de Pisan, Matteo Maria Boiardo,
     Gaspara Stampa, and Agrippa d'Aubigné." Ph.D. Oregon 1979.
     DAI, XL (1979), 3344A.
        Examines the different ways in which male and female poets
     use the topos of the eyes. In CH's case the eyes function as
     catalyst for the first stirrings of love. See also Price 535.

534 Garey, Howard B. "The Variable Structure of the Fifteenth-
     Century Rondeau." The Sixth LACUS Forum 1979 [Linguistic
     Association of Canada and the U.S.] Ed. William C. McCormack
     and Herbert J. Izzo. Columbia, SC: Hornbeam Press, 1980.
     pp. 494-501.
        Uses CH and Alain Chartier (801) as study examples in dis-

cussion on the structure and rhyme scheme of rondeaux. CH
thought to be less conservative than Chartier in shortening refrain.

535 Price, Paola Malpezzi. "Masculine and Feminine Personae in the
Love Poetry of Christine de Pisan." Women and Literature,
n.s., I (1980: Gender and Literary Voice), 37-53.
     Thinks CH's importance as a writer lies in her ability to
bring feminine perspective to courtly love poetry.

536 Wolfzettel, Friedrich. "La poésie lyrique en France comme mode
d'appréhension de la realité: remarques sur l'invention du sens
visuel chez Machaut, Froissart, Deschamps et Charles d'Orléans."
In Mélanges de langue et littérature françaises du Moyen Âge
et de la Renaissance offerts à Charles Foulon, I. Rennes: In-
stitut de français, Univ. de Haute-Bretagne, 1980. pp. 409-19.
     Identifies elements in CH and above poets which contributed
to development of the modern lyric and explains how these poets
made lyric poetry into vehicle for perceiving existential reality.
The "interjection of a physical self" thought to be a particularly
important factor in CH's work.

537 Françon, Marcel. "Notes sur les 'Rondeaux.'" In SMSRQF
(1981), 53-70.
     Discusses recent editions of CH's poetry (pp. 58-67) and
reflects on the special problems editors have in deciphering
scribal abbreviations.

538 Tabarlet-Schock, Marie Dominique. "La souffrance et la joie
dans les Cent Ballades et Rondeaux de Christine de Pisan: tradition littéraire et expérience personnelle." Ph.D. Rice 1981.
DAI, XLII (1981), 696-97A.
     Suggests that CH contributed to French lyric poetry and the
revitalization of the French language by restoring emotional and
psychological elements to it.

539 Willard, Charity Cannon. "Lovers' Dialogues in Christine de
Pizan's Lyric Poetry from the Cent ballades to the Cent ballades
d'amant et de dame." FCS, IV (1981), 167-80.
     Explains how CH used love debates and dialogues to explore
male-female relationships. Willard feels these give more accu-
rate picture of relations between the sexes than do CH's more
popular letters on the Roman de la Rose. CR: 786.

540 Calvez, Daniel. "La Structure du rondeau: mise au point."
FR, LV (1982), 461-70.
     Argues for the view that CH deliberately shortened her re-
frains.

541 Huot, Sylvia Jean. "Lyric Poetics and the Art of Compilatio in
the Fourteenth Century." Ph.D. Princeton 1982. DAI, XLIII
(1982), 1142A.

Deals with the poetic compilations of individual medieval
poets like CH, Petrarch (822), Deschamps (804), and Froissart
(806).

542 Margolis, Nadia. "An Enigmatic Necessity: Poetry as Journalism
in Eustache Deschamps and Christine de Pizan." Paper presented at MLAA Centennial Convention, Sheraton Centre, New
York City, December 1983. 16 pp.
   Defines what "journalistic poetry" is and shows how CH and
Deschamps (804) used it to project their views of themselves
and of the world.

543 Mühlethaler, Jean-Claude. Poétiques du Quinzième Siècle: Situation de François Villon et Michault Taillevent. Paris: A.-G.
Nizet, 1983. CdP: p. 15, 19, 25-26, 28, 54, 77, 142, 171.
   References to CH in various poetical contexts. Cites CH on
her image of poverty in the Mutacion and prints an excerpt
from it, p. 142.

544 Wolfzettel, Friedrich. "Zur Poetik Subjektivität bei Christine
de Pisan." In Lyrik des Ausgehenden 14. und 15. Jahrhunderts.
Ed. Franz V. Spechtler. Amsterdam: Rodopi, 1984. pp. 379-
97.
   Puts CH into historical perspective and analyzes what is per-
ceived as a fundamental ambiguity in her courtly poetry. Uses
the Dit de la pastoure, Cent ballades d'amant et de dame and
the Duc des vrais amans to make his point.

545 Bagoly, Suzanne. "Christine de Pizan et l'art de 'dictier' ballades." MA, XCII (1986), 41-67.
   Examines the structural elements in CH's verse, discussing
rhyme schemes, meters, and syllabication of her ballades dialoguées and single ballades to learn how she composed her poems.
CR: SF, 92 (1987), 271.

(d) Political and Educational Ideas

See also Bornstein 303, Laigle 267, Lynn 365, Thomassy 701.

546 Nys, Ernest. Christine de Pisan et ses principales oeuvres.
The Hague: Martinus Nijhoff, 1914.
   Eighty-three page monograph that deals with CH's political
thought and explains how Honoré Bouvet (Bonet 795) influenced
her attitude towards war. CH's contributions to political science
seen as modest though she is generally regarded as having had
good effect upon her age.

547 Temple, Maud Elizabeth. "The Fifteenth Century Idea of the
Responsible State." RR, VI (1915), 402-33.

Comments on CH's political attitude toward proletarian democracy but reaches no definite conclusions.

548 Gabriel, Astrik Ladislas. "The Educational Ideas of Christine de Pisan." JHI, XVI (1955), 3-21.

Focuses on CH's teachings and didactic writings. Author sees CH as one of greatest moralists in Christian literature.

549 Lewis, Peter S. Later Medieval France: The Polity. New York: St. Martin's Press, 1968.

CH cited throughout on various social and political issues: p. 92, 111-12 royal processions; p. 112 oligarchical suppression of urban disorder; p. 168 unity in society; p. 246 the bourgeoisie; p. 248n social responsibility.

550 Grandeau, Yann. "Les Enfants de Charles VI: Essai sur la vie privée des princes et des princesses de la maison de France à la fin du Moyen Âge." Bulletin Philologique et Historique du Comité des travaux et scientifique, Année 1967. Paris: Bibliothèque Nationale, 1969. II, 809-49.

Suggests that Isabeau of France (811) was influenced by CH's ideas on raising well-informed daughters, p. 832.

551 Edmonds, Barbara P. "Aspects of Christine de Pisan's Social and Political Ideas." Ph.D. Maryland 1972. DAI, XXXIII (1972), 2369A.

Thoughtful study on CH's efforts to rehabilitate society. Covers CH's life and works (pp. 24-25), her role as historian (pp. 46-85), her political thought (pp. 86-133), her views on chivalric ideals and the nobility (pp. 134-67), and her treatment of personal relationships (pp. 168-205). Edmonds sees CH's overreliance on the nobility (as a social catalyst) as the greatest weakness in her thinking.

552 Gauvard, Claude. "Christine de Pisan, a-t-elle en une pensée politique? A propos d'ouvrages récents." RH, CCL (1973), 417-30.

Reviews recent editions of CH's political writings--Lucas (296), Solente (201), Towner (286), Willard (337)--and tries to explain why her works are so often misinterpreted or misunderstood.

553 Mombello, Gianni. "Quelques aspects de la pensée politique de Christine de Pizan d'après ses oeuvres publiées." In CPFEHR (1974), 43-153.

Extensive investigation of CH's political thought based on a close analysis of Charles V, Corps de Policie, the Livre de la paix, and on a review of earlier criticism. Mombello's notion of CH as a compiler of received ideas has more recently been challenged by Earl Jeffrey Richards (234, p. xxxi). CR: 773.

114 Christine de Pizan

554 Mühlethaler, Jean-Claude. "Le Poète et le Prophète: littérature et politique au XVe siècle." MF, XIII (1983), 37-57.

Examines texts that shed light on fifteenth-century French politics by drawing on the Bible. Cites CH's Ditié and Lamentacion, which allude to third chapter of Book of Jonah, and Chartier's Quadrilogue Invectif (801), which uses Book of Isaiah. The author calls attention to the "narrateur-prophète" who was part of the literary scene in CH's day. CR: SF, 94 (1988), 132.

555 Blanchard, Joël. "'Vox poetica, vox politica,' l'entrée du poète dans le champ politique au XVe siècle." In Actes du Colloque International sur le Moyen Français, Milan, 6-8 mai 1985. (Scienze filologiche e letteratura, XXXI). Milan: Vita e Pensiero, 1986. pp. 39-51.

Examines the strategies of writers commenting on political unrest with special focus on CdP, Jean Gerson (807), and Alain Chartier (801).

(e) Chivalry and Courtly Love

See also Dulac 226, Monter 136, Steinberg 414, Willard 189, 311.

556 Piaget, Arthur. "La cour amoureuse dite de Charles VI." Romania, XX (1891), 417-54.

Publishes the names of members belonging to the "Cour amoureuse" and prints what CH had to say about antifeminist writers like Matheolus and Jean de Meun.

557 Baerwolff, Carl. "Christine von Pisan, ihre Auflösung und Weiterbildung der Zeitkultur." ASNSL, CXLI (1921), 93-110.

General discussion of CH and her milieu with a look at her courtly poetry and the chivalric tradition. Also comments on her feminism.

558 Prestage, Edgar, ed. Chivalry: A Series of Studies to Illustrate its Historical Significance and Civilizing Influence. New York: Alfred A. Knopf, 1928. CdP: p. 54, 79, 191-92.

Discusses CH and her opposition to the corruption of chivalric ideals.

559 Kilgour, Raymond L. The Decline of Chivalry as Shown in French Literature of the Late Middle Ages. (Harvard Studies in Romance Languages, XII). Cambridge, MA: Harvard Univ. Press, 1937. CdP: p. 124, 128-40, 141, 145, 155, 163, 180-81, 231, 233, 281.

Suggests that CH's "militant feminism" is indicative of a change in chivalric standards but feels her writings do not generally reflect a decline of chivalry.

560 Painter, Sidney. French Chivalry: Chivalric Ideas and Prac-
tices in Mevieval France. Baltimore: Johns Hopkins Univ.
Press, 1940. CdP: p. 29, 117, 133, 147.
Makes comments on the Livre du duc des vrais amans and
CH's concept of chivalry.

561 Lazar, Moshe. Amour Courtois et 'Fin Amors' dans la littérature du XIIe siècle. Paris: C. Klincksieck, 1964.
Suggests that Dante, Petrarch (822), and CH all used terms
like amour courtois and courtoisie interchangeably even though
they actually have different meanings.

562 Sims, Robert. "La Sincérité chez Christine de Pisan et Alain
Chartier." Chimères: A Journal of French and Italian Literature. (Fall 1976-Spring 1977), 39-48.
Places CH and Chartier (801) within courtly love tradition
but finds that in giving courtly themes "un nouveau visage plus
sincère" (p. 47), they have in fact transcended it.

563 Benson, Larry D. "Courtly Love and Chivalry in the Later Middle Ages." In Fifteenth-Century Studies: Recent Essays. Ed.
Robert F. Yeager. Hamden, CT: Archon Books, 1984. pp.
237-57.
Thinks CH may have attacked courtly love on basis of its
abusive language.

564 Willard, Charity Cannon. "Concepts of Love according to Guil-
laume de Machaut, Christine de Pizan and Pietro Bembo." In
The Spirit of the Court. Selected Proceedings of the Fourth
Congress of the International Courtly Literature Society, Toronto
1983. Ed. Glyn S. Burgess and Robert A. Taylor et al. Exeter,
Devon: Short Run Press, 1985. pp. 386-92.
Analyzes how the above poets handled theme of courtly love--
in Trois jugemens, the Dit de Poissy, and the Débat de deux
amans. Although CH was influenced by Machaut (816) and
French poetic tradition her Italian background also played a part
in shaping her ideas. CR's:
FS, XL (1986), 317-18
MA, XCIII (1987), 522-23
MAe, LVII (1988), 85-86

(f) Humanism

See also Bornstein 302, 303; Coville 117; Furr 137; Steinberg
414; Willard 275.

565 Combes, André. Jean de Montreuil et le chancelier Gerson.
Contribution à l'histoire des rapports de l'humanisme et de la
théologie en France début du XVe siècle. (Études de Philosophie

Médiévales, XXXII). 1942; rpt. Paris: J. Vrin, 1973. CdP:
p. 9, 15, 16, 21, 27, 40, 83-109, 113-16, 119, 125, 126, 129-37,
138, 141-50, 156-58, 161, 162, 164, 165, 168, 169, 170, 172,
173, 177, 183, 196, 197, 226, 234, 249, 261, 269.
     Numerous references to CH as prominent figure in Rose de-
bate and as one of early French humanists. Discussion cen-
ters on relationship between de Montreuil (820) and Gerson (807),
as title indicates, but the CH-Gerson connection is also explored.
On question of whether or not Gerson was CH's "notable clerc,"
Combes concludes that "rien ne permet de supposer que Christine ... pense à Gerson en écrivait notable clerc" p. 104. More
on this problem in 134, 135.

566 Simone, Franco. Il Rinascimento francese. Studi e ricerche.
     (Biblioteca di studi francesi. Istituto di lingua e letteratura
     francese della facoltà di lettere e filosofia dell'Università di
     Torino). 1961; 2nd ed. Turin: Società Editrice Internationale,
     1965. English ed., The French Renaissance: Medieval Tradition
     and Italian Influence in Shaping the Renaissance in France, a
     partial trans., H. G. Hall, London, 1969.
          Landmark study on French letters and ideas, with a discus-
     sion on CH and the early French humanists.

567 Willard, Charity Cannon. "Isabel of Portugal, Patroness of
     Humanism?" In Miscellanea di studi e ricerche sul Quattrocente
     francese. Ed. Franco Simone. Turin: Giappichelli, 1967. pp.
     519-44.
          As wife of Philip the Good of Burgundy, Isabel supported
     the early French humanists and apparently showed a special
     interest in CH's Livre des trois vertus, which had been acquired
     by the Burgundian library.

568 Gundersheimer, Werner L., ed. French Humanism, 1470-1600.
     (Harper Torch Books). New York: Harper & Row, 1970.
          CH cited as imitator of Dante, p. 42.

569 Ouy, Gilbert. "Paris l'un des principaux foyers de l'humanisme
     en Europe au début du XVe siècle." Bulletin de la Société de
     l'Histoire de Paris et de l'Ile-de-France (1967-1968 [1970]), 71-
     98.
          CH's involvement with humanism explored on pp. 85-90.

570 _____. "Humanisme et propaganda politique en France au
     début du XVe siècle: Ambrogio Migli et les ambitions impériales
     de Louis d'Orléans." In Culture et politique en France à l'épo-
     que de l'humanisme et de la Renaissance. Ed. Franco Simone.
     (Atti del Convegno Internazionale promosso dall' Accademia delle
     Scienze di Torino in collaborazione con la Fondazione Giorgio
     Cini di Venezia, 29 Marzo-3 Aprile 1971). Turin: Accademia
     delle Scienze, 1974. pp. 13-42.
          This study on French humanism includes references to CH.

571   Bell, Susan Groag. "Christine de Pizan (1364-1430): Human-
      ism and the Problem of a Studious Woman." Feminist Studies,
      III (1976), 173-84.
         Evaluates CH's humanism in terms of how she handled Boc-
      caccio's De claris mulieribus. Also considers her unique posi-
      tion as a medieval woman writer, with conclusion that she did
      not recommend her scholarly life to other women because it led
      to solitude and a "painful" estrangement from society. Cf.
      Bornstein 637, p. 17.

572   Wisman, Josette A. "L'Humanisme dans l'oeuvre de Christine
      de Pisan." Ph.D. Catholic Univ. of America 1976. DAI, XXXVI
      (1976), 961A.
         To determine whether CH can justly be considered one of
      first French humanists Wisman surveyed her complete works from
      five different perspectives analyzing (1) her use of the verna-
      cular; (2) her interpretation of Christianity; (3) her social
      views; (4) her feminism; and (5) her participation in the inter-
      nationalization of humanism. Appendix A is an edition of the
      Ditié de Jehanne d'Arc. Appendix B lists CH's manuscripts
      and editions--rpt. in Wisman 485.

573   Ullman, Walter. Medieval Foundations of Renaissance Humanism.
      Ithaca: Cornell Univ. Press, 1977.
         CH seen as important link between Italy and France in devel-
      opment of humanism and as one of earliest women to have made
      "intelligent use of Aristotle's Politics and Ethics" p. 184. Au-
      thor considers the Livre du corps de policie valuable for trying
      to offer solutions to contemporary problems.

574   Ouy, Gilbert. "La ponctuation des premiers humanistes fran-
      çais." In La ponctuation. Recherches historiques et actuelles.
      (Actes de la Table ronde internationale CNRS de mai 1978).
      Paris/Besançon: GTM-CNRS-HESO, 1979. pp. 56-89.
         This article on the early French humanists discusses Pierre
      d'Ailly, Jean Gerson (807), Nicholas de Clamanges, Jean de
      Montreuil (820), and CH. CR: SF, 71 (1980), 319.

575   Favier, Jean. Les Fastes du Gothique, le siècle du Charles V.
      Paris: Éditions de la Reunion des musées nationaux, 1981.
         The Introduction (p. 15) makes passing reference to CH's
      humanism.

576   Jordan, Constance. "Feminism and the Humanists: The Case
      of Sir Thomas Elyot's Defence of Good Women." RQ, XXXVI
      (1983), 181-201; rpt. in 255.
         Suggests that the Cité des dames eliminates Boccaccio's
      humanistic perspective.

FEMINIST STUDIES, CHRISTINE DE PIZAN
IN "WOMEN'S" TITLES

See also Batany 128, Chap. IV; Bell 274, 571; Boldingh-Goemans 407; Bornstein 35, 279; Guth 424; Laigle 267; Lynn 365; Price 535; Reno 251; Willard 275, 278.

577 Le Roux de Lincy, Antoine Jean Victor. Les Femmes célèbres de l'ancienne France: mémoires historiques sur la vie publique et privée des femmes françaises depuis le cinquième siècle aux dix-huitième. Paris: Leroi, 1848.
     Considers CH of special interest to historians and antiquarians but sees her primarily as a poet of light verse rather than as a serious prose writer (I, 558-63). Does not discuss her feminism.

578 Minto, William. "Christine de Pisan, a Medieval Champion of Her Sex." Macmillan's Magazine, LIII (1886), 264-75.
     Survey of CH's life and work with focus on her feminism.

579 Gröber, Gustav. "Die Frauen im Mittelalter und die erste Frauenrechtlerin." Deutsche Revue, IV (1903), 343-51.
     CH recognized as first champion of women.

580 Hentsch, Alice A. De la littérature didactique du Moyen Âge s'adressant spécialement aux femmes. Cahors: A. Coueslant, 1903.
     Includes a section on CH's feminist writings, pp. 154-61, 238.

581 Butler, Pierre. Women in all Ages and in all Countries: Women of Medieval France. Philadelphia: Rittenhouse Press, 1907.
     General survey of CH, pp. 345-59, but no comments on her feminism.

582 Kemp-Welch, Alice. "A Fifteenth-Century Feministe, Christine de Pisan." The Nineteenth Century, LXI (1907), 602-10.
     Analyzes CH's feminist arguments in L'Epistre au dieu d'Amours, discusses her views on the Roman de la Rose, and reflects on the philosophical meaning of the Livre de la mutacion de Fortune.

583 Kastenberg, Mathilde. Die Stellung der Frau in den Dichtungen
der Christine de Pisan. Darmstadt: G. Otto's Hof-Druckerei,
1909.
Heidelberg doctoral dissertation with feminist focus.

584 Broc, Hervé de. Les Femmes auteurs. Paris: Plon Nourrit,
1911.
Includes general survey of CH with special reference to the
Cité des dames and Epistres sur le Roman de la Rose, pp. 40-
48.

585 Rigaud, Rose. Les Idées féministes de Christine de Pisan.
Neuchâtel: Attinger, 1911; rpt. Geneva: Slatkine, 1973.
Sees the rehabilitation of women as a major theme in CH's
works and views CH herself as "la théoricienne du féminisme
moderne" (p. 142). This 151-page monograph includes lengthy
discussions of the Epistre au dieu d'Amours, the Epistres sur
le Roman de la Rose, the Cité des dames, and Trois vertus.

586 Kemp-Welch, Alice. Of Six Medieval Women. London: Macmillan,
1913; rpt. Williamstown, MA: Corner House, 1972.
The chapter on CH, pp. 116-46, focuses on her feminism
and patriotism. The author talks about the "psychological unity"
of CH's writings and examines such works as the Dit de Poissy,
Duc des vrais amans, and Livre des trois vertus.

587 Melegari, Dora. Les Victorieuses: ames et visages de femmes.
1914; rpt. Paris: Payot, 1923.
CH is one of the "victorieuses" who had to overcome great
obstacles to vindicate herself and her sex. An analysis of her
feminism, the Epistre au dieu d'Amours, Cité des dames, and
Trois vertus is given on pp. 48-80.

588 Riesch, Helene. Frauengeist der Vergangenheit: Biographisch
literarische Studien. Freiberg: Herdersche, 1915.
CH cited as "first suffragette," in a study dealing with outstanding women from the past. Focus is on her handling of
chivalric love as reflected in the Dit de la pastoure, Débat de
deux amans, Livre des trois jugemens, and Livre du duc des
vrais amans, pp. 29-48.

589 Abensour, Léon. Histoire générale du féminisme des origines
à nos jours. Paris: Delagrave 1921; reissued Geneva: Slatkine, 1979.
Implies that Mlle de Gournay's Egalité des hommes et des
femmes (1622) was influenced by CH's Cité des dames (1405),
p. 153.

590 _____. La Femme et le féminisme avant la Révolution. Paris:
Leroux, 1923.
Briefly discusses CH's place in the history of feminism, p.
v, vi.

591 Power, Eileen Edna. "The Position of Women." In The Legacy
     of the Middle Ages. Ed. C. G. Crump and E. F. Jacobs. 1926;
     rpt. Oxford: Clarendon Press, 1962. CdP: p. 406, 409, 416,
     418, 419, 423, 428, 433.
         Power credits CH with leading the revolt against the abuse
     of women; sees both realism and idealism in the Livre des trois
     vertus, p. 409.

592 Richardson, Lula McDowell. The Forerunners of Feminism in
     French Literature of the Renaissance. Part I: From Christine
     de Pisan to Marie de Gournay. (The Johns Hopkins Studies in
     Romance Literatures and Languages, XII). Baltimore: Johns
     Hopkins University Press, 1929. CdP: pp. 12-34, 42, 49, 57,
     58, 90, 91, 116, 117, 160.
         This feminist survey includes an assessment of CH and her
     didactic works for women. Devotes Chap. I to the Rose debate
     and CH's defense, arguing that although feminism as a move-
     ment did not flourish until the sixteenth century, its basic tenets
     were laid down with CH and the Quarrel. CR: 779.

593 Rohrbach, Martha. Christine von Pisan: Ihr Weltbild und ihr
     Geistiger Weg. Paris: Droz, 1934.
         Münster doctoral dissertation with feminist focus.

594 Dow, Blanche Hinman. The Varying Attitude toward Women in
     French Literature of the Fifteenth Century: The Opening Years.
     New York: Publications of the Institute of French Studies,
     1936. CdP: p. 8, 31, 33-34, 140-49, 159-68, 172-98, 225-63.
         Lengthy discussions on CH and her feminism. Dow deals
     with the Dit de la Rose, Trois vertus, Duc des vrais amans and
     with the Roman de la Rose. She sees the Quarrel and CH's role
     in it as a crucial social event leading to a new conception of
     women.

595 Blum-Erhard, Anna. "Christine von Pisan, eine Bahnbrecherin
     geistigen Frauensberufs." Die Literatur, XLI (1938-1939), 540-
     43.
         Gives general account of CH's background and comments on
     her writings on women. Includes German translation of "Seulete
     suy."

596 De Koven, Anna. Women in Cycles of Culture. New York:
     Putnam, 1941. CdP: Preface; p. 14, 65, 67-69, 81, 84, 87,
     162, 172, 260, 303.
         Repeated references to CH as strong moral force in her so-
     ciety. Uses CH's lyric poetry to illustrate theme of courtly
     love.

597 Hughes, Muriel Joy. Women Healers in Medieval Life and Litera-
     ture. New York: King's Crown, 1943. CdP: p. 37, 41-42.
         CH cited as example of an educated fourteenth-century woman
     whose writings incorporate her knowledge of medicine and healing.

598 Defourneaux, Marcelin. La Vie quotidienne au temps de Jeanne
     d'Arc. Paris: Hachette, 1952. CdP: p. 141, 144, 156, 157.
        Chapter VIII discusses the Rose quarrel and CH's attempt
     to restore women to a position of dignity and honor.

599 Lehmann, Andrée. Le Rôle de la femme dans l'histoire de France
     au Moyen Âge. Paris: Berger-Levrault, 1952.
        The chapter on "La Vie Intellectuelle," pp. 410–14, is devoted
     to Héloise, Marie de France, and CH.

600 Beauvoir, Simone de. The Second Sex. Ed. and trans. H. M.
     Parshley. New York: Alfred A. Knopf, 1953.
        With reference to the querelle des femmes, de Beauvoir notes
     that "for the first time we see a woman take up her pen in de-
     fense of her sex when Christine de Pisan ... attack[s] ...
     clerics in her Épître au Dieu d'Amours," p. 128.

601 Davis, Natalie Zemon. Society and Culture in Early Modern
     France. 1965: 4th ed. Stanford, CA: Stanford Univ. Press,
     1975. CdP: p. 73, 126, 131, 144, 215, 219n.
        This collection of essays on the interaction of society and
     culture cites CH, p. 126, as example of early feminist thought.
     CR: Signs, I, 4 (Summer 1976), 983–85.

602 Jackson, W. T. H. Medieval Literature: A History and Guide.
     New York: Collier Books, 1966.
        Briefly mentions CH as defender of women and author of the
     Mutacion, p. 114, 119.

603 Bardèche, Maurice. Histoire des femmes. Paris: Firmin-Didot,
     1968.
        Includes a few scattered remarks about CH--in Vol. I, 92,
     96--but does not specifically comment on her feminism.

604 Desplantes, F., and P. Pouthier. Les Femmes de lettres en
     France. Geneva: Slatkin, 1970.
        This survey of twenty-four women writers features CH in
     first chapter.

605 Utley, Francis Lee. The Crooked Rib: An Analytical Index to
     the Argument about Women in English and Scots Literature to
     the End of the Year 1568. New York: Octagon, 1970. CdP:
     p. 6, 20, 24, 25, 31, 37, 44, 51, 56–60, 64, 71, 76, 82, 84,
     85, 86, 111, 120, 121, 219, 246, 271.
        Makes various generalizations about CH's feminism placing
     her "somewhere between" being a reformer and an apologist for
     the status quo, p. 57.

606 Herlihy, David. Women in Medieval Society. (The Smith History
     Lecture, 1971). Houston: Univ. of St. Thomas, [1971].
        Seventeen-page paper on the status of medieval women which

contains references to CH and her importance as a social commentator.

607 Davis, Judith M. "Christine de Pisan and Chauvinist Diplomacy." In Female Studies VI: Closer to the Ground. Ed. Nancy Hoffman, Cynthia Secor, and Adrian Tinsley. Old Westbury, NY: Feminist Press, 1972. pp. 116-22.
     Explains what "chauvinist diplomacy" is, how CH used it (to challenge male authority), and why she eventually abandoned it.

608 Finkel, Helen Ruth. "The Portrait of the Woman in the Works of Christine de Pisan." Ph.D. Rice 1972. DAI, XXXII (1972), 1679-80A.
     Sensitive study of CH and her ideas on women. In Foreword, pp. 1-9, the author suggests that CH's main contribution to the feminist cause was opening up new areas of human relations. In the Conclusion, pp. 197-203, she argues that CH's contradictions were ultimately never resolved but that they appear less paradoxical when viewed through her own philosophy. Appendix, pp. 204-14, gives brief critical summaries of CH's works. Includes bibliography of primary and secondary sources, pp. 215-28. See also Finkel 612.

609 Kelly, F. Douglas. "Reflections on the Role of Christine de Pisan as a Feminist Writer." Sub-Stance, II (Winter 1972), 63-71.
     Attributes CH's failure to question the inferior social position of women to her conservatism and challenges idea of accepting her as a genuine feminist.

610 Brée, Germaine. Women Writers in France: Variations on a Theme. New Brunswick, NJ: Rutgers Univ. Press, 1973. CdP: p. ix, 5, 10, 11, 16-22, 23.
     In the "Querelles des Femmes 'Old and New'," p. 16-22, Brée discusses CH's contributions to the Debate. Sees CH as a major creative force in medieval letters.

611 O'Faolian, Julia, and Lauro Martines, eds. Not in God's Image. New York: Harper and Row, 1973. CdP: p. xix, 181-82.
     Prints extracts from the Livre de la cité des dames to show that what was considered assertive and avant-garde in CH's time would be regarded as timid today.

612 Finkel, Helen Ruth. "The Portrait of the Woman in the Works of Christine de Pisan." BF, III (Fall 1974), 138-51.
     Based on the author's doctoral dissertation by same title (608), this article explores CH's teachings and examines the rationale behind her theories on women. CR: SF, 57 (1975), 527.

613 Harksen, Sibylle. <u>Women in the Middle Ages</u>. New York: Abner Schram, 1975.
    Pages 54-56 give general overview of CH. Harksen does not comment on CH's feminism but feels nevertheless that she was ahead of her times.

614 Lehrman, Sara. "The Education of Women in the Middle Ages." In <u>The Roles and Images of Women in the Middle Ages and Rennaissance</u>. Ed. Douglas Radcliff-Umstead. (Univ. of Pittsburgh Publications on the Middle Ages and Renaissance, III). Pittsburgh: Center for Medieval and Renaissance Studies, 1975. pp. 133-44.
    Page 144 n. 24 suggests that CH's ideas on the education of women were influenced by Vincent of Beauvais. See also p. 140 on CH.

615 Power, Eileen Edna. <u>Medieval Women</u>. Ed. M. M. Postan. Cambridge: Cambridge Univ. Press, 1975. CdP: pp. 12-13, 28, 31-34, 41, 43, 47, 75, 80, 85.
    Significant references to CH as unique personality and champion of her sex.

616 Beard, Mary Ritter. <u>Woman as Force in History: A Study in Traditions and Realities</u>. New York: Octagon, 1976.
    Includes some general observations on CH's life and work; no discussion of her feminism (pp. 267-68).

617 Casey, Kathleen. "The Cheshire Cat: Reconstructing the Experience of Medieval Woman." In <u>Liberating Women's History: Theoretical and Critical Essays</u>. Ed. Berenice A. Carroll. Chicago: Univ. of Illinois Press, 1976. pp. 224-49.
    Provocative piece on CH as groundbreaker and enigma with Cheshire-Cat-Syndrome: being bold and confident one minute, fading into nothing but a grin the next.

618 Crossland, Margaret. <u>Women of Iron and Velvet: French Women Writers after George Sand</u>. New York: Taplinger, 1976.
    Pages 44-46 devoted to CH and her feminism. The author sees the Cité as the equivalent of today's women's movement but is critical of CH for not recommending the professions to women.

619 Erickson, Carolly. <u>The Medieval Vision: Essays in History and Perception</u>. New York: Oxford Univ. Press, 1976.
    Comments on the querelle des femmes and on CH as an "ambivalent feminist," p. 201.

620 Albistur, Maïté, and Daniel Armogathe. <u>Histoire du féminisme français du Moyen Âge à nos jours</u>. 2 vols. Paris: Éditions des Femmes, 1977. CdP: I, 43, 48, 58-62, 63-65, 67, 93-94, 103, 125, 476.
    Chapter 2 (in Vol. I) discusses CH and fifteenth-century

feminism but authors are not up to date on Christine scholarship.

621 Schmitz, Betty Ann. "French Women Writers and their Critics:
     An Analysis of the Treatment of Women Writers in Selected His-
     tories of French Literature." Ph.D. Wisconsin 1977. DAI,
     XXXVIII (1977), 3547-48A.
         Argues that a writer's gender is a determining factor in his
     or her reception by critics. CH discussed pp. 155-63.

622 Davis, Natalie Zemon. "Women on Top: Symbolic Sexual Inver-
     sion and Political Disorder in Early Modern Europe." In The
     Reversible World: Symbolic Inversion in Art and Society. Forms
     of Symbolic Inversion Symposium, Toronto 1972. Ed. and with
     an Introduction by Barbara A. Babcock. Ithaca, NY/London:
     Cornell Univ. Press, 1978. pp. 146-90; rpt. with minor revi-
     sions from 601.
         Thinks CH used examples of ancient female conquerors to
     call attention to women of strength and courage, pp. 173-74.

623 Gies, Frances and Joseph. Women in the Middle Ages. New
     York: Crowell, 1978. CdP: pp. 10-12, 90-91, 162, 198.
         CH seen as eloquent, early feminist with unique insight into
     the special role and condition of women.

624 Ignatius, Mary Ann. "A Look at the Feminism of Christine de
     Pizan." Proceedings of the Pacific Northwest Conference on
     Foreign Languages. XXIX, 2 (1978), 18-21.
         Discusses both the personal and literary aspects of CH's
     feminism and tries to explain how it relates to today's women's
     movement.

625 Marks, Elaine. "Women and Literature in France." Signs, III,
     4 (Summer 1978), 832-42.
         Finds that French criticism approaches major women writers
     such as CH, Marie de France, Colette, and others from a psy-
     chological standpoint rather than from a feminine perspective.

626 Rabant, Jean. Histoire du féminisme français. Paris: Stock,
     1978.
         Characterizes CH as "la première féministe connue," p. 19.

627 Chicago, Judy. The Dinner Party: A Symbol of our Heritage.
     Garden City, NY: Doubleday, Anchor Press, 1979.
         Pictorial tribute to feminism. In this unusual book women
     who are considered good role-models are honored with symbolic
     place-settings. CH represented with a "dinner plate" and brief
     write-up explaining her significance in women's history, pp. 78-
     79.

628 Rieger, Dietmar. "Die französische Dichterin im Mittelalter:

Marie de France--die trobairitz--Christine de Pisan." In Die
französische Autorin vom Mittelalter bis zur Gegenwart. Ed.
Renate R. Baader and Dietmar Fricke. Wiesbaden: Akademische
Verlagsgesellschaft Athenaion, 1979. pp. 24-48.
      The German critic Dietmar Rieger gives CH low marks on
her feminism but admits that she did some consciousness-raising
in her time.

629   Roos, M. de. "Hee, Feminin sexe! Christine de Pisan en de
      vrouwenopvoeding." In Excursiones mediaevales: Opstellen
      aangeboden aan Prof. Dr. A. G. Jongkees door zijn leerlingen.
      Ed. H. Schulte Nordholt. Groningen: Vakgroep Middeleeuwse
      Geschiedenis van de Rijksuniversiteit te Groningen, 1979. pp.
      175-95.
            In response to recent studies portraying CH as the foremost
      medieval feminist, Roos argues that she was in fact more of a
      moralist than feminist inasmuch as she seemed to place women's
      duties above their rights.

630   Schulenburg, Jane Tibbetts. "Clio' European Daughters: Myo-
      pic Modes of Perception." In The Prism of Sex: Essays in the
      Sociology of Knowledge. Ed. Julia S. Sherman and Evelyn Tor-
      ton Beck. Madison: Univ. of Wisconsin Press, 1979. pp. 33-
      53.
            Discusses CH's significance as first feminist in Western tradi-
      tion.

631   Altman, Leslie. "Christine de Pisan: First Professional Woman
      of Letters." In Female Scholars: A Tradition of Learned Women
      before 1800. Ed. J. R. Brink. Montreal: Eden Press, 1980.
      pp. 7-23.
            Finds CH's works valuable for providing a "fresh insight
      from a uniquely female perspective into the actual social position
      of women ..." (p. 8).

632   Bornstein, Diane, ed. The Feminist Controversy of the Ren-
      aissance. Delmar, NY: Scholars' Facsimiles Reprint, 1980.
            The Introduction points out (p. vi) that CH's Cité des dames
      makes assertions about women's abilities that were not again
      made until the Renaissance.

633   Davis, Natalie Zemon. "Gender and Genre: Women as Histori-
      cal Writers, 1400-1820." In Beyond Their Sex: Learned Women
      of the European Past. Ed. Patricia H. Labalme. New York:
      New York Univ. Press, 1980. pp. 153-82.
            Examines historical writing-process in such female authors
      as CH, Catharine Macauly and Madame de Staël, noting that
      there was a connection for all of them between their work and
      gender. Although CH never became a model for women histori-
      ans her career illustrates how women could come to write history.

634   Pernoud, Régine. La Femme au temps des cathédrals. Paris:
      Stock, 1980.
         Prints two stanzas from L'Epistre au dieu d'Amours and
      briefly discusses the querelle and CH as observer of the con-
      temporary scene, pp. 271-72.

635   Reno, Christine M. "Feminist Aspects of Christine de Pizan's
      Epistre d'Othea a Hector." SF, 71 (1980), 271-76.
         Argues that CH modified her sources in favor of her female
      figures in order to expand her culture's view of women.

636   Bornstein, Diane, ed. Ideals for Women in the Works of Chris-
      tine de Pizan. (Medieval and Renaissance Monograph Series,
      I). Series' ed. Guy R. Mermier and Edelgard E. Du Bruck.
      Detroit: Michigan Consortium for Medieval and Early Modern
      Studies, 1981.
         Contains six original essays by four scholars: D. Bornstein
      277, 637; M. S. Durley 290; C. Reno 251; and C. C. Willard
      148, 278. The papers deal with "Christine's attitudes toward
      herself, other women, and the role of women in society. The
      first two articles [pp. 11-50] focus on the psychology of Chris-
      tine ... the other four [pp. 51-128] discuss Christine's views
      of the moral, sexual, and practical roles of women ..." (back-
      cover). Includes critical Introduction by the editor, pp. 1-9;
      biographical notes on the contributors, pp. 129-30; a chronolo-
      gical list of CH's writings, pp. 131-32; and a lengthy biblio-
      graphy, pp. 133-39. CR's: 749.

637   _____. "Self-Consciousness and Self-Concepts in the Work
      of Christine de Pizan" In IFW (1981), 11-28.
         Sensitive psychological study of CH's attitude toward her
      own feminism, suggesting that her strong sense of insecurity
      stemmed from a "consciousness of herself as a woman in a man's
      world..." (p. 24). Includes discussion of the Avision and Muta-
      cion. Bornstein does not consider CH a true feminist. CR:
      SF, 78 (1982), 529.

638   Reno, Christine M. "Christine de Pizan: Feminism and Irony."
      In SMSRQF (1981), 125-33.
         Shows how CH used irony (in her ballades, letters, prose
      works) to defend women and express her feminist beliefs. CR:
      777. See also SF, 79 (1983), 125.

639   Bell, Susan Groag. "Medieval Women Book Owners: Arbiters
      of Lay Piety and Ambassadors of Culture." Signs, VII, 4 (Sum-
      mer 1982), 742-68.
         Casual references to CH as author of a book on moral instruc-
      tions (93) and as one of the most scholarly laywomen of Middle
      Ages, p. 754, 756-58.

640   Kelly, Joan. "Early feminist theory and the querelle des femmes,
      1400-1789." Signs, VIII, 1 (Autumn 1982), 4-28.

Comments on CH's role as initiator of the querelle des femmes
and as first theoretical feminist articulating what was later to
become the modern feminist sensibility (pp. 8-9). For expanded
version of this paper, see Kelly 654.

641 Quilligan, Maureen. "For Women, A.D. 1405." NYTBR (25
     July 1982), p. 6, 18.
     This provocative review article (see 778-a) of Richards' trans-
     lation (234) describes the Book of the City of Ladies as an ori-
     ginal and militantly feminist work. The BCL seen as constitut-
     ing an early chapter in women's revisionary history.

642 Richards, Earl Jeffrey. "Introduction". In Richards, trans.,
     The Book of the City of Ladies. New York: Persea, 1982.
     pp. xix-xlvi (234).
     See pp. xix-li for timely and perceptive discussion of CH's
     feminism. Richards thinks CH was "profoundly feminist" and
     considers her ideas on women original.

643 Berriot-Salvador, Evelyn. "Les femmes et les pratiques de
     l'écriture de Christine de Pisan à Marie de Gournay 'femmes
     scavantes et scavoir féminin.'" Réforme, Humanisme, Renais-
     sance, XVI (1983), 52-69.
     Discusses the part CH played in development of feminism.

644 Delany, Sheila. "The Conservatism of Christine de Pizan."
     Paper presented at the Centennial Convention of the MLAA,
     Sheraton Centre, New York City, December 1983. 15 pp.
     Canadian scholar questions trend of making CH into literary
     role-model for modern women writers. See also Delany 662.

645 King, Margaret L., and Albert Rabil, Jr., eds. Her Immaculate
     Hand: Selected Works by and about the Women Humanists of
     Quattrocento Italy. (Medieval and Renaissance Texts and Studies,
     XX). Binghamton, NY: Center of Medieval and Early Renais-
     sance Studies, State Univ. of New York at Binghamton, 1983.
     CH mentioned on p. 133, n.28, in connection with Cassandra
     Fedele, an Italian writer of lesser talents.

646 Kleinbaum, Abby Wettan. The War Against the Amazons. New
     York: McGraw-Hill, 1983. CdP: pp. 64-68, 159-60, 220, 223-
     25.
     Makes various comments on CH's handling of Amazon tales.
     Kleinbaum thinks CH was probably the first woman ever to write
     about the Amazons and to make them into symbol of transcend-
     ence for women.

647 Lucas, Angela M. Women in the Middle Ages: Religion, Mar-
     riage, and Letters. New York: St. Martin's Press, 1983. CdP:
     P. 132, 138-39, 161-69.
     Includes good survey of CH for nonspecialist but errs in stat-
     ing (p. 138) that CH's parents were against educating girls.

Only her mother was. CH's father actually encouraged his daughter to acquire an education.

648   McMillan, Ann Hunter. "The Angel in the Text: Christine de Pizan and Virginia Woolf." Paper presented at the MLAA Centennial Convention, Sheraton Centre, New York City, December 1983. 12 pp.
        Both CH and Virginia Woolf attempted to change women's perception of themselves through a female figure McMillan calls the "angel in the text."

649   Patterson, Lee. "'For the Wyves love of Bathe': Feminine Rhetoric and Poetic Resolution in the Roman de la Rose and the Canterbury Tales." Speculum, LVIII (1983), 656-95.
        Cites the story of Novella d'Andrea in the Cité des dames (Richards 234, II, 36.3) to show that CH considered feminine beauty as a potential problem for women.

650   Richards, Earl Jeffrey. "Christine de Pizan and the Question of Feminist Rhetoric." Teaching Language Through Literature (Modern Language Association Conference, XXII). 2 April 1983, pp. 15-24.
        On rhetoric and its relationship to feminism. CR: SF, 88 (1986), 113.

651   Schibanoff, Susan. "Early women writers: in-scribing, or, reading the fine print." Women's Studies International Forum, VI, 5 (1983), 475-89.
        Deals with Marie de France, Margery Kemp, Julian of Norwich, and CH.

HM

652   _____. "Comment on Kelly's 'Early Feminist Theory and the Querelle des Femmes, 1400-1789'." Signs, IX, 2 (Winter 1983), 320-26.
        Questions Joan Kelly's interpretation of CH's feminism (in 640), noting that the latter had contradictory attitude toward female literacy.

653   Shahar, Shulamith. The Fourth Estate: A History of Women in the Middle Ages. Trans. Chaya Galai. New York: Methuen, 1983. CdP: p. 4, 9, 47, 48, 73, 98, 109, 110, 142, 143, 151, 155, 157, 158, 166-70, 172, 245.
        CH repeatedly cited on the social condition of women and to support author's thesis that medieval women constituted a fourth estate. CR: Signs, XI, 2 (Winter 1986), 189-90.

654   Kelly, Joan. Women, History, and Theory: The Essays of Joan Kelly. London/Chicago: Univ. of Chicago Press, 1984.
        Chapter IV is an elaboration of Kelly 640. Deals with early feminist thought and CH's contribution to it.

655 Gottlieb, Beatrice. "The Problem of Feminism in the Fifteenth
Century." In Women of the Medieval World. Essays in Honor
of John H. Mundy. Ed. Julius Kirshner and Suzanne F. Wemple.
New York/Oxford, U.K.: Basil Blackwell, 1985. pp. 337-62.
Explores the question of how medieval women generally viewed
themselves and what misogyny meant to CH.   *Hq1143.W6*

656 Huot, Sylvia Jean. "Seduction and Sublimation: Christine de
Pizan, Jean de Meun and Dante." RN, XXV (1985), 361-73.
Thoughtful analysis of the paradoxes underlying CH's femin-
ism, with close look at her poetic identity and political values.
Huot sees CH as a "marginal" figure because she never really
explored the implications of a feminist poetics, calling for a
social order that had no place in it for someone like herself.
CR: RR, LXXVIII (1987), pp. 240-41, parag. 4.

657 Williamson, Joan B. "Philippe de Mézières' Book for Married
Ladies: A Book from the Entourage of the Court of Charles
VI." In The Spirit of the Court. Selected Proceedings of the
International Courtly Literature Society, Toronto 1983. Ed.
Glyn S. Burgess and Robert A. Taylor et al. Exeter, Devon:
Short Run Press, 1985. pp. 393-408.
CH believed to have rejected the kind of generalizations de
Mézières made about women in his Livre de la vertu du sacre-
ment de mariage et réconfort des dames mariées; see p. 399,
407, 408.

658 Wilson, Katharina H. "Figmenta vs. veritas: Dame Alice and
the medieval literary depiction of women by women." Tulsa
Studies in Women's Literature, IV (Spring 1985), 17-32.
On Hrotsvit of Gandersheim and CH, with comments on latter's
attitude toward Matheolus and Jean de Meun.

659 Delany, Sheila. "Rewriting Woman Good: Gender and the Anx-
iety of Influence in Two Late-Medieval Texts." In Chaucer in   *pr1924.*
the Eighties. Ed. Julian N. Wasserman and Robert J. Blanch.   *c4*
Syracuse, NY: Syracuse Univ. Press, 1986. pp. 75-92.
Uses the Cité des dames and Legend of Good Women to gauge   *p75-92*
CH's and Chaucer's response to the misogynistic tradition in
western literature. Also explores question of woman as "written
object" (in Legend) as opposed to "writing subject" (in Cité).
CR: MAe, LVII (1988), 107-08.

660 Labarge, Margaret Wade. A Small Sound of the Trumpet: Women
in Medieval Life. Boston: Beacon Press, 1986. CdP: p. xi,
19, 41-43, 65, 69, 76, 95, 111, 112, 113, 143-46, 156, 157, 198,
232, 235-38; the writings, pp. 41-42, 65, 111-13, 143-44, 156-
57, 235-38.
On the daily life of women in the feudal societies of France,
England, Low Countries and southern Germany from 1100 to
1500. Deals largely with the lives of unknown women but also

covers such personalities as Mahaut of Artois, Hildegard of
Bingen, and CdP. The latter cited, among other things, on
the duty of a noble wife, p. 19; Jeanne de Bourbon, p. 65;
peasant women, pp. 156-57. Includes a bio-literary survey of
CH, pp. 41-43, and a reproduction of the author and the Three
Virtues from BN f.fr. 1177.

661 Schibanoff, Susan. "Taking the Gold out of Egypt: The Art
     of Reading as a Woman." In Gender and Reading: Essays on
     Readers, Texts, and Contexts. Ed. Elizabeth A. Flynn and
     Patrocinio P. Schweickart. Baltimore/London: Johns Hopkins
     Univ. Press, 1986. pp. 83-106.
         Breezy piece about how CH learned to read "as a woman" by
     approaching old, critical texts from new direction.

662 Delany, Sheila. "Mothers to Think Back Through: Who Are
     They? The Ambiguous Example of Christine de Pizan." In
     Medieval Texts and Contemporary Readers. Ed. Laurie A.
     Finke and Martin B. Shichtman. Ithaca, NY/London: Cornell
     Univ. Press, 1987. pp. 177-97.
         This expanded version of 644 describes CH as a medieval
     "Phyllis Schlafly" and questions her relevance for contemporary
     women writers. For a more sympathetic view of CH, see Delany
     252.

663 Wayne, Valerie. "Zenobia in Medieval and Renaissance Litera-
     ture." In Ambiguous Realities: Women in the Middle Ages and
     Renaissance. Ed. Carol Levin and Jeanie Watson. Detroit:
     Wayne State Univ. Press, 1987. pp. 48-65.
         The thirteen essays in this collection reinterpret specific
     literary, historical, and theological texts to illuminate issues con-
     cerning medieval and Renaissance women. Wayne examines CH's
     concept of "moral nature" and suggests that her arguments for
     women's superiority represent a historical change in the thinking
     about women, pp. 54-56.

• V •

MISCELLANEA

664 Tiraboschi, Girolamo. Storià della letteratura italiana. 16 vols.
Milan: Società tipogr. de' classici italiani, 1822-1823. (Vols.
V-XV are divided into 2 parts).
    Vol. V, 318-21 and p. 460 deal with Thomas de Pizan and
Charles V (798).

665 Malet, Gilles. Inventaire ou catalogue des livres de l'ancienne
Bibliothèque du Louvre fait en l'année 1373. Paris: Librairie
de la Bibliothèque Royale, 1836.
    This volume contains Malet's 1373 inventory of Charles V's
(798) book collection; a Preface by Boivin; and extracts from
CH's works, pp. xv-xvi. CH also mentioned in notes, p. xxviii,
and in entries No. 165, 194, 496.

666 Quicherat, Jules. "Recherches sur le chroniqueur Jean de
Castel." BEC, II (1840-1841), 461-77.
    Suggests that CH's grandson, Jean de Castel, was Louis XI's
secretary not his chronicler, as claimed by Lacroix du Main.
See Willard 450, pp. 207-08, on reason for frequent confusion
over de Castel.

667 Paris, Gaston. "Chronique." Romania, IX (1880), 492-93.
    Announces decision not to award Bordin Prize and outlines
requirements for new study on CH to be based on a literary,
historical, and bibliographical approach.

668 Luce, Simeon. La France pendant la guerre de cent ans. Paris:
Hachette, 1890.
    Contains reference to Thomas de Pizan as "père de la célèbre
Christine..." p. 174.

669 Prost, B. "Quelques acquisitions des manuscrits par les ducs
de Bourgogne Philippe le Hardi et Jean sans Peur." Archives
historiques, artistiques et littéraires. II (1890-1891), 337-53.
    Reprints Burgundian records showing that CH received 100
crowns from John the Fearless (814) for her Charles V and another, unidentified work.

670 Meyer, Paul. "Les anciens traducteurs français de Végèce et

en particulier Jean de Vignai." Romania, XXV (1896), 401-
23.
Makes brief reference to CH and her knowledge of Vegetius.

671 Toynbee, Paget, ed. The Letters of Horace Walpole. Oxford:
Clarendon Press, 1903-1905.
CH cited in a number of Walpole letters: letter dated 28
February 1780 (in Vol. XI, p. 133); letter dated 1 January 1787
(in Vol. XIII, p. 434); letter dated 23 February 1787 (in Vol.
XIII, 446); letter dated 15 September 1787 (in Vol. XIV, p. 54).
Letters of 28 February 1780 and 9 July 1788 suggest that it
was Walpole who circulated the rumor that CH and the Earl of
Salisbury were in love--Mombello discusses this question in 434.
For additional letters citing CH, see 674.

672 Doutrepont, Georges. Inventaire de la librairie de Philippe le
Bon (1420). Brussels: Kiessling, 1906.
Lists six items for CH: Nos. 8, 98, 109, 117, 124, 130.
Doutrepont states that she was one of best represented authors
in Burgundian library.

673 Temple, Maud Elizabeth. "Christine de Pisan and the Victorine
Revival." Ph.D. Radcliffe, 1912.
This dissertation served as basis for Temple 547.

674 Toynbee, Paget, ed. Lettres de la marquise Du Deffand à
Horace Walpole (1766-1780). Édition complète, augm. d'environ
500 lettres inédites, pub. d'après les originaux, avec une introduction, des notes, et une table des noms. 3 vols. London:
Methuen, 1912.
Vol. III includes four letters with references to CH: letter
dated 10 January 1780 (p. 572); letter dated 25 January 1780
(p. 574); letter dated 3 February 1780 (p. 577); and letter
dated 11 February 1780. See also Toynbee 671.

675 Champion, Pierre, ed. Charles d'Orléans: poésies. (Les
Classiques français du Moyen Age, XXXIV, LVI). 2 vols.
1923-1929; rpt. Paris: Champion, 1966.
Here is what Champion had to say about CH's influence on
Orleans (800): "...Christine a pu lui enseigner la tendresse...
Et surtout elle avait évoqué, dans le Débat de deux amants,
l'atmosphère de sa cour dont on retrouvera, sous l'allégorie,
comme l'écho affaibli dans la Retenue d'Amour" (II, 552).

676 Lone, Emma Miriam. Some Bookwomen of the Fifteenth Century.
New York: n. pub., 1932; first pub. in Colophon, Pt. II, no.
10, 1932.
This eight-page Colophon offprint on fifteenth-century women
authors, book collectors, and printers briefly comments on CH
and Dame Juliana Berners.

677 Thorndike, Lynn. A History of Magic and Experimental Science.
     Vol. III. New York: Columbia Univ. Press, 1934.
        Contains good material on Thomas de Pizan. See especially
     Chap. XXXVI and pp. 32-33, 165, 183, 585, 635, 676 where
     author discusses his practice of alchemy and the strange rituals
     he engaged in. Also offers fascinating look at his correspond-
     ence with fourteenth-century alchemist Bernard of Treves.

678 Patch, Howard Rollin. The Tradition of Boethius: A Study of
     his Importance in Medieval Culture. 1935; reissued New York:
     Russell & Russell, 1970. CdP: p. 25, 107, 135.
        Discusses CH as part of Boethian tradition.

679 Legge, Mary Dominica. Anglo-Norman in the Cloisters: The
     Influence of the Orders upon Anglo-Norman Literature. Edin-
     burgh: Univ. of Edinburgh Press, 1950.
        The editor of CH's Epistre à la reine (282) calls attention
     here (p. 48) to CH as well-known French author writing in an
     age when women were not given to writing.

680 Coopland, George William. Nicole Oresme and the Astrologers:
     A Study of his 'Livre de Divinacions.' Liverpool: Univ. of
     Liverpool Press, 1952.
        Wonders whether Oresme and Philippe de Mézières (819) were
     among the learned men who visited the Pizan household, as CH's
     writings suggest.

681 Brunelli, Giuseppe A. "Jean de Castel et Mirouer des dames."
     MA, LXII (1956), 93-117.
        Good source of information for CH's grandchildren, especially
     for writer and chronicler Jean de Castel. His "Mirouer" printed
     pp. 110-16; also part of his poem to Charles de Gancourt, p.
     95.

682 Bossuat, André. "Jean Castel, chroniqueur de France." MA,
     LXIV (1958), 284-304; 499-538.
        I. Deals with the life of French chronicler Jean de Castel
     who was one of CH's grandsons. II. Prints extracts from his
     Chronique du Mont-Saint Michel.

683 Nardis, Luigi de. "La 'Harparesse' di Valentina." In Il Sor-
     riso di Reims e attri saggi di cultura francese. (Saggi e mono-
     grafie di letteratura). Rocca San Casciano: Capelli editore,
     1960.
        Mentions CH p. 79, 80, in connection with Louis (815) and
     Charles of Orleans (800).

684 Vaughan, Richard. Philip the Bold: The Formation of the
     Burgundian State. Cambridge, MA: Harvard Univ. Press, 1962.
        Includes discussion on Philip the Bold (823) and CH as im-
     portant figure in author-patron relationship, p. 198.

685 Willard, Charity Cannon. "The Remarkable Case of Clothilde
     de Surville." EC, VI (1966), 108-16.
        Deals with the literary hoax that tried to pass off Clothilde
     de Surville as a fifteenth-century poet. Author calls attention
     to the similar biographies of the bogus Clothilde and the genuine
     CH.

686 Cookshaw, Pierre. "Mentions d'auteurs, de copistes, d'enlumi-
     neurs et de libraires dans les comptes généraux de l'état Bour-
     guignon (1384-1419)." Scriptorium, XXIII (1969), 122-24.
        Items No. 52, 64, 68, 72, 76, and 81 of Burgundian records
     reproduced here pertain to CH.

687 Mollat, Michel. Genèse Médiévale de la France Moderne XIVe-
     XVe siècles. Paris: B. Arthaud, 1970.
        Contains excellent background material on CH's comtemporaries
     but only casual reference to CH herself. Illustration of CH and
     Louis of Orleans (815), p. 80; of Cité des dames, p. 115.

688 Walravens, C. J. H. Alain Chartier: études biographiques
     suivies de pièces justificatives, d'une description des édi-
     tions et d'une édition des ouvrages inédites. Amsterdam:
     Meulenhoff-Didier, 1971. CdP: p. 49, 51, 52, 79.
        Makes observations on the similarities and differences between
     CH and Chartier (801).

689 Calin, William C. A Poet at the Fountain: Essays on the Nar-
     rative Verse of Guillaume de Machaut. Lexington: Univ. of
     Kentucky Press, 1974. CdP: p. 36, 44, 131, 156, 226, 246.
        This comprehensive work on Machaut's (816) long dits dis-
     cusses his influence on Chaucer, Froissart (806) and CH.

690 Laidlaw, J. C., ed. The Poetical Works of Alain Chartier. Cam-
     bridge: Cambridge Univ. Press, 1974. CdP: p. 23, 29, 36;
     notes p. 443, 448, 456, 467.
        CH cited as possible influence on Chartier (801), probably
     in the Breviaire de Nobles, Débat de deux Fortunés d'Amours,
     and in his sequential poems.

691 Vale, Malcolm Graham Allan. Charles VII. Berkeley/Los Angeles:
     Univ. of California Press, 1974.
        Brief comment on CH and Charles VII, p. 5.

692 Vaughan, Richard. Valois Burgundy. Hamden, CT: Archon
     Books, 1975.
        Cites CH on Philip the Bold (823), p. 77.

693 Hughes, Muriel Joy. "The Library of Philip the Bold and Mar-
     garet of Flanders, first Valois duke and duchess of Burgundy."
     JMH, IV (1978), 145-88.
        Various references to CH concerning the duke's (823) patronage

and his collection of her works in Burgundian library, p. 181.

694 Lyttle, Guy Fitch, and Stephen Orgel, eds. Patronage in the Renaissance. Princeton, NJ: Princeton Univ. Press, 1981.
      This study on Tudor patronage reports that Henry VII's predominantly French book collection was filled with works by CH, Froissart (806), and Chartier (801), p. 124.

695 Gripari, Pierre. "Christine de Pisan, ou la cité des dames." le spectacle du monde, CCXLIX (December 1982), 108-09.
      Article announcing publication of Régine Pernoud's biography (447).

696 Krynen, Jacques. Idéal du prince et pouvoir royal en France à la fin du Moyen Âge 1380-1440. Paris: Picard, 1982.
      Includes vernacular writers such as CH and Froissart (806).

697 Hogetorn, C. "Christine de Pizan, auteur à la mode?" Rapports, LIII (1983), 141-53.

698 Bodenham, C. H. L. "The Nature of the Dream in late mediaeval French Literature." MAe, LIV (1985), 74-84.
      Situates CH, Chartier (801), and Villon within the genre of medieval dream literature.

699 Spence, Sarah, ed. and trans. The French Chansons of Charles d'Orléans, with the corresponding Middle English chansons. (Garland Library of Medieval Literature, XLVI, Ser. A). London/New York: Garland, 1986.
      The Introduction briefly comments on CH's and Deschamps' (804) influence on Orleans (800), p. xxiii.

COLLECTED WORKS, ANTHOLOGIES, SELECTIONS

700 Kéralio, Louise Guinement de. Collection des meilleurs ouvrages françois, composés par des femmes, dediée aux femmes
françoises. Paris: Lagrange, 1787. II, 109-467; III, 1-132.
Kéralio contributed to CH's literary revival by publishing
many of her works here. Vol. II includes extracts from the
Livre des fais et bonnes meurs du sage roy Charles V, Grou-
leau's prose text of the Livre du chemin de long estude (155),
and Janot's ed. of the Livre des trois vertus (262); also contains reprints on CH's life by Boivin (373) and the abbé Sallier (58). Volume III includes: extracts from L'Avision-Christine, Livre de la cité des dames, Cent ballades, Rondeaux,
Jeux à vendre, Epistre au dieu d'Amours, Epistres sur le Roman
de la Rose, Dits moraux, Livre des fais d'armes et de chevalerie,
and the Livre de la mutacion de Fortune.

701 Thomassy, Raimond Marie Joseph. Essai sur les écrits politiques de Christine de Pisan suivi d'une notice littéraire et de
pièces inédites. Paris: Debécourt, 1838. pp. 87-199.
This study was instrumental in reviving interest in CH and
her works. Publishes editions of L'Epistre à la reine, L'Oroyson
Nostre Dame, Lamentacion, and excerpts from Le Livre de la
paix and Le Livre des trois vertus. Texts are preceded by
lengthy Introduction, pp. i-lxxxiv, dealing with CH's political
views and influence on her contemporaries and on the sixteenth
century.

702 Roy, Maurice, ed. Oeuvres poétiques de Christine de Pisan.
(SATF) 3 vols. Paris: Firmin Didot, 1886-1896; rpt. New
York: Johnson Reprint, 1985.
The only anthology to publish all of CH's poetic works except three: Le Livre du chemin de long estude (see Eargle
157), Le Livre de la mutacion de Fortune (see Solente 175),
and the Ditié de Jehanne d'Arc (see Kennedy and Varty 358).
Volume I comprises the Cent ballades (pp. 1-100), Virelais (pp.
101-18), Ballades d'estrange façon (pp. 119-24), Lais (pp. 125-
45), Rondeaux (pp. 147-85), Jeux à vendre (pp. 186-205),
Autres ballades (pp. 207-69), Encore autres ballades (pp. 271-
79), Complaintes amoureuses (pp. 281-95). Volume II contains

the Epistre au dieu d'Amours (pp. 1-27), Dit de la Rose (pp. 29-48), Débat de deux amans (pp. 49-109), Livre des trois jugemens (pp. 111-57), Dit de Poissy (pp. 159-222), Dit de la pastoure (pp. 223-94), Epistre à Eustache Morel (pp. 295-301). Volume III encompasses L'Oroyson Nostre Dame (pp. 1-9), Les XV Joyes Nostre Dames (pp. 11-14), L'Oroyson Nostre Seigneur (pp. 15-26), Enseignemens moraux (pp. 27-44), Proverbes moraux (pp. 45-57), Livre du duc des vrais amans (pp. 59-208), Cent ballades d'amant et de dame (pp. 209-317).   Each of the three volumes has an Introduction, notes, and table of contents.   The first also includes a four-page biographical survey of CH and a table identifying the various manuscript families on which the text is based, namely, BN f.fr. 835, 836, 605, with variants from BN 604, 606, 12779, and BL Harley 4431 for the Cent ballades d'amant et de dame.   The third volume carries a Note on Harley 4431 by P. Meyer, pp. xxi-xxiv.

703   Clédat, Léon, ed.   Morceaux choisis des auteurs français du Moyen Âge.   Paris: Garnier, 1889.
        Prints CH's ballade "Seulete suy" (Roy 702, I, p. 12) together with explanatory note, pp. 367-77.

704   Du Bos, Maurice, ed.   Christine de Pisan: Un carteron de balades.   (Petite Bibliothèque Surannée).   Paris: Chiberre, 1921.
        Includes ballades from the Cent ballades, Autres ballades, and Cent ballades d'amant et de dame, pp. 19-68.

705   Pernoud, Régine, ed.   La Poésie Médiévale française.   Paris: Du Chêne, 1947.
        Publishes two of CH's Jeux à vendre, pp. 33-36, and a biographical note, 271.

706   Savill, Mervyn, ed.   Anthology of European Poetry.   I. From Machault to Malherbe, 13th to 17th Century.   Trans. William Stirling.   London: Allan Wingate [1947].
        Features poems--with parallel English translations--by CH, Machaut (816), Froissart (806), Deschamps (804), Charles of Orleans (800), Oliver Basselin, and Villon.

707   Martin, Charlotte H., trans.   A few early French verses done into English.   Albany, NY: Argas Press, 1949.
        Prints the works of six French poets, including CdP and Marie de France, pp. 4-37.

708   Currey, R. N.   Formal Spring: French Renaissance Poems of Charles d'Orléans, Villon, Ronsard, du Bellay and others.   (Granger Index Reprint Series) 1950; rpt. Freeport, NY: Books for Library Press, 1969.
        Includes two of CH's rondeaux and a biographical note, pp. 15-17.

709 Jones, Charles W., ed. Medieval Literature in Translation.
New York: Longmans, Green, 1950.
     Gives English rendition of one of CH's rondeaux, p. 688.

710 Wallis, Cedric, ed. and trans. Charles d'Orléans and other
French Poets: Rondels. London: Caravell Press, 1951. No.
31 of an edition limited to 150 numbered copies. CdP: pp. 20-
21, 28, 31, 56-57.
     Prints twenty-five rondeaux in French and English by Or-
leans (800), Machaut (816), Deschamps (804), Villon, Marot,
Héroët, Voiture, and CdP.

711 Pauphilet, Albert. Poètes et Romanciers du Moyen Âge. (Bibliothèque de la Pléiade). Paris: Gallimard, 1952.
     Includes two of CH's ballades and a Jeux à vendre, pp.
1001-07. Biographical note, p. 999.

712 Fouchet, Max-Pol. De l'amour au voyage: anthologie thémati-
que de la poésie française. Paris: Seghers, 1958.
     Page 540 prints a chanson by CH on solitude.

713 Moulin, Jeanine. "Christine de Pisan." Les Annales-Conferencia,
LXVII, 116 (June 1960), 41-43.
     Presents a selection of CH's poems in Modern French. CR:
LF, 996 (1963), 2.

714 _____. Christine de Pisan: introduction, choix et adaptation.
Paris: Seghers, 1962.
     Publishes seventeen Ballades, fifteen Rondeaux, six Dits et
Débats, four Virelais, a Lais mortel, and three religious poems
all in Modern French. Texts preceded by a critical Introduction
(pp. 11-36) that traces CH's writings from her early courtly
lyrics to the later feminist works. Contains plates from BN
f.fr. 835, 605, 836, 606. CR: SF, 19 (1963), 132-33.

715 Varty, Kenneth, ed. Christine de Pisan's Ballades, Rondeaux
and Virelais: An Anthology. Leicester, Eng.: Leicester Univ.
Press, 1965.
     Collection of 119 short poems arranged by subject. The text,
pp. 3-125, is based on Harley 4431. It is preceded by an Introduction, pp. ix-xxxvii, and bibliography, pp. xxxviii-xl. Varty
gives no variants but a list of rejected readings is provided on
pp. 126-27. The notes, pp. 128-64, deal primarily with imagery,
rhetoric, and vocabulary although some are explanatory. Has
glossary, index of first lines, and a list of proper names, pp.
165-88. CR's: 782. See also:
     SF, 29 (1966), 328
     FS, XXI (1967), 56-57
     CN, XXVII (1967), 194-95

716 Ferrier, Janet MacKay. French Prose Writers of the Fourteenth

and Fifteenth Centuries. (The Commonwealth and International
Library. Pergamon Oxford Series). New York: Pergamon,
1966.
    Includes extracts from CH's writings, pp. 191-94. Also an
analysis of her various prose styles, pp. 98-111. The autobiographical works written in simple reporting style considered
more successful than the treatises using style clergial. For
more on CH's prose style, see Bornstein 299, 304, and Burnley
507.

717 Kanters, Robert, and Maurice Nadeau, eds. Anthologie de la
     poésie française. II. Le Moyen Âge. Paris: Editions Recon-
     tre, 1966.
        CH represented with two ballades, a Ballade a reponses, and
     jeux à vendre. Introductory comments, pp. 338-49.

718 Pernoud, Régine. Joan of Arc: By Herself and Her Witnesses.
     Trans. Eduard Hyams. New York: Stein & Day, 1966.
        Includes four stanzas from the Ditié with brief comment, p.
     94.

719 Mary, André, ed. Anthologie poétique française: Moyen Âge.
     II. Paris: Garnier-Flammarion, 1967.
        CH represented with seven poems, pp. 173-80.

720 Moulin, Jeanine. La Poésie feminine du XIIe au XIXe siècle.
     Paris: Seghers, 1969.
        Poems by CH on pp. 94-100.

721 Wilkins, Nigel, ed. One Hundred Ballades, Rondeaux and Vire-
     lais from the Late Middle Ages. Cambridge: Cambridge Univ.
     Press, 1969.
        CH represented with fifteen poems and explanatory note, pp.
     81-95. CR: SF, 38 (1969), 324-25.

722 Bonnefoy, Claude, ed. La Poésie française des origines à nos
     jours: anthologie. Paris: Seuil, 1975.
        CH represented with three poems and brief introduction, pp.
     16-17.

723 Moulin, Jeanine. Huit siècles de poésie feminine: anthologie.
     Paris: Seghers, 1975.
        Reprints CH's poems from 720, pp. 44-50.

724 Aspland, Clifford W., ed. A Medieval French Reader. Oxford:
     Clarendon Press, 1979.
        An introduction to medieval French literature for university
     students. It includes CH's poems "Com turtre suis sans per
     toute seulete" and "Seulete suy." Glossary and notes on CH,
     pp. 174-77.

725 Sullerot, Evelyne. <u>Women On Love: Eight Centuries of Feminine</u>
     <u>Writings</u>. Trans. Helen R. Lane. Garden City, NY: Double-
     day, 1979.
        French sociologist prints some of CH's poems in attempt to
     trace evolution of the "feminine love cult." Short biography of
     CH, p. 296.

726 Bankier, Joanna, and Deirdre Lashagari, eds. <u>Women Poets of</u>
     <u>the World</u>. New York: Macmillan, 1983. CdP: p. 149, 160-61.
        Prints two of CH's poems and discusses CH and Marie de
     France in terms of their importance as medieval women poets.

727 Dezon-Jones, Elyane. <u>Les écritures féminines</u>. Préface de Ger-
     maine Brée. Paris: Magnard, 1983.
        Works by twenty-eight French women writers, from Marie
     de France to Simone de Beauvoir. Section on CH, pp. 24-29,
     prints two of her ballades and an excerpt from the <u>Lamentacion</u>.
     The accompanying bibliography wrongly lists Pinet's (398) date
     of publication as 1912 instead of 1927. Brée's Preface is re-
     print, in French, of 610.

728 Willard, Charity Cannon. "The Franco-Italian Professional
     Writer Christine de Pizan." In <u>Medieval Women Writers</u>. Ed.
     Katharina M. Wilson. Athens: Univ. of Georgia Press, 1984.
     pp. 333-63.
        Well-balanced overview of CH's life and ideas, with represen-
     tative selections from the writings. Includes part of her impor-
     tant letter to Jean de Montreuil (820) translated here by Willard
     for the first time into Modern English (pp. 342-46); extracts
     from the <u>City of Ladies</u> (pp. 346-50) and the <u>Book of Three</u>
     <u>Virtues</u> (pp. 350-58). Notes to the translation (pp. 358-60) are
     followed by a bibliography (pp. 360-63). References to CH
     also in Wilson's Introduction, p. viii, xvii-xviii, xix, xx, xxi.
     CR: <u>SF</u>, 91 (1987), 98.

729 Wisman, Josette A., ed. and trans. '<u>The Epistle of the Prison</u>
     <u>of Human Life</u>,' with '<u>An Epistle to the Queen of France</u>,' and
     '<u>Lament on the Evils of the Civil War</u>.' (Garland Library of Medi-
     eval Literature, XXI, Ser. A). London/New York: Garland,
     1984.
        Scholarly new edition of the hitherto unedited <u>L'Epistre de</u>
     <u>la prison de vie humaine</u>, pp. 1-69; the previously edited <u>Epi-</u>
     <u>stre a la Royne de France</u>, pp. 70-83; and <u>La Lamentacion sur</u>
     <u>les maux de la guerre civile</u>, pp. 84-95. French texts and edi-
     tor's line-by-line English translation appear on facing pages.
     An Introduction, pp. ix-xxxii, deals with CH's life and milieu;
     sources and influences; editorial policy. Wisman's bibliography
     is classified and extensive listing modern editions and transla-
     tions of CH's works, over ninety critical studies with brief an-
     notations, and study aids, pp. xxxiii-xlv. Includes index of
     proper names, pp. 97-99. CR's: 791.

730 Gally, Michèle, and Christiane Marchello-Nizia. Littérature de
     l'Europe Médiévale. (Collection, Textes et Contextes). Paris:
     Magnard, 1985.
         Handsomely produced book with nice section on CH, pp. 392-
     96. Provides biographical sketch, a chronological survey of
     the writings, ballades from the Cent ballades d'amant et de dame,
     extracts from the Mutacion and Avision, and illustrations from
     the Cité. Section on the Roman de la Rose prints part of CH's
     1401 letter to Jean de Montreuil (820), pp. 398-99. Also, stan-
     zas from the Ditié, p. 537.

731 Petroff, Elizabeth A., ed. Medieval Women's Visionary Litera-
     ture. New York/Oxford: Oxford Univ. Press, 1986.
         Features the works of twenty-eight women writers from late
     antiquity to fifteenth century. Selections for CH, pp. 337-46,
     include parts of the Avision; her letter to Jean de Montreuil
     (820); and ballades from the Cent ballades, all translated into
     Modern English by Nadia Margolis. CH also discussed in "Women
     Writers of the late Fourteenth Century--Seeking Models," pp.
     299-303. (Margolis's trans. of CH's letter to de Montreuil to
     be rpt. in Laurie Finke and Robert Con Davis, Critical Texts:
     Literary Theory from the Greeks through the Present, Long-
     mans, 1989).

732 Thiébaux, Marcelle, trans. The Writings of Medieval Women.
     (Garland Library of Medieval Literature, XIV, Ser. B). New
     York/London: Garland, 1987.
         Includes the works of CdP, Egeria of Spain, Hrotsvit of
     Gandersheim, Marie de France, Julian of Norwich, and others.
     Each chapter has an introduction and bibliography on the writer
     featured. The chapter on CH (XV, pp. 235-50) prints her
     "Letter of Lady Sebille de la Tour" from the Livre du duc des
     vrais amans and eleven poems, all in Modern French.

• VII •

BIBLIOGRAPHICAL MATERIAL

733 Farrar, Clarissa P., and Austin P. Evans, eds. Bibliography
of English Translations from Medieval Sources. (Records of
Civilization Sources and Studies, XXXIX). New York: Columbia Univ. Press, 1946.
     Nos. 3192-95 are entries for CH.

734 Cabeen, David C., general ed. A Critical Bibliography of
French Literature. I. The Medieval Period. Ed. Urban T.
Holmes, Jr. 6 vols. Syracuse, NY: Syracuse Univ. Press,
1947; rev. 2nd ed., 1952.
     This selected, annotated list includes several items on CH:
no. 303, 1696-1705, 1744, 2403.

735 Bossuat, Robert. Manuel bibliographique de la littérature française du Moyen Âge. (Bibliothèque Elzévirienne. Nouvelle
Série. Etudes et Documents). Melun: Librairie d'Argences,
1951.
     A basic reference work with numerous entries for CH: nos.
4437-82, 5115; Supplement I (1949-1953), nos. 6834-45; Supplement II (1954-1960), nos. 7888-92, 7900.

736 Klapp, Otto. Bibliographie der französischen Literaturwissen-
schaft. Frankfurt am Main: Vittorio Klostermann, 1965-1984.
     Entries for CH in following vols.: I (1956-1958), p. 70.
II (1959-1960), p. 108. III (1961-1962), pp. 96-97. IV (1963-
1964), p. 57, 85. V (1965-1966), p. 86, 124-25. VI (1967-
1968), pp. 126-27. VII (1969), p. 69. VIII (1970), p. 120.
IX (1971), p. 124. X (1972), pp. 154-55. XI (1973), pp. 145-
46. XII (1974), pp. 178-79. XIII (1975), p. 156. XIV (1976),
p. 153. XV (1977), p. 162. XVI (1978), p. 160. XVII (1979),
p. 160. XVIII (1980), p. 172. XIX (1981), p. 161. XX (1982),
p. 162. XXI (1983), p. 160. XXII (1984), pp. 157-58. XXIII
(1985), pp. 170-71. XXIV (1986), pp. 175-76. None of the
listings above are annotated.

737 Knudson, Charles A., and Jean Misrahi. The Medieval Literature of Western Europe: A Review of Research, Mainly 1930-
1960. General ed. John H. Fisher. New York: Pub. for MLAA
by New York Univ. Press, 1966.

142

Lists four items for CH: Pinet (398), Towner (286), Solente (201), Willard (337).

738 Ferguson, Mary Ann Heyward. Bibliography of English Translations from Medieval Sources, 1943-1967. New York: Columbia Univ. Press, 1974.
Main entry for CH is no. 1608; items relating to her, no. 717, 722-23, 728; CH and Bouvet (Bonet 795), no. 328. Most entries have brief annotations.

739 Erickson, Carolly, and Kathleen Casey. "Women in the Middle Ages: A Working Bibliography." MS, XXXVII (1975), 340-59.
Lists four items for CH, pp. 355-56.

740 Cooke, Thomas D., ed. The Present State of Scholarship in Fourteenth-Century Literature. Columbia: Univ. of Missouri Press, 1982.
Many useful bibliographical citations on medieval French literature. CH, Froissart (806), and Machaut (816) named as example of great writers flourishing during this period, p. 66, 95.

741 Burgoyne, Lynda, and Renée Gélinas. "Christine de Pisan, Alain Chartier, Charles d'Orléans: Cinq ans d'études (1976-1980)," MF, VIII-IX (1983), 291-308.
Bibliographical and statistical study, with most extensive treatment given CH, pp. 295-300.

742 Kennedy, Angus J. Christine de Pizan: a bibliographical guide. (Research Bibliographies and Checklists, XLII) London: Grant & Cutler, 1984.
Critical bibliography with coverage to November 1981. Containing 502 numbered items, a brief Introduction, and three indexes, this excellent 131-page manual is divided into five parts, the last and longest dealing with CdP's individual works. Many entries have citations to critical reviews. Especially useful is list of Manuscript Catalogues and Reference Works on Early Printed Editions, pp. 20-30, as these are not covered in present volume (i.e., Yenal, 2nd ed.). CR's:
SF, 87 (1985), 552-53
MAe, LIV (1985), 347
FR, LIX (1986), 608-09
MA, XCII (1986), 325-29
Speculum, LXII (1987), 770-71
FS, XLI (1987), 319

743 Krueger, Roberta L., and E. Jane Burns. "A Selective Bibliography of Criticism: Women in Medieval French Literature." RN, XXV (1985), 375-90.
Focuses on critical studies treating the literary representation of women from 1100-1500, with emphasis on recent scholarship. Section IV, pp. 385-88, has over fourteen items on or relating to CH.

CRITICAL REVIEWS TO WORKS CITED
(arrangement is alphabetical by author)

744   CR of 138. P.-Y. Badel, Le 'Roman de la Rose' au XIVe siècle:
      étude de la reception de l'oeuvre. In SF, 79 (1983), 122-23
      (G. Mombello).
         Thinks author's interpretation of Quarrel is original.

745   CR of 112. J. L. Baird and J. R. Kane, trans., La Querelle
      de la Rose: Letters and Documents. In FR, LIII (1980), 737
      (L. S. Crist).
         Translation considered workmanlike but de Montreuil's Epistle
      103 (on p. 40) thought to have lost its original flavor, especially
      when compared to Hicks 111, pp. 28-29.

746   CR of 443. J. Beck and G. Mombello, eds., Seconda Miscellanea
      di Studi e Ricerche sul Quattrocento Francese. In Speculum, LX
      (1985), 228-30 (D. Fraioli).
         Reviewer focuses primarily on essays by Willard (37), Reno
      (638), and Hicks (141), the latter important because of his Rose
      research.

747   CR of 299. D. Bornstein, ed., The Middle English Translation
      of CdP's "Livre du corps de policie." In MAe, XLVIII (1979),
      298-300 (J. M. Ferrier).
         Considers this ME edition not only an interesting contribution
      to late medieval renderings of French texts but feels Bornstein
      has "considerably increased our knowledge and understanding
      of the original" (p. 298).

748   CR of 279. _____, The Lady in the Tower. In MLR, LXXX
      (1985), 111-12 (J. W. Nicholls).
         Feels book would have been more valuable if author had
      limited her scope.

749   CR's of 636. _____, ed., Ideals for Women in the Works of
      CdP. In:
      (a) SF, 78 (1982), 529-30 (G. Mombello). Each essay in collec-
           tion reviewed separately under contributor's name.
      (b) Speculum, LVIII (1983), 437 (D. Fraioli). Wonders if the

conflicting views represented by essays in collection are ultimately resolvable.
(c) FCS, IX (1984), 249–53 (J.-L. Picherit). Finds the various contributions of uneven quality.

750 CR of 241. C. Bozzolo, "Il Decameron come fonte del Livre de la cité des dames di CdP." In SF, 33 (1967), 519–20 (S. Cigada). Discusses Bozzolo's findings on CH's use of the Decameron.

751 CR's of 56. C. F. Bühler, ed., The Epistle of Othea. In:
(a) SF, 45 (1971), 524-25 (G. Mombello). Considers this critical edition valuable tool for Pizan specialists and scholars of late medieval French literature.
(b) Speculum, XLVII (1972), 803–04 (M. W. Bloomfield). Calls Bühler's Introduction "solid," the notes "excellent," the glossary "selective."
(c) MAe, III (1972), 274-76 (D. Pearsall). Regards this an excellent work but finds editor's literary parallels "curiously arbitrary" sometimes.

752 CR's of 319. A. T. P. Byles, ed., The Book of Fayttes of Armes and of Chyualrye. In:
(a) MAe, II (1933), 217-18 (P. G. C. Campbell). Makes suggestions as to where Byles's Introduction could use modification, amplification, or correction.
(b) MAe, III (1934), 214-17 (G. D. B.) Calls attention to Byles's errors and omissions but commends editor for revealing the strengths and weaknesses of Caxton's style.

753 CR of 61. P. G. C. Campbell, L'Epître d'Othéa: étude sur les sources de CdP. In Romania, LII (1926), 239 (M. Roques). Considers this well-executed and successful study.

754 CR's of 265. D. Carstens-Grokenberger, ed., Buch von den drei Tugenden in portugiesicher Übersetzung. In:
(a) RR, LV (1964), 119-20 (D. W. McPheeters). Thinks Carstens-Grokenberger's printed text is "meticulously" edited.
(b) RPh, XVIII (1964-1965), 133-34 (B. Maler). Finds that the editor's numerous errors (some listed on p. 34) make this text virtually useless.

755 CR of 444. G. M. Cropp, "Boèce et CdP." In SF, 81 (1983), 539-40 (G. Mombello). Calls this an important contribution.

756 CR's of 433. F. Du Castel, Damoiselle CdP, veuve de Me Etienne de Castel 1364-1431. In:
(a) MAe, XLIII (1974), 202-04 (K. Chesney). Finds this study superior to author's previous work, 403.

146 Christine de Pizan

(b) Speculum, L (1975), 488-89 (J. V. Fleming). Though lack-
ing in formal scholarship, this book considered best general
work on CH to date.

757 CR of 247. L. Dulac, "Une mythe didactique chez CdP: Sémiramis ou la veuve héroïque (Du De mulieribus claris de Boccace à la Cité des dames.)" In SF, 65-66 (1978), 458 (G. Mombello).
General discussion of Dulac's findings.

758 CR of 366. _____, "Un écrit militant de CdP, Le Ditié de
Jehanne d'Arc." In SF, 76 (1982), 122 (G. Mombello).
Feels author has made intelligent observations on the Ditié.

759 CR of 135. E. Hicks and E. Ornato, "Jean de Montreuil et le
débat sur le Roman de la Rose." In SF, 68 (1979), 337-38 (G.
Mombello).
Calls this an interesting contribution.

760 CR of 141. E. Hicks, "La tradition manuscrite des épîtres sur
la Rose." In SF, 79 (1983), 124 (G. Mombello).
Hicks praised for his accuracy, precision, presentation.

761 CR's of 111. _____, ed., Le Débat sur le 'Roman de la Rose.'
In:
(a) MAe, XLVII (1978), 363-64 (J.-C. Payen). Rave review.
Is impressed with Hicks's clarity, precision, exhaustiveness.
(b) Speculum, LIV (1979), 146-48 (C. C. Willard). Commends
editor for excellent arrangement of documents; for showing
development of Quarrel; for scrupulously establishing the
chronology; and for editing texts with great care.
(c) Romania, C (1979), 126-32 (G. Hasenohr). Main interest
of this work lies in method in which texts have been presented, says reviewer.
(d) FR, LIII (1980), 736-38 (L. S. Crist). Suggests that
Hicks's edition is essential to any understanding of the
French history of ideas.
(e) RPh, XXXIV (1980-1981), 562-66 (P. H. Stäblein). Hicks's
texts considered superior to those of Beck 108, and Ward
109.

762 CR of 82. M. A. Ignatius, "CdP's Epistre Othea: An Experi-
ment in Literary Form." In SF, 74 (1981), 333 (G. Mombello).
Thinks this is an interesting study.

763 CR of 357. A. J. Kennedy and K. Varty, eds., "CdP's Ditié
de Jehanne d'Arc." In Romania, XCVII (1976), 142-43 (F. Lecoy).
Feels the inclusion of photographic plate of MS Berne 205
is of great value.

764 CR's of 358. _____, eds., <u>Ditié de Jehanne d'Arc</u>: CdP.
     In:
     (a) <u>Speculum</u>, LIV (1979), 559-60 (N. B. Smith). Describes
          edition as "paragon of convenience and scholarship" (p.
          559).
     (b) <u>MAe</u>, XLVIII (1979), 297-98 (J. Fox). Sees more than a
          little irony in fact that final work of a feminist and anti-
          English writer should "find its best edition at the hands
          of two British male editors" (p. 298).
     (c) <u>MLR</u>, LXXV (1980), 397 (A. H. Diverres). Thinks this
          is carefully and conservatively edited text.

765 CR's of 345. A. J. Kennedy, ed., <u>Epistre de la prison de vie</u>
     <u>humaine</u>. In:
     (a) <u>SF</u>, 88 (1986), 113 (G. Mombello). Calls this an excellent
          edition.
     (b) <u>MA</u>, XCIII (1987), 127-29 (S. Bagoly). Has highest praise
          for Kennedy's scholarship. Comments on his careful tran-
          scription, clear and logical punctuation, and precise descrip-
          tion of the MSS.
     (c) <u>MAe</u>, LVI (1987), 145-46 (K. Varty). Considers edition a
          "model of scholarly precision."

766 CR of 267. M. Laigle, '<u>Le Livre des trois vertus</u>' de CdP et
     <u>son milieu historique et littéraire</u>. In <u>BEC</u>, LXXIV (1913), 143-
     44 (E. Langlois).
          Found many errors but considers this nevertheless an ele-
     gently written book.

767 CR of 266. S. Lawson, trans., <u>The Treasure of the City of</u>
     <u>Ladies; or, The Book of Three Virtues</u>. In <u>Choice</u> (October
     1985), 85 (M. R. Bonfini).
          Finds text eminently readable despite its "fidelity to the
     pietistic tone of the author."

768 CR of 240. R. Lievens, "Kerstine van Pizen." In <u>SF</u>, 24
     (1964), 524 (S. Cigada).
          Presents useful French summary of Lievens' Dutch article.

769 CR's of 296. R. H. Lucas, ed., '<u>Le Livre du corps de policie</u>'
     of CdP: <u>A Critical Edition</u>. In:
     (a) <u>BEC</u>, CXXVI (1968), 248-50 (C. F. Ward). Because of
          misprints and awkward transcription, reviewer advises
          philologists to approach this edition with caution.
     (b) <u>MA</u>, LXXVI (1970), 156-61 (S. Solente). Suggests edition
          could be more complete noting lack of index for proper
          names and inadequate bibliography.
     (c) <u>RPh</u>, XXIX (1975-1976), 110-14 (P. Ménard). Considers
          edition unsatifactory citing poor establishment of text, mis-
          readings, and faulty punctuation. Errors listed p. 43.

770   CR of 365. T. B. Lynn, "The <u>Ditié de Jeanne d'Arc</u>: Its Po-
      litical, Feminist, and Aesthetic Significance." In <u>SF</u>, 77 (1982),
      322 (G. Mombello).
         Notes that Lynn's reading of <u>Ditié</u> differs from that of Ken-
      nedy and Varty, 357.

771   CR's of 436. E. McLeod, <u>The Order of the Rose: The Life
      and Ideas of CdP</u>. In:
      (a) <u>FR</u>, L (1976-1977), 760-61 (G. Mermier). Describes <u>Order</u>
           as a "rich, learned, and thoroughly researched book" but
           finds bibliography weak.
      (b) <u>SF</u>, 64 (1978), 139-40 (G. Mombello). Is critical of McLeod's
           handling of the <u>Ditié</u> and of her failure to acknowledge
           Campbell's contribution to chapter on CH and England.
      (c) <u>Speculum</u>, LIII (1978), 167-70 (C. C. Willard) Raises ques-
           tions about responsibilities of a popular biographer and
           cautions scholars against relying on older sources.
      (d) <u>Signs</u>, III, 3 (Spring 1978), 700-01 (S. Delany). Attacks
           McLeod for writing in "frustratingly bland tone" and for
           not revealing what was socially significant about CH. This
           review provoked sharp response from feminist critics (see
           below) who objected to Delany's calling CH a "literary hack"
           and applying other pejorative epithets to her (on p. 701).
      (e) <u>Signs</u>, IV, 3 (Spring 1979), 592-93 (S. G. Bell). Agrees
           with Delany's allegation that McLeod does not show reader
           what was interesting about CH but totally rejects her
           characterization of the latter as a "pompous reactionary
           sycophant."
      (f) <u>Signs</u>, IV, 3 (Spring 1979), 593-96 (A. Diamond). Objects
           to Delany's "contemptuous dismissal" of McLeod and defends
           CH against charge of toadying and being a reactionary.
      (g) <u>Signs</u>, IV, 3 (Spring 1979), 596 (S. Delany). Answers
           critics who have accused Delany of arrogantly writing off
           both McLeod and CH.

772   CR's of 75. G. Mombello, <u>La tradizione manoscritta dell' 'Epis-
      tre Othea' di CdP</u>. In:
      (a) <u>MA</u>, LXXVI (1970), 594-99 (S. Solente). Calls this a
           "brilliante thèse" (p. 599) and comments on Mombello's
           careful execution of the work.
      (b) <u>SF</u>, 40 (1970), 131-32 (G. Bernadelli). General review of
           Mombello's exhaustive work.
      (c) <u>RPh</u>, XXV (1971-1972), 467-69 (C. C. Willard). Acknowl-
           edges Mombello's contribution but wonders why he casts
           "so little light" on the still many unresolved problems of
           his chosen period (p. 469).

773   CR of 553. _____, "Quelques aspects de la pensée politique
      de CdP d'après ses oeuvres publiées." In <u>SF</u>, 56 (1975), 331
      (A. Stramignoni).
         Feels this study sheds light on CH's political thought.

774   CR's of 447.   R. Pernoud, CdP.   In:
   (a)   BTAM, XIII (January-December 1982), 892 (G.M.)   Con-
         siders Pernoud's study "une monographie originale...."
   (b)   FR, LVII (1984), 549-50 (M. J. Ward).   Is impressed with
         scope of Pernoud's historical research but finds no new
         revelations about CH.

775   CR's of 398.   M.-J. Pinet, CdP...étude biographique et littéraire.
      In;
   (a)   RBPH, VIII (1929), 350-39 (S. Solente).   Updates Pinet's
         manuscript listing and corrects errors but still considers
         this a valuable work.
   (b)   MLR, XXIV (1929), 489-92 (F. C. Johnson).   Thinks the
         author has succeeded in presenting life-like picture of CH.
   (c)   ZFSL, LIV (1930-1931), 129-64 (Ph. A. Becker).   Romanist
         Becker has expanded this review article into complete sur-
         vey of CH and her works.   Includes chronology, criticism,
         documentation.   Reprinted in Becker 422.

776   CR's of 313.   R. R. Rains, ed., 'Les sept psaumes allegorisés'
      of CdP.   In:
   (a)   MLR, LXII (1967), 331-32 (K. Varty).   Finds chapters pre-
         ceding Psalsm informative and well-written.
   (b)   RPh, XXI (1967-1968), 129-33 (C. C. Willard).   Thinks
         Rains's text gives evidence of insufficient revision between
         original presentation as Illinois master's thesis and subse-
         quent publication.
   (c)   SF, 34 (1968), 68-73 (B. Richter).   Calls this "a sober
         piece of scholarship" (p. 72) and presents lengthy analysis
         of CH's text.

777   CR of 638.   C. Reno, "CdP: Feminism and Irony."   In SF, 79
      (1983), 125 (G. Mombello).
      Briefly comments on author's presentation of ironic passages
      in CH's work.

778   CR's of 234.   E. J. Richards, trans., The Book of the City of
      Ladies.   In:
   (a)   NYTBR (25 July 1982), 6, 18 (M. Quilligan).   Provocative
         review article on the originality of the BCL.   Thinks Rich-
         ards' translation lets CH come through as the very model
         of a modern woman.   See also Quilligan on CH's feminism,
         641.
   (b)   Washington Post, "Book World" (8 August 1982) (G. Pool).
         Considers this an "excellent, readable translation."   Also
         has highest praise for Richards' Introduction.
   (c)   Women's Studies, X(1984), 339-42 (S. Delany).   Argues
         against Richards' presentation (in Introduction) of CH as
         a revolutionary thinker.   The translation itself only briefly
         dealt with in last paragraph of review; calls it "somewhat
         insensitive" and "occasionally anachronistic" (pp. 341-42).

(d) RPh, XXXIX (1985-1986), 125-28 (P. F. Dembowski).
     Thinks this is a "highly readable" translation and suggests
     that all future students of the BCL will have to reckon
     with it.

779 CR of 592. L. McDowell Richardson, The Forerunners of Fem-
     inism in French Literature of the Renaissance. Part I: From
     CdP to Marie de Gournay. In MLN, XLVI (1931), 556-59 (M.
     de Schweinitz).
          Feels Richardson's discussion of CH should have taken into
     account the earlier studies of Piaget 113, and Rigaud 585.

780 CR's of 201. S. Solente, ed., Le Livre des fais et bonnes meurs
     du sage roy Charles V. In:
     (a) BEC, XCVII (1936), 406-07 (H. Moranvillé). Considers
          this text superior to earlier editions.
     (b) RH, CLXXXIV (1938), 397-98 (E. Perroy). Finds Introduc-
          tion first-rate, the treatment of CH's textual sources
          thorough, and analysis of the text enlightening. Only
          first two parts of edition reviewed here.

781 CR of 73. R. Tuve, Allegorical Imagery: Some Mediaeval Books
     and their Posterity. In RPh, XXII (1968-1969), 216-22 (C. C.
     Willard).
          Considers Tuve's section on the Epistre d'Othea instructive
     and her explanation of epistle's popularity illuminating.

782 CR's of 715. K. Varty, ed., CdP's Ballades, Rondeaux, and
     Virelais: An Anthology. In:
     (a) MAe, XXXV (1966), 279-82 (K. Chesney). Finds list of
          works on p. ix "something of a jumble" (p. 280) and thinks
          editor should have told readers that as mature writer CH
          usually turned from verse to prose.
     (b) FR, XL (1966-1967), 424-25 (A. L. Cohen). An "intelli-
          gently selected collection" of some of CH's best poetry
          (p. 425).
     (c) MLR, LXII (1967), 722-23 (J. Fox). A "comparison of the
          text of the forty-four ballades reproduced from the Cent
          Ballades with the MS shows ... departures from the original
          not included in the rejected readings or notes" (p. 723).
     (d) RR, LIX (1968), 214-15 (H. Watson). Considers this an
          exemplary anthology, valuable textbook, and good reference
          tool.
     (e) RPh, XXIV (1970-1971), 664-66 (C. C. Willard). Is criti-
          cal of editor for rejecting certain readings in Harley, for
          correcting scribal errors, and for changing order of CH's
          poems.

783 CR of 519. N. Wilkins, "The Structure of Ballades, Rondeaux
     and Virelais in Froissart and in CdP." In SF, 40 (1970), 131
     (N. Mann).
          Comments on Wilkins' theory of musicology.

784 CR's of 337. C. C. Willard, ed., The 'Livre de la Paix' of
CdP: A Critical Edition with Introduction and Notes. In:
(a) Speculum, XXXIV (1959), 147-49. (U. T. Holmes, Jr.).
Expresses concern that readers will not be able to tell
whether "strange spellings, lack of agreement, etc., are
misprints, misreadings on the part of the editor, or care-
lessness due to the copyist or Christine herself" (p. 148).
List of suggested corrections on p. 148.
(b) RPh, XIII (1959-1960), 101-02 (K. G. Bottke). Considers
this an admirable edition with pertinent notes and carefully
proofread text.
(c) MAe, XXIX (1960), 44-46 (K. Chesney). Thinks Introduction is an adequate preparation for text but feels it would
have been better to keep readings from Brussels, BR
10366 correcting from BN f.fr. 1182 "without purporting
to give us variants which are manifestly unreliable" (p.
46).
(d) MLR, LV (1960), 443 (H. P. Clive). Calls this a satisfac-
tory edition.

785 CR of 275. _____, "A Fifteenth Century View of Women's
Role in Medieval Society: CdP's Livre des trois vertus." In
Speculum, LII (1977), 717 (H. A. Kelly).
Sums up essay as a "good, straightforward account of the
life and teachings..." of CdP.

786 CR of 539. _____, "Lovers' Dialogues in CdP's Lyric Poetry
from the Cent ballades to the Cent ballades d'amant et de dame."
In SF, 78 (1982), 530 (G. Mombello).
Feels article sheds light on CH's ideas on courtly love.

787 CR of 37. _____, "A New Look at CdP's Epistre au dieu
d'Amours." In SF, 79 (1983), 124 (G. Mombello).
Considers this an interesting study on the source, content,
and posterity of the Epistre.

788 CR's of 450. _____, CdP: Her Life and Works. In:
(a) NYTBR (24 February 1985), 15 (J. M. Ferrante). Thinks
medievalists might object to book's lack of reference to all
earlier female writers and scholars.
(b) Choice, XXII (May 1985), 1340 (M. R. Bonfini). Sees this
as distinctive literary biography and as important addition
to the work on CdP.
(c) FR, LIX (1986), 607-08 (M. J. Ward). Finds book "highly
informative and pleasant to read" (p. 607) and praises
author for "striking a rare and judicious balance between
erudition and popularization..." (p. 608).
(d) FS, XL (1986), 315-16 (A. J. Kennedy). Calls this timely
and important work, placing it alongside Pinet's 1927 classic,
398.
(e) Speculum, LXII (1987), 222-25 (S. L. Hindman). Suggests

Willard's study does not give readers the kind of analysis that would let them make a reassessment of CH. Also, finds level of analysis "superficial and ... conclusions uninteresting, misleading, or incorrect" (p. 223).

789 CR of 364. A. J. Wisman, "L'éveil du sentiment national au Moyen Âge: la pensée politique de CdP." In SF, 67 (1979), 139 (G. Mombello).

Considers this useful article but sees nothing new in it.

790 CR of 485. _____, "Manuscrits et éditions des oeuvres de CdP." In SF, 68 (1979), 339 (G. Mombello).

Calls the author's work a useful bibliographical and codicological study.

791 CR's of 729. _____, ed. and trans., 'The Epistle of the Prison of Human Life' with 'An Epistle to the Queen of France' and 'Lament on the Evils of the Civil War'. In:

(a) Choice, XXII (July-August 1985), 204 (C. Reno). Thinks Wisman's translation of Vie humaine is faithful to CH's prose and her punctuation easier to follow than that of A. J. Kennedy in 345.

(b) Speculum, LXII (1987), 121-23 (C. Reno). Finds complexity of CH's thought and syntax well rendered; her "labyrinthine" prose made accessible to modern readers; and the punctuation of French text most often impeccable. However, some errors in transcription and inaccuracies in spelling are noted.

CHRISTINE DE PIZAN'S CONTEMPORARIES:
A SELECTED LIST

792 BERNARD VII, count of Armagnac (d. 1419)
Armagnac leader who took over Orleanist party and gave it
his name after Louis of Orleans's (815) assassination--in 1407
by an agent of John the Fearless of Burgundy (814). Bernard
later married his daughter Bonne to the victim's son, Charles
of Orleans (800). Louis' murder subsequently led to civil war
between the Burgundians and Armagnacs, the two rival factions
that dominated French politics during first two decades of fifteenth century. The Burgundians had the support of part of
nobility and lower classes, notably the Cabochians (796). They
were particularly strong in Paris. The Armagnacs became the
national party after the French civil war and Hundred Years'
War merged in 1415. They tried to turn back the invading army
of Henry V of England (809) but suffered a reversal in Battle
of Agincourt (1415). The count of Armagnac and his sympa-
thizers were massacred by the Burgundians a year after the
latter seized control of Paris in 1418. Allusions to these events
are made in CH's Lamentacion sur les maux de la France, 334,
and Livre de la paix, 336. (J. D'Avout, La Querelle des Armagnacs et des Bourguignons, Paris, 1945; M. Nordberg, Les
Ducs et la royauté: étude sur la rivalité des ducs d'Orléans
et de Bourgogne, 1392-1407, Stockholm, 1964).

793 BOCCACCIO, Giovanni (1313-1375)
Italian poet and prose writer. Born in Paris, France; died
in Certaldo, Tuscany. Was one of the founders of Italian Renaissance. Most famous work is the Decameron (1349-1353), a
collection of one hundred earthy tales portraying Italian society.
Also wrote biographies of Livy and Petrarch, whom he met in
1351. Produced the prose work Filocolo (c. 1340); the psychological romance La Fiammetta (c. 1344); and in his final period
the Latin work De claris mulieribus ("On Famous Women") from
which CH borrowed in her Livre de la cité des dames, 227. (N.
Avril and F. Callu, Boccace en France, Paris, 1975; V. Branca,
Boccaccio: The Man and His Work, trans. R. Monges, New York,

1978; J. Powers Serafini-Sanli, Giovanni Boccaccio, Boston,
1982). See also 246.

794 BOUCICAUT, Marshal of France (c. 1366-1421)
     French crusader (fought at Constantinople) whose real name
was Jean II le Maingre. Founded a chivalric order, L'Ordre de
l'Escu vert à la Dame Blanche, and rallied to CH's defense in
Rose debate. She in turn composed the Autres ballades XII in
the Order's honor. Le Livre des fais du bon messire Jehan le
Maingre, dit Bouciquaut was once thought to have been written
by her (see Picherit 448) but Bouciquaut's editor, Denis Lalande,
does not attribute it to CH, in 446, 452. (Histoire de Maréchal
de Boucicaut, ed. T. Godefroy, Paris, 1620--this was first publication of Boucicaut from MS BN f.fr. 11432 of which there is
only one copy; J. Delaville Le Roux, La France en Orient au
XIV siècle: expéditions du Maréchal Boucicaut, vol. I Paris,
1886; Livre des fais du bon messire Jehan le Maingre, dit Bouciquaut, ed. D. Lalande, Paris, 1985--452).

795 BOUVET (Bonet), Honoré (c. 1345-c. 1405)
     French poet and prose writer born in Provence. His treatise
L'Arbre des batailles, based on John of Legnano's De Bello,
became the principal source for last two books of CH's Livre des
fais d'armes et de chevalerie, 315. Written probably around
1387, Arbre deals with warfare and topics of contemporary interest. It was widely read during later Middle Ages. (The
Tree of Battles of Honoré Bonet, ed. and trans. G. W. Coopland, Liverpool, U.K./Cambridge, MA, 1949--324; N. A. R.
Wright, "The Tree of Battles of Honoré Bouvet and the Laws of
War," in War, Literature, and Politics in the Late Middle Ages,
ed. C. T. Allmand, New York, 1976, pp. 12-31). See also
Nys 322, 546.

796 CABOCHE, Simon (Simon Lecoustellier) fl. early 15th century
     Parisian skinner and head of butchers' guild who led the
Cabochian Revolt. The Cabochians were composed of small
tradespeople whose demand for radical administrative reform had
been ignored by the government. Their riots--on 22 April and
on 22 May 1413--finally led to passage of the Ordonnance Cabo-
chienne. It provided for a Chambre des Comptes and for the
election of a French council, the Parlement. The Cabochians'
excesses turned the Parisian bourgeoisie against them however,
bringing about the downfall of John the Fearless (814) whose
cause they espoused. Eventually Louis of Guyenne had to ask
the Armagnacs (792) to step in and suppress the rioters. The
Ordinance was subsequently withdrawn and by the end of August
both the Cabochians and Burgundians were driven from Paris
(until 1418). CH mentions these events in Book III of her Livre

de la paix (1412-1413), 336. (A. Coville, Les Cabochiens et
l'ordonnance de 1413, Paris, 1888; rpt. Geneva, 1974--this is
still the standard work on the Cabochian Revolt).

797 CAXTON, William (1422?-1491)
      Pioneering printer, first to print in English language. Was
also a translator, publisher, advertiser, bookseller, and textile
merchant. Probably learned technique of printing in Cologne
around 1471 or 1472. In 1476 set up a printing press near
Westminster Abbey and thereafter brought out close to a hundred titles including the works of Boethius, Chaucer, and Malory.
His Recuyell of the Historyes of Troy (1474 or 1475) was first
book ever printed in English and the Dictes or Sayengs of the
Philosophers the first English book with a definite date, 18
November 1477. Also printed Anthony Woodville's translation
of CH's proverbs, The Morale Proverbes of Christyne (1478),
97, and later translated and printed her manual on warfare,
The Boke of the Fayt of Armes and of Chyualerie (1489 or 1490),
318. (N. F. Blake, Caxton and his World, London, 1969; G. D.
Painter, William Caxton: A Biography, New York, 1977--106).

798 CHARLES V (The Wise), king of France (1338-1380)
      Valois king who ruled from 1364 until his death. Assumed
regency when his father, John II, was taken prisoner by the
English in Battle of Poitiers (1356). As regent had to deal with
a popular peasant revolt, the Jacquerie, and the reformist movement of Etienne Marcel. Successfully reversed the disastrous
Anglo-French settlement of 1360 and brought about the country's
recovery from first phase of Hundred Years' War (1337-1453).
A bibliophile and man of learning Charles promoted the arts
and sciences, especially astrology, and encouraged manuscript
production. His enormous book collection, which numbered over
900 volumes at a 1373 inventory, formed the nucleus of the Bibliothèque du Roy later the Bibliothèque Nationale, Paris. Thomas
de Pizan became his court astrologer and CH his official biographer when she was commissioned to write the Livre des fais
et bonnes meurs du sage roy Charles V (1404), 192. (L. Delisle,
Recherches sur la librairie de Charles V, 2 vols., Paris, 1907,
rpt. Amsterdam, 1967--204; R. Delachenal, Histoire de Charles
V, 5 vols., Paris, 1909-1931--205; J. Calmette, Charles V,
Paris, 1945--209; Paris, Bibliothèque Nationale, La Librairie de
Charles V, Paris, 1968; C. R. Sherman, The Portraits of Charles
V of France, New York, 1969--211; J. Quillet, Charles V: le
roi lettré, Paris, 1984--223.

799 CHARLES VI (The Mad), king of France (1368-1422)
      Ruled France from 1380 to 1422 but a debilitating mental ill-
ness forced him to remain a figurehead for much of his reign.

Married Isabelle of Bavaria (queen Isabeau, 811) on 17 July
1385. In 1388 decided to rule without Council of Twelve. After
dismissing his uncles, recalled his father's old officials the Mar-
mousets. During his attacks of insanity, the rivaling dukes of
Orleans (815) and Burgundy (814) each sought control over the
regency. Charles's sovereignty was further threatened by the
invasion of Henry V of England (809), who defeated his army
at Agincourt in 1415. The Treaty of Troyes (1420), an agreement made under Burgundian influence between Charles and
Henry V, recognized Henry as heir of France. (Le Religieux
de Saint-Denis. Chronique du religieux de Saint-Denys, con-
tenant le règne de Charles VI, de 1380 à 1422, ed. F. L. Bellag-
net, 6 vols., Paris, 1839-1852; J. Juvenal des Ursins, Histoire
de Charles VI, ed. J. A. C. Buchon, Paris, 1875--see 207; M.
Heim, Charles VI le Fol, Paris, 1955; A. Denieul-Cormier, Wise
and Foolish Kings: The First House of Valois, 1328-1498, Garden City, NY, 1980; R. C. Famiglietti, Royal Intrigue: Crisis
at the Court of Charles VI, 1392-1420, New York, 1986).

800   CHARLES OF ORLEANS (1394-1465)
      Poet-prince, son of Louis of Orleans (815) and Valentina
Visconti (825), father of king Louis XII. As an Armagnac
leader he sought to avenge his father's 1407 murder--by an
agent of John the Fearless (814). Was captured at Agincourt
(1415) and spent twenty-five years in English prison writing
verse. Upon his return to France he established a court of
poetry at Blois and devoted himself to perfecting his art. Left
a total of 123 ballades, 400 rondeaux and some 89 chansons. Is
today regarded as one of the major courtly poets of his time.
Charles acquired several of CH's manuscripts from his mother's
library. His love poems are thought to have been influenced
by her. (Charles d'Orléans: poésies, ed. P. Champion, 2
vols., 1923-1927, rpt. Paris, 1956; The English Poems of Charles
of Orleans, ed. R. Steele and M. Day, Oxford, 1941-1946; D.
Poirion, Le poète et le prince: l'évolution du lyrisme courtois
de Guillaume de Machaut à Charles d'Orléans, Paris, 1969--518;
D. A. Fein, Charles d'Orléans, Boston, 1983; E. Yenal, Charles
d'Orléans: A Bibliography of Primary and Secondary Sources,
New York, 1984; The French Chansons of Charles d'Orléans,
ed. and trans. S. Spence, New York, 1986--699.

801   CHARTIER, Alain (1385?-1433?)
      One of leading French poets of the period. Diplomat under
Charles VII. The style of his prose writings marks a resurgence
of classicism in French literature. First important poetic work
was a collection of lyrics about four ladies lamenting their lovers'
fate at Agincourt, the Livre des quatre dames (1414 or 1416).
His best-known prose work, Quadrilogue Invectif (1422), is an
anti-English pamphlet describing the confused conditions in

France after Agincourt. His celebrated poem on unrequited love, La Belle Dame sans merci (1424), inspired John Keats. His other works include the Traité de l'ésperance, the Curial, Bréviaire des nobles, and Lay de Plaisance. Chartier's love poems were influenced by CH's ideas on courtly love. (C. J. H. Walravens, Alain Chartier: études biographiques suivies de pieces justificatives, d'une description des éditions et d'une édition des ouvrages inédites, Amsterdam, 1971--688; The Poetical Works of Alain Chartier, ed. J. C. Laidlaw, Cambridge, U.K., 1974--690; François Rouy, L'Esthétique du traité moral d'après les oeuvres d'Alain Chartier, Geneva, 1980--217).

802 CHASTELLAIN, Georges (1405?-1474)
     Burgundian poet and chronicler. His Chronique des ducs de Bourgogne (1419-1474, with gaps) gives history of Burgundy and France. CH's grandson, Jean de Castel, exchanged ballades with him. (Oeuvres, ed. H. K. de Lettenhove, 7 vols., Brussels, 1863-1865; K. Urwin, ... Georges Chastellain: la vie, les oeuvres, Paris, 1937).

803 COL, Gontier (1354?-1418); Pierre (fl. early 15th century)
     Early French humanists today best remembered for their correspondence with CH in the debate over the Roman de la Rose (c. 1236-1276). Both held appointments at the royal Chancellery: Gontier as secretary to Charles VI and ambassador to the Pope in Avignon; his brother Pierre as a royal secretary. The latter was also Canon of Notre Dame. (A. Coville, Gontier et Pierre Col et l'humanisme en France au temps de Charles VI, Paris, 1934--117).

804 DESCHAMPS, Eustache (Eustache Morel) c. 1346-c. 1406
     Leading fourteenth-century French poet and diplomat, disciple of Guillaume de Machaut (816). Held administrative posts under Charles V (798) and Charles VI (799). He composed caustic ballades and rondeaux; drafted the first ars poetica ever written in French, L'Art de dictier (1392); and left a long, unfinished satire on women, Le Miroir de mariage. Also produced dramatic works such as the Farce de Maître Trubert et d'Antroignart. CH corresponded with Deschamps, addressing him as "dear brother and friend." He in turn called her "handmaid of learning" and "eloquent muse," signing as her "disciple and well-wisher." See her letter to him, 191. (Oeuvres complètes, ed. Marquis de Queux de Saint-Hilaire and G. Raynaud, 11 vols., Paris, 1878-1901; J. G. Bruins, Observation sur la langue d'Eustache Deschamps et de Christine de Pisan, Dordrecht, 1925--500).

805 DU GUESCLIN, Bertrand (1320?-1380)
     Popular French hero and legendary warrior known for his
martial skills and loyalty to French crown. Constable of France
from 1370 to 1380. Was in service with Charles V (798), dying
while on a military expedition in Languedoc. CH pays homage
to him in her Livre des fais et bonnes meurs du sage roy Charles
V (192), Pt. 2, chaps. XIX, XX, XXIII-XXV and Pt. 3, chap.
LXX. (J. Cuvelier, Chronique de Bertrand du Guesclin, ed.
E. Charrière, 2 vols., Paris, 1839; S. Luce, Histoire de Bertrand du Guesclin et son époque, Paris, 1876).

806 FROISSART, Jean (1337?-1400?)
     Poet, scholar, court historian. Born in Flanders, he traveled
widely throughout Europe holding appointments at various royal
courts and in the Church. His journeys to England, Scotland,
Belgium, France, and Italy provided him with the material for
his historical writings. Spent twelve years compiling his famous
Chroniques (ed. G. Raynaud, Paris, 1894). In it he records
events of the Hundred Years' War from 1325 to 1400, giving detailed account of 14th-century feudal society. (Oeuvres, ed.
H. K. de Lettenhove, 25 vols., Brussels, 1870-1875; F. S.
Shears, Froissart, London, 1930; J. N. Palmer, Froissart, historian, Totowa, NJ, 1981).

807 GERSON, Jean (1363-1429)
     Prominent French theologian. Important writer, scholar,
mystic, and court preacher to Charles VI (799). Chancellor
of the University of Paris. Was renowned for his outstanding
sermons in both French and Latin. He strove to end schism
in the Church becoming delegate to the Councils of Pisa and
Constance (1415-1418). His writings deal with theology, morals,
philosophy, and education. Was an outspoken critic of the Roman de la Rose (c. 1236-1276), denouncing it as a threat to
public morality. Gerson backed CH during Quarrel and bestowed
upon her the epithet, femina ista virilis. His own contribution
to the Rose debate was the Traité contre le Roman de la Rose--
see 110. (J. L. Connolly, Jean Gerson: Reformer and Mystic,
Louvain, 1894; L. Mourin, Jean Gerson prédicateur français,
Bruges, 1952--121; J. B. Morrall, Gerson and the Great Schism,
Manchester, U.K., 1960). See also Hicks 111.

808 GUTENBERG, Johann (c. 1397-1468)
     CdP was a contemporary of the German printer Johann Guten-
berg who invented moveable, metal type in 1436 or 1437. (V.
Scholderer, Johann Gutenberg: the Inventor of Printing, London, 1963).

809   HENRY V, king of England (1387-1422)
      Ruled from 1413 to 1422, holding the title of Duke of Lan-
caster and Prince of Wales.   He made England one of strongest
kingdoms in medieval Europe.   Two years after his victory in
Battle of Agincourt (1415) he conquered Normandy, then Rouen
(1417-1418).   In 1420 concluded the Treaty of Troyes with
Charles VI (799) and queen Isabeau of France (811).   Under
its terms he received regency of France along with promises of
succession to French throne; also, in marriage, Charles's eldest
daughter.   (S. H. Wylie, The Reign of Henry the Fifth, 3 vols.,
Cambridge, U.K., 1919; E. F. Jacob, Henry V and the Invasion
of France, New York, 1950; H. F. Hutchison, King Henry V:
A Biography, New York, 1967).

810   HOCCLEVE (Occleve), Thomas (1368?-1450?)
      English poet, imitator of Chaucer.   Composed ballads and
versified moral tales.   His longest work is a didactic poem on
the virtues and vices of a ruler, The Regiment of Princes; his
earliest, "The Letter of Cupid" (1402), is a paraphrase of CH's
Epistre au dieu d'Amours (1399), 16.   (J. Mitchell, Thomas
Hoccleve: A Study in Early 15th Century Poetic, Urbana,
1968--28).   See also 18-23, 27, 30, 31, 35, 36, and 38.

811   ISABELLE OF BAVARIA (queen Isabeau) 1370-1435
      Daughter of the German House of Wittelsbach, French queen
and consort of Charles VI (799) who was married to the king on
17 July 1385 at age fourteen.   After the king went insane she
was appointed regent (in 1408) but had no real authority.   Fri-
volous and pleasure-loving, she is said to have had liaison with
brother-in-law Louis of Orleans (815).   Helped bring about the
disgraceful Treaty of Troyes (1420) which disinherited her own
son, the future Charles VII.   CH sought her patronage, addressing the Epistre à la reine (280) and other works to her.
At queen's request she presented Isabeau with a beautifully illuminated manuscript of her collected works, the famed Harley
4431.   (M. Thibault, Isabeau de Bavière: la jeunesse, 1370-
1405, Paris, 1903; H. Kimm, Isabeau de Bavière, reine de France
1370-1435, Beitrag zur Geschichte einer bayerischen Herzogs-
tochter und des französischen Königshauses, Munich, 1969;
J. Verdon, Isabeau de Bavière, Paris, 1981--283).

812   JEAN OF FRANCE, duke of Berry (1340-1416)
      Third son of king John II of France, brother of king Charles
V (798).   Powerful and wealthy prince who controlled one-third
of French territories during middle phase of the Hundred Years'
War (1338-1453).   Sat on dauphin's Council of Twelve and acted
as peacemaker between Burgundians and Armagnacs at Auxerre
(1412) and Pointoise (1413).   Leading patron of the arts, he

spent vast sums acquiring illuminated manuscripts and collecting
rare treasures. His artistically illustrated Très Riches Heures
du duc de Berry is preserved at the Musée Condé in Chantilly.
The duke and his daughter, Marie of Berry, were important patrons of CH's. (F. Lehoux, Jean de France, duc de Berri: sa
vie, son action politique, 1340-1416, 4 vols., Paris, 1966-1968;
M. Meiss, French Painting in the Time of Jean de Berry, 2 vols.,
New York, 1967--474).

813 JOAN OF ARC (c. 1412-1431)
French saint and national heroine who led resistance against
the English and Burgundians in second period of the Hundred
Years' War. Is said to have heard "voices" telling her to help
dauphin regain French throne. Lifted siege of Orleans on 8
May 1429, then routed the English at Patay. This paved way
for dauphin's coronation as Charles VII at Reims Cathedral to
which Joan personally escorted him on 17 July 1429. Was subsequently captured (in 1430) by the Burgundians at Compiègne
and turned over to their English allies. Tried by French ec-
clesiastical court for witchcraft, Joan was condemned as a heretic and burned at the stake in Rouen on 30 May 1431. She was
officially rehabilitated at new trial in 1456 and canonized in
1920. CH's poem, Le Ditié de Jehanne d'Arc (1429), 349, was
first long literary work written in her honor. (J. Quicherat,
Procès de condamnation et de réhabilitation de Jeanne d'Arc, 5
vols., Paris, 1841-1849--352; M. Warner, Joan of Arc, New York,
1981--370; A. Barstow, Joan of Arc: Heretic, Mystic, Shaman,
1984).

814 JOHN THE FEARLESS (Jean sans Peur), duke of Burgundy
        (1371-1419)
Son of Philip the Bold (823) and one of four Burgundian
dukes from House of Valois who controlled large parts of the
Netherlands and Burgundy between 1384 and 1477. Inheriting
the title from his father in 1404, he played significant role in
maintaining Burgundian power in Europe. His strong political
and military machinery enabled him to exert considerable influence on France's internal affairs. But his bid for control of
French regency led to bitter rivalry with king's younger brother,
Louis of Orleans (815), whom he had assassinated in 1407. John
was himself killed during dispute with the Armagnacs (792) in
1419. He was one of CH's benefactors. (E. Petit, Itinéraires
de Philippe le Hardi et de Jean sans Peur, Paris, 1888; O. Cartellieri, The Court of Burgundy, 1929, rpt. New York, 1970--
399; R. Vaughn John the Fearless, New York, 1966--421; M.
Nordberg, Les Ducs et la royauté: études sur la rivalité des
ducs d'Orléans et de Bourgogne, 1392-1407, Stockholm, 1964).

815 LOUIS I OF FRANCE, duke of Orleans (1372-1407)
       Son of Charles V (798); younger brother of Charles VI (799);
father of poet-prince Charles of Orleans (800). In 1386 was
granted Touraine which he exchanged in 1392 for duchy of Orleans. Through his marriage in 1387 to cousin Valentina Visconti (825), inherited the rights to duchy of Milan. Had ambitions for founding a kingdom there but was more immediately
concerned with controlling the French regency during the king's
(Charles VI) attacks of insanity. His intense rivalry with dukes
of Burgundy (first with Philip 823, then John 814) became major
factor in the internal affairs of early fifteenth-century France.
Was assassinated in Paris on 23 November 1407 by Raoul d'An-
quentonville, a Norman knight hired by John the Fearless.
Louis had a reputation for an extravagant lifestyle and extramarital affairs, most notably with sister-in-law Isabeau of Bavaria (811). CH made her literary debut at his court and sought
his patronage, dedicating to him the Epistre d'Othea, 46; the
Débat de deux amans, 39; and the Dit de la Rose, 146. (E.
Jarry, La Vie politique de Louis de France, duc d'Orléans, 1372-
1407, Paris, 1889; F. M. Graves, Quelques pièces relatives à la
vie de Louis I d'Orléans et de Valentine Visconti, Paris, 1913;
M. Nordberg, Les Ducs et la royauté: étude sur la rivalité
des ducs d'Orléans et de Bourgogne, 1392-1407, Stockholm, 1964).

816 MACHAUT, Guillaume de (1300?-1377)
       Major French poet and composer in Ars Nova style. Took
holy orders and enjoyed patronage of powerful protectors such
as kings of Bohemia (1323) and Navarre (1349). Popularized
the ballade. His lyric poems are founded on courtly love themes.
He left 19 lais, 33 virelais, 21 rondeaux, 42 ballades and music
preserved in 32 manuscripts. Among his better-known works
are Le Prise d'Alexandrie (c. 1370) and Le Livre du voir dit
(1361-1365), an account of a young girl of high rank falling in
love with the old poet because of his fame. He influenced Chaucer and fourteenth- and fifteenth-century French poets. CH
based part of her Débat de deux amans (c. 1400) on his Jugement du Roy de Navarre (c. 1349); see 42. (Oeuvres, ed. E.
Hoepffner, 3 vols., unfinished, SATF, 1908-1921--40; D. Poirion,
Le poète et le prince: l'évolution du lyrisme courtois de Guillaume de Machaut à Charles d'Orléans, Paris, 1969--518; Guillaume de Machaut: The Judgment of the King of Bohemia, ed.
and trans. R. Barton Palmer, New York, 1984; B. Hosington,
Guillaume de Machaut: fontienne amoureuse, New York, 1986).

817 MARTIN LE FRANC (c. 1410-1461)
       French poet. Secretary to Popes Felix V and Nicholas V,
and to ducal house of Savoy. Also Provost of Lausanne and
Canon of Geneva. Wrote moralizing and allegorical verse, his
principal works being L'Estrif de fortune et de vertu (1447-1448)

and Le Champion des dames (1440-1442). The latter is lengthy
poem devoted to the defense of women in which he pays tribute
to CH by comparing her to Cicero and Cato. Is ranked, after
Villon, with Alain Chartier (801) and Charles of Orleans (800).
(A. Piaget, Martin Le Franc, prévot de Lausanne, 1888).

818   MESCHINOT, Jean (1422?-1491)
      French writer associated with the Grands Rhétoriqueurs.
His verse is allegorical and moralizing. The Lunettes des princes,
one of his best-known works, is both in verse and prose. Is
said to have been inspired by CdP.

819   MÉZIÈRES, Philippe de (c. 1327-1405)
      French writer and crusader. Chancellor of Peter I, king of
Cyprus. After Peter's death served on royal council of Charles
V (1373) and was appointed preceptor to his son, the future
Charles VI (799) for whom he wrote the Songe du vieil pelerin,
1389 (ed. G. W. Coopland, 2 vols., Cambridge, U.K., 1969--
327). In 1392 bought a property from CH, the Château de
Mémorant, and is thought to have been possible influence on
her writings--see 449. (N. Jorga, Philippe de Mézières, 1327-
1405, et la croisade au XIVe siècle, Paris, 1896).

820   MONTREUIL, Jean de (c. 1354-1418)
      Early French humanist, member of royal chancellery, Provost
of Lille. Played major role in quarrel over the Roman de la Rose
(c. 1236-1276), defending it against CH's and Jean Gerson's (807)
charges of immorality and misogyny. Recent studies by Hicks
(below) have shown that it was de Montreuil rather than CH
who initiated the famous debate. (E. Ornato, Jean Muret et
ses amis, Nicolas de Clamanges et Jean de Montreuil, Paris,
1969; E. Hicks and E. Ornato, "Jean de Montreuil et le débat
sur le Roman de la Rose," Romania, XCVIII, 1977, pp. 34-64,
pp. 186-219--135; E. Hicks, Le Débat sur le 'Roman de la Rose,'
critical edition, Paris, 1977--111). See also Hicks 133.

821   ORESME, Nicole (1325-1382)
      Fourteenth-century savant who wrote in both French and
Latin. Became adviser to Charles V (798), for whom he made
French translations of Aristotle's Politics and Ethics. Produced
a celebrated treatise on coinage, De Moneta (c. 1369) and a com-
mentary on Aristotle's cosmology, De Caelo (1377). In his two
works on judicial astrology, Contra judiciarios astronomos and
Des divinations, he tried to warn Charles V against putting too
much trust in his Italian advisers--for instance, Thomas de
Pizan. (G. W. Coopland, Nicole Oresme and the Astrologers,
Liverpool, U.K., 1952--680; Le Livre du ciel et du monde, ed.
E. D. Menut and A. S. Denomy, Madison, 1968).

822 PETRARCH (Francesco Petrarca) 1304-1374
     Great Italian poet and humanist who helped pave the way
for the Renaissance. Renowned for his erudition and scholarship, he is considered by many as the first modern poet. Among
his writings in the vernacular are the Rime, or Canzonieri,
Italian lyrics telling of his love for the Lady Laura. His Latin
works include a series of biographies of ancient celebrities, De
viris illustribus; the epic poem Africa; the prose dialogue Se-
cretum; and such treatises as Rerum memorandarum libri, De
vita solitaria, De otio religioso, and De remediis utriusque for-
tunae. Also left twelve Eclogues and important Letters. His
last work, I Trionfi, is a poem describing allegorical processions
or "triumphs" of Love, Chastity, Death, Fame, Time and Eter-
nity. In CH's allegorical prose work, L'Avision-Christine (284),
there is evidence of Petrarch's influence. (E. H. Wilkins, The
Life of Petrarch, Chicago, 1963; M. Bishop, Petrarch and His
World, Bloomington, 1963).

823 PHILIP THE BOLD (Philippe le Hardi), duke of Burgundy
     (1342-1404)
     Youngest son of John II of France, brother of Charles V
(798), father of John the Fearless (814). He controlled large
territories including Burgundy, Flanders, Nevers, and Franche-
Comté. Together with his brothers was appointed regent for
his nephew, the future Charles VI (799). Upon latter's acces-
sion to French throne in 1380 Philip became virtual ruler of
France until 1388 and again after 1392 when Charles went insane. In 1396 imposed an alliance with England on French
government and drained large sums from royal treasury. This
led to conflict with nephew Louis of Orleans (815), his chief
rival for power and influence. Philip was a collector of illuminated books and manuscripts and champion of the arts. It
was at his request that CH wrote the Livre des fais et bonnes
meurs du sage roy Charles V (1404), 192. (E. Petit, Itinéraires
de Philippe le Hardi et de Jean sans Peur, Paris, 1888; O. Cartellieri, The Court of Burgundy, 1929, rpt. New York, 1970--
399; H. David, Philippe le Hardi, duc de Bourgogne et co-
régent de France de 1392 à 1404...Dijon, 1947--this book contains unique material; R. Vaughan, Philip the Bold, Cambridge,
MA, 1962--684; M. Nordberg, Les Ducs et la royauté: étude
sur la rivalité des ducs d'Orléans et de Bourgogne, 1392-1407,
Stockholm, 1964).

824 VISCONTI, Gian Galeazzo (Giangaleazzo), duke of Milan (1351?-
     1402)
     Italian nobleman and member of prominent Ghibelline family
who ruled Milan from the thirteenth to the fifteenth century.
Made alliance with ruling house of France by marrying daughter
of French king John II; then giving his own daughter, Valentina

Visconti (825), in marriage to Louis of Orleans (815). Visconti
invited CdP to Milan to become his court poet but died before
she could reply. (E. R. Chamberlin, The Count of Virtue:
Giangaleazzo Visconti, Duke of Milan, New York, 1965).

825 VISCONTI, Valentina, duchess of Milan (c. 1370-1408)
       Daughter of Gian Galeazzo Visconti (824), whose marriage in
1387 to Louis of Orleans (815) established close link between
duchy of Milan and royal House of Valois. She was the mother
of French poet-prince Charles of Orleans (800) and grandmother
of kings Louis XII and Francis I of France. Her book collection included many of CH's manuscripts which her son, Charles
of Orleans, inherited upon her death. (E. Collas, Valentine de
Milan, Paris, 1911; F. M. Graves, Quelques pièces relatives à
la vie de Louis I d'Orléans et de Valentine Visconti, Paris, 1913).

• Appendix B •

FORTHCOMING STUDIES AND ADDENDA
(Items are listed in the order in which they have come to my attention.)

826 Cosman, Madeleine P., ed. A Medieval Woman's Mirror of Honor:
The Treasury of the City of Ladies. Trans. from the Old French
and with an Introduction by Charity Cannon Willard. New York:
Persea. c. 256 pp. To be published Spring 1989.
     This volume contains an English translation of the Livre des
trois vertus (259) by Charity Cannon Willard, an Introduction
by Willard, a glossary, bibliography, and 20 black-and-white
illustrations. Also, an introductory essay by editor Cosman.

827 McLeod, Glenda K., ed. Visitors to the City: The Readers of
Christine de Pizan. Ann Arbor, MI: Medieval and Renaissance
Consortium, 1989.
     This volume contains an Introduction by the editor and seven
original essays:

(1) Charity Cannon Willard, "Antoine de la Salle, Reader of
Christine de Pizan."
     "deals with ... la Salle's knowledge of Christine's works,
specifically her Epistre d'Othéa, the Cité des Dames, the Livre
des Trois Vertus, and possibly Livre du Duc des Vrais Amants.
It also questions whether the widow of de la Salle's Jehan de
Saintré might have been modelled on Christine de Pizan." Citing
Glenda K. McLeod.

(2) Glenda K. McLeod, "A Case of Faulx Semblance: L'Epistre
au Dieu d'Amours and the Letter of Cupid."
     "...compares Christine's L'Epistre au Dieu d'Amours with
Thomas Hoccleve's Letter of Cupid and suggests how and where
Hoccleve might have made changes." Citing Glenda K. McLeod.

(3) Francis Teague, "Christine de Pizan's Book of War."
     "examines how Le Livre des Faites d'Armes et de Chevalerie
came to England and how and why William Caxton published its
translation, The Boke of Fayttes of Armes and of Chyualrye."
Citing Glenda K. McLeod.

(4) Paula Sommers, "Marguerite de Navarre's Reading of Christine de Pisan."
"...essay ranges widely over the entire body of work of
Christine and Marguerite, concluding that Marguerite's appreciation of Christine as a writer was confined to Christine's work
in the courtly tradition. Here, like Marguerite herself, Christine
was a writer combining the talented manipulation of casuistique
amoureuse with an outspoken defense of women." Citing Glenda
K. McLeod.

(5) John Rooks, "Sufficient to Stand Or Free to Fall: The Boke
of the Cyte of Ladyes and Its Audience."
"...looks at problems in the 16th century reception of the
English translation of Cité des Dames." Citing Glenda K. McLeod.

(6) Bob Bernard, "Isabel, Duchess of Burgundy and the Portuguese Translation of Le Livre des trois vertus."
"...explains why Le Livre des Trois Vertus interested Isabella, Duchess of Burgundy, who sent a copy to her niece, the
queen of Portugal. Queen Leonora later commissioned the Portuguese translation." Citing Glenda K. McLeod.

(7) Earl Jeffrey Richards, "The Medieval 'femme auteur' as a
provocation to Literary History: Eighteenth Century Readers
of Christine de Pizan."
"...ranges over a wide variety of material, bringing together
a lengthy list of references to Christine from the 18th century,
establishing that she was not totally forgotten in this age ...
and illustrating the kinds of difficulties which Christine has presented to readers separated in time from her own epoque." Citing Glenda K. McLeod.

(Source of Reference: Glenda K. McLeod, Univ. of Georgia,
Athens, GA--typed, signed letter to E. Y. dated 2 October
1988).

828 Brownlee, Kevin. "Structure of Authority in Christine de Pizan's
     Ditié de Jehanne d'Arc." In Discourses of Authority in Medieval
     and Renaissance Literature. Ed. Kevin Brownlee and Walter
     Stephens. Hanover/London: Univ. Press of New England. To
     be published Fall 1989.

829 Margolis, Nadia, ed. and trans. The Lyric Poetry of Christine
     de Pizan. Work-in-Progress.

830 Person, James E., Jr., ed. Literature Criticism from 1400 to
     1800. Vol IX. Detroit: Gale Research, (November) 1988.
     "Presents significant passages from the most noteworthy

published criticism" (p. vii) as introduction to authors of the
fifteenth through eighteenth centuries. The section on CdP,
pp. 20-51, provides a good overview of CH, a list of Principal
Works, and previously published material (in chronological order)
by William Minto, Frederick P. Henry, Alice Kemp-Welch, A. T.
P. Byles, Rosemond Tuve, Susan Groag Bell, Enid McLeod,
Mary Ann Ignatius, Charity Cannon Willard, and Edith Yenal.
Bibliography, with brief annotations, pp. 50-51.

831 Revue des Langues Romanes. XCII, 2 (1988).
    No. 2 is a special issue on CdP. Contains a Foreword by
Liliane Dulac and Jean Dufournet and the following articles:

(1) Jacqueline Cerquiglini, "L'Etrangère." pp. 239-51.
    On CH as an outsider (by birth, sex, other factors).

(2) Angus J. Kennedy, "Christine de Pizan's Epistre à la reine
(1405)." pp. 253-64.
    First critical ed. of the epistre based on all six known manu-
scripts. Includes rejected readings and notes on the establishment of base text, pp. 258-64.

(3) Gilbert Ouy and Christine M. Reno, "Les hésitations de
Christine: Etude des variantes de graphies dans trois manuscrits autographes de Christine de Pizan." pp. 265-86.
    A study of CH's writing style in Chantilly., Musée Condé
XX.B 5; Paris, BN fr. 12779; London, BL Harley 4431. Includes graphs, pp. 282-86.

(4) Teddy Arnavielle, "Structuration personelle du Ditié de
Jehanne d'Arc (1429)." pp. 287-93.
    Expands on Kennedy and Varty's analysis, in 358, of the
structure of the Ditié.

(5) Rosalind Brown-Grant, "Décadence ou progrès? Christine
de Pizan, Boccace et la question de 'l'âge d'or.'" pp. 295-306.
    Examines CH's attitude towards the "golden age" of Boccaccio.

(6) Liliane Dulac, "Unité et variations de la sagesse dans le
Livre des fais et bonnes meurs du sage roy Charles V." pp.
307-15.
    Explains how CH modified the word sagesse and its various
meanings to express her personal vision.

(7) Claude Gauvard, "De la théorie à la pratique: Justice et
miséricorde en France pendant le règne de Charles VI." pp.
317-25.
    Tries to show how CH arrives at a balance between "miséri-
corde" and the strict application of justice--in such works as
the Livre de la paix, Chemin de long estude.

(8) Eric Hicks, "Discours de la toilette, toilette du discours: De l'idéologie du vêtement dans quelques écrits didactiques de Christine de Pizan." pp. 327-41.

Sees CH's feminism in terms of her humanism. The Epistres sur le Roman de la Rose, the Cité des dames, Trois vertus, are among the didactic works discussed.

(9) Sylvie Lefevre, "Le poète ou la pastoure." pp. 343-58.

On the Dit de la pastoure and CH's identification with the suffering of the shepherd girl.

(10) Marie-Thérèse Lorcin, "Pouvoirs et contre-pouvoirs dans le Livre des trois vertus." pp. 359-68.

Analyzes the positive and negative values in Vertus, considering how the latter might be detrimental to women.

(11) Shigemi Sasaki, "Le poète et Pallas, dans le Chemin de long estude (1402-1403) (vv. 787-1170 et 1569-1780)." pp. 369-80.

In Chemin Pallas is identified with the image of Philosophy and the contemplative life.

832 Blanchard, Joël. "Compilation et légitimation au XVe siècle." Poetique, LXXIV (1988), 139-57. Reprinted in English in 836.

Gives reasons why the Livre de la cité des dames should not be read as a book on women and indicates why the act of compiling was meaningful for CH.

833 Slerca, Anna. "La Louenge de mariage di Pierre de Lesnauderie (1523) e le sue fonti." SF, 94 (1988), 1-14.

Discussion of the Cité des dames' influence on Louenge on pp. 8-9.

834 Schryver, Lauren, ed. and comp. "Dissertations in Progress." FR, LXII (1988), p. 20.

Lists the following items for CH:

(1) Bernadette Tchen, "Christine de Pisan." (Univ. SC).

(2) Christine Laennec, "Christine de Pisan antygrafe: l'écriture inavouée." (Yale).

(3) Andrea Tarnowski, "Christine de Pisan and the Late Medieval View of Learning." (Yale).

835 Zeeman, Nicolette. "The Lover-Poet and Love as the most pleasing 'matere' in Medieval French Love Poetry." MLR, LXXXIII (1988), 820-42.

On CH's and Machaut's love poems. Tries to explain why CH thought love was the most appealing subject for readers. References to the Cent ballades and Epistre d'Othea.

836 Richards, Earl Jeffrey, ed., with Nadia Margolis, Christine M. Reno and Joan Williamson. Reinterpreting Christine de Pizan: Essays in Honor of Charity Cannon Willard. With an Introduction and Bibliography of the Writings of Charity Cannon Willard by the editor. Athens, GA: Univ. of Georgia Press. Date not set.
Contains fifteen original essays and one previously published in French, 832:

(1) Barbara K. Altmann, "Reopening the Case: Machaut's Jugement Poems as a Source in Christine de Pizan."

(2) Jeanette M. A. Beer, "Stylistic Conventions in Le Livre de la Mutacion de Fortune."

(3) Joël Blanchard, "Compilation and Legitimation in the Fifteenth Century: Le Livre de la Cité des Dames." (Article trans. into English by Earl Jeffrey Richards; previously pub. in French, see 832).

(4) Maureen Cheney Curnow, "La Pioche d'Inquisicion: Legal-Judicial Content and Style in Christine de Pizan's Livre de la Cité des Dames."

(5) Lilian Dulac, "The Representation and Function of Female Speech in the Livre des Trois Vertus of Christine de Pizan." (Article trans. from the French by Christine M. Reno).

(6) Thelma Fenster, "Did Christine Have A Sense of Humor? The Evidence of the Epistre au dieu d'Amours."

(7) Allison Kelly, "Christine de Pizan and Antoine de la Sale: The Dangers of Love in Theory and Fiction."

(8) Angus J. Kennedy, "A Selective Bibliography of Christine de Pizan Scholarship, c. 1980-87."

(9) Nadia Margolis, "Elegant Closures: The Use of the Diminutive in Christine de Pizan and Jean de Meun."

(10) Glenda McLeod, "Poetics in Action: Misogyny and Genre in Le Livre de la Cité des Dames."

(11) Gianni Mombello, "Christine de Pizan and the House of Savoy." (Article trans. from the Italian by Nadia Margolis).

(12) Christine M. Reno, "The Preface to the Avision-Christine
in ex-Phillipps 128."

(13) Earl Jeffrey Richards, "Christine de Pizan, the Conventions of Lyric Poetry and Italian Humanism."

(14) Patricia Stäblein-Harris, "Orleans, the Epic Tradition and
the Sacred Texts of Christine de Pizan."

(15) Elena Stecapoulas, with Karl D. Uitti, "Christine de Pizan's
Le Livre de la Cité des Dames: The Reconstruction of Myth."

(16) Lori Walters, "Fathers and Daughters: Christine de Pizan
as Reader of Male Chivalric Order and Traditions of Clergie in
the Dit de la Rose."

837   Willard, Charity Cannon. "Punishment and Reward in Christine
de Pizan's Lyric Poetry." In Rewards and Punishments in the
Arthurian Romances and Lyric Poetry of Medieval France. Essays presented to Kenneth Varty on the occasion of his sixtieth
birthday. Ed. Peter V. Davies and Angus J. Kennedy. (Arthurian Studies XVII) Woodbridge, Suffolk, U.K.: D. S. Bre-
wer, 1987. pp. 165-74.
      On CH's treatment of the subjects of love, Fortune, Divine
Will, showing how she developed independent views on society's
system of rewards and punishment.

838   Willard, Charity Cannon. "Christine de Pizan on Chivalry."
In The Study of Chivalry: Resources and Approaches. Ed.
Howell Chickering and Thomas H. Seiler. Kalamazoo, MI: Medieval Institute Publications, Western Michigan Univ., 1988. pp.
511-28.

839   O Espelho de Cristina (1518). With an Introduction by Maria
Manuella Cruziero. Lisbon: Biblioteca Nacional, 1987.
      Facsimile edition of 264.

840   Quilligan, Maureen. "Allegory and the Textual Body: Female
Authority in Christine de Pizan's Livre de la Cité des Dames."
RR, LXXIX (1988), 222-48. 12 figs.
      Deals with CH's idiosyncrasies in rewriting a masculine tradi-
tion of textuality.

841   Willard, Charity Cannon, ed. Selected Writings of Christine
de Pizan. New York: Persea. Forthcoming, Fall 1990.

• INDEX TO INDIVIDUAL WORKS •

(numbers refer to entries, not pages)

• INDEX TO MANUSCRIPTS •

174   Christine De Pizan

DURHAM III.9: 20.

ERLANGEN, Universitätsbibliothek 2361: 46, 484.

GENEVA, Bibliothèque Publique et Universitaire fr. 180: 227.
GRENOBLE, Bibliothèque Municipale 871 (MS 319): 96, 103; ----U.
909 Rés.: 349, 351, 356-58.

LEIDEN, Bibliothek der Rijksuniversität Ltk 1819: 227.
LENINGRAD, Bibliothek Saltykov Chtchédrine F.II, 96: 315.
LILLE, Bibliothèque Municipale 175: 46; ----335: 46; ----390: 227;
----fonds Godefroy 152: 259.
LONDON, BL Cotton Otho D II: 490.
LONDON, BL Harley 219: 46; ----838: 55; ----4410: 295; ----4431:
1, 11-16, 39, 45, 46, 51, 54, 93, 96, 107, 132, 149, 150, 153,
154, 157, 171, 185, 191, 224, 227, 229, 234, 253, 291, 307-09,
457, 463, 466, 468, 481, 484, 492-94, 520, 702 (see pp. xxi-xxiv),
715, 831.3; ----4605: 315.
LONDON, BL Royal 14.E.11: 46; ----15.E.VI: 315; ----17.E.VI:
46; ----19.A.XIX: 227, 243; ----19.B.XVIII: 315.
LONDON, BL Add. 15641: 259; ----17446: 93; ----20698: 230;
----31841: 259.
LONDON, Westminster Abbey Library 21: 16, 185.

MADRID, Biblioteca Nacional 11515: 265, 270, 271.
MANCHESTER, John Rylands Library M 3 3EH: 102.
MODENA, Biblioteca Estense α .n.8.7: 192, 459.
MOUCHET, Bibliothèque Royale 6: 2.
MUNICH, Bayerische Staatsbibliothek Cod. Gall. 8: 227; ----11:
174.

NEW HAVEN, Yale Univ., Beinecke Library 318: 227; ----427: 259,
482.
NEW YORK, Pierpont Morgan Library 48: 482; ----929: 46.
NEW YORK, Public Library, Spencer Collection 17: 295.

OXFORD, All Souls 182: 280, 282.
OXFORD, Bodley, D5: 259; ----421: 46, 464; ----824: 315; ----
Laud. misc. 570: 46, 67, 464, 471, 475.

PARIS, Arsenal 2681: 295; ----2686: 227; ----3172: 174; ----3182:
227; ----3295: 1, 11-16, 39, 45, 46, 85, 93, 107, 146, 150, 153,
171, 185, 307; ----3356: 259.

• INDEX TO NAMES •

(Includes authors, editors, translators, reviewers,
illustrators, and recipients of Festschriften)